INVESTING ABROAD

Investing Abroad

A GUIDE TO FINANCIAL EUROPE

BY Gerald Krefetz AND Ruth Marossi

HARPER & ROW, PUBLISHERS

NEW YORK, EVANSTON, AND LONDON

TO OUR PARENTS

FIRST EDITION

LIBRARY OF CONGRESS CATALOG CARD NUMBER: 64-25150

C-P

CONTENTS

FOREWORD

by HERBERT V. PROCHNOW

President, The First National Bank of Chicago

There is a surprising lack of authoritative studies which combine in a single volume the information needed to invest abroad intelligently. This book gives a thoughtful analysis from the investor's viewpoint of the economies of the nations of Europe, their financial structures, and their methods of operation. Furthermore, it describes the functions and operations of the bourses, brokers, and bankers abroad. This work represents comprehensive research both in this country and in all the major financial centers of Europe.

The history of American economic progress is a remarkable record of achievement. Through the decades after the establishment of the nation the conditions necessary to individual security for all men became better established. The American people steadily accumulated savings and increased the capital available for domestic investment.

By the end of World War I the United States was in a position to export capital and began to look abroad for profitable investment. Since that time many billions of dollars have been invested by Americans in all parts of the world.

As the nations of the world become molded into a close financial and international community all investments become increasingly international. This book should be invaluable to businessmen and bankers, as well as to college and university teachers, who wish a better understanding of the important subject of investing abroad.

PREFACE

This survey of the Wall Streets of Western Europe attempts an appraisal of the Continent's financial centers. In the belief that it is increasingly important for Americans to understand the business environment within the European Continent, we have described the economic and financial forces of fifteen countries as well as the workings of the American foreign securities market.

In the two years it took to complete this project, we held extensive interviews with several hundred prominent bankers, brokers, economists, and other informed observers both in the United States and Europe. Thanks to their frankness and cooperation, we were afforded insights into the spirit and workings of Europe's financial structure which research alone could not have evoked. The resulting approach entails both a description and a critical appraisal of each country's financial community, its principle institutions and their role vis-à-vis each other.

Our primary focus, however, is on the securities exchanges. We hope thus to provide a helpful guide for those with a professional interest in the subject, for those thinking of investing abroad, for holders of foreign securities, or for students simply curious as to the function and operation of Wall Street's European counterparts. Needless to say, the subject is a vast one; indeed, each nation easily deserves a separate volume. Consequently, we were occasionally forced to compress or delete relevant but peripheral material. In this we can take comfort in the words of one Latin grammarian who knowingly remarked: "Since all things have been said by men of sense,/ The only novelty is, to condense."

We tried to sketch a comprehensive panorama, but at the same time concentrate on assessing the major financial and governmental institutions that bear most directly on a nation's Stock Exchange. At all times we have kept American practice in mind when comparing or describing foreign procedure.

In order to avoid constant explanations we have used the term Europe to include Great Britain, realizing full well that the British think of themselves as more than Europeans and the Europeans think of the British as less than Continentals. Finally, the reader will not find any information on Ireland, Luxembourg, or the minuscule European states since their part in international finance is as yet quite small.

Though we had the cooperation and assistance of central banks, stock market officials, and private bankers and brokers, the final analysis is based solely on our own judgment. We alone must take full responsibility for the conclusions. However, we would like to thank everyone who cooperated in this venture. Their interests are probably best served in remaining anonymous.

We should particularly like to thank Andries Woudhuysen, a partner of Burnham and Company, for his kindness in undertaking our appenticeship at the start of this project. Finally, much gratitude goes to John Macrae, our editor, who had the patience and the foresight to see us through to the book's completion.

G. K.
R. M.

New York City
January 1965

INVESTING ABROAD

INTRODUCTION

"The merchant has no country."
—Thomas Jefferson

Dollars only recently ventured abroad though sterling, guilders, and francs have poured into the United States since the discovery of the continent. Indeed, investments by foreigners have been closely tied to America's history and development. Perhaps the bargain of beads for Manhattan was the first and best, but throughout the next three hundred years, foreign money played a decisive role industrializing the economy, enabling it to skip painful stages that Europe had to experience. In fact, investments by foreigners in the United States helped to conserve human and physical resources which would have been spent in the process of capital accumulation.

America's turn to reverse the process and try its hand at foreign investments came after Sarajevo; World War I marked a change in direction. United States funds had accumulated to the point where it became more profitable—or so it seemed—to invest abroad rather than domestically. Working on the assumption that the return on dollars is always greener elsewhere, America became on balance, an exporter of capital. Rapidly, she pre-empted Great Britain's role to become the world's investment banker.

However, the first substantial private purchases by Americans of foreign securities were not notably successful. Attracted by high yields, many investors in the 1920s bought 7 per cent and 8 per cent over-

1

seas bond issues. The ensuing worldwide depression turned many of these loans sour, often returning to their purchasers no more than ten cents on a dollar. Analysts and professors of finance thereafter agreed with Benjamin Graham's remark that "investors with even small experience know that foreign bonds, as a whole, have had a bad investment history since 1914."

In 1933 a Foreign Bondholders Protective Council was established to bring some redress. By exerting a variety of pressures, the council has negotiated permanent settlements on bonds totaling more than $1.2 billion. The council was instrumental in settling the last Western European prewar debt—that of Greece in 1964.

Today, the American stake in foreign lands is vast, productive, and profitable. Besides economic and military assistance on a governmental level, it consists of both direct and portfolio investments. Indeed, private investments overseas exceed $66 billion; holdings of foreign stocks and bonds are variously estimated to be between $12 billion and $15 billion. The bulk of these investments were made after 1950, largely in the Western Hemisphere and Western Europe. American commitments abroad reflect modern economic thought, the unifying factors of world trade, and, of course, enlightened self-interest.

United States interest in Europe dates from her independence from the Old World. Besides a kindred ancestry, similar language, mutual traditions, Europeans and Americans share a Western ideology, a frame of mind. The Atlantic community is perhaps doubly favored, for besides enjoying common points of reference, there is enough diversity of thought and action to stimulate and cross fertilize. This hybridization has been a boon to both sides of the Atlantic as well as to the rest of the world.

It became clear in the early 1950s that most Europeans had recovered from the traumas of war with surprising rapidity. It was also apparent that the Continent's energy had not been expended but was going on to a period of sustained growth. This remarkable transformation of nations wrecked by history's most devastating war attested to the strength of the renascent Western spirit. That spirit is impossible to define but it would seem a compound of history and technology, faith and foresight, geography and environment. One historian placed the Continent in perspective by remarking that "the resources of the continent are sufficiently modest to exact effort and forethought and sufficiently ample to reward them. They have neither the luxuriance that makes man lazy and improvident nor the barrenness that makes him niggardly and takes away his hope."*

On a pragmatic level, interest in Europe was more than academic or nostalgic. Given the spiritual and material strengths of Western Europe, many observers were also impressed by the pursuit of sound political and economic policies in European countries. With the assistance of American aid, democratic institutions were maintained and strengthened in the face of the Cold War. Even the game of musical chairs of the Fourth French Republic could not disrupt the underlying vitality of the French state. Expanding trade and a spirit of liberalization ushered in almost complete currency convertibility and a lifting of restrictions against foreigners. Though governments covered the political gamut, from Falangist Spain to Socialist Sweden, free enterprise in a market economy found a dominant if occasionally regulated role in every European nation. Some nationalization took place but probably more industries were returned to the ranks of private corporations. In brief, investors both in and out of Europe in the 1950s had reason to be pleased with the resources, strengths, spirit, and direction of European economies.

At first investors were solely nationals; Americans were simultaneously afraid of foreign commitments and totally immersed in the rapidly expanding investment possibilities after the Korean War. A few sophisticated Americans had very early in the postwar recovery thought of Europe as an area for diversification. By and large, they were either refugees, or expatriates long familiar with native economies, or widely traveled Americans who had more than a passing acquaintance with Europe before World War II.

By 1955 and 1956 some of the cleverer Wall Street professionals began to investigate the potentials of European securities and cautiously undertook investments. It was a curious period, for no sooner had Americans become aware of Europe's possibilities than the

* Solomon F. Bloom, *Europe and America: The Western World in Modern Times* (New York: Harcourt, Brace and World, 1961), p. 4.

Europeans began to consider American purchases. European governments began to free currencies little by little and America seemed a logical place for putting money to work.

One of the first professionals to think of Europe as a place to "double your money" was George Nelson. During the initial stages of the Nelson Fund, a small but highly successful mutual fund, Mr. Nelson arrived in Paris with his pot of gold. "French bankers thought I was quite mad; they were taking their pots to the States."

As soon as Americans began to think seriously of European commitments, the European economies began to suffer a surfeit of investment. For the first time since the start of the enormous postwar expansion, it appeared that Europe was running out of steam in 1957–1958. In retrospect, however, the Continent was only catching its breath for another extended rise that was to last at least half a dozen years. An American recession also slowed buying for a while, but late in 1958 investment activities picked up. It was joined by an almost frantic deluge of American money. From 1958 to 1962 money invested abroad flowed in a quasi-algebraic progression; for five years the amount of U.S. money venturing to Europe nearly doubled year after year.

Throughout this boom, many Americans made considerable sums of money through judicious European investments. Some Swiss drug companies quintupled their market values. Other instances, though not hard to find, are obviously singular in their occurrence. But one can achieve an appreciation of the potential of foreign securities by comparing a few foreign indexes with the Dow-Jones Industrial Average. From 1953, a year that is commonly thought of as a "normal" postwar year, until the market highs of 1962, the *Financial Times'* Industrial Ordinary Index of British shares appreciated a little better than two and one-half times. The French index prepared by a government agency, the National Institute of Statistics, appreciated over five times. In Germany, the index of the Herstatt Bank rose seven times above the 1953 average. In Italy the average as compiled by the financial newspaper, *24 Ore,* appreciated by over four times. The Swiss registered a gain of over three and one-half times according to the Swiss National Bank measurement. In America the Dow-Jones Industrial Average appreciated only two and a half times. Foreign indexes are not quite comparable, but they do serve as rough indicators.

The investing public, and indeed America as a whole, did not have to face the ominous fact that Western European industrial expansion was roughly twice as rapid as the United States' until the 1960 election campaign. The Democrats pointed to the sobering growth rates of European countries as compared to the U.S.'s laggardly level. By any standards—productivity, employment, capital formation, gross national product—Europe was progressing at a faster pace than Americans could have imagined a decade before. Candidate Kennedy stressed he would "get the country moving again." Whether this argument garnered votes is problematic, but it did alert both the general public and the investing public. To the latter, it spelled potential opportunities. After all, not only did Europe offer the possibility of faster capital gains, but interest rates on bonds, and demand deposits and even a few equity dividends were somewhat higher. By the end of the fifties and the beginning of the sixties the money dealers, who professionally and on a fulltime basis seek havens of higher interest, were no longer alone. The small investors were also running their dollars from one country to another. The U.S. government became increasingly unhappy about the situation—for private enterprise was undercutting the balance-of-payments position. The government did not at that point take any concrete steps to end this flight of investment dollars but it did take other measures to keep the dollar at home, such as cutting down the duty free allowances from $500 to $100 per person.

With the plunge in May 1962, some of the glamour had worn off European investment possibilities. European stock prices, as had those in the United States, had lost sight of economic reality. The spring sell-off which saw American securities lose one-fifth of their inflated values, saw comparable falls abroad. Though the greatest period of European expansion was not over, prices dawdled and proved recalcitrant in 1963 and 1964 due to profit squeezes and inflation.

A precise correlation between European and American security prices does not exist for the same reason that adding oranges and apples is impossible without making fruit salad. As long as national economies and characteristics differ, whether in or out of trade blocs, national Stock Exchanges will follow their own destinies. American influences on European nations cannot be denied, but on the other hand should not be overemphasized. International political or financial crises will always act pervasively since the world diminishes in size daily. However, the old saw of Europe catching cold when the United States sneezes is simply no longer true.

While the U.S. markets staged an impressive climb from the 1962 Cuban crisis to the present, some countries' financial marts likewise rallied, such as Sweden's and Germany's. Others treaded water—France's and Switzerland's. While still other markets fell, such as Italy's and Austria's. Even though European integration has made major strides, decisive market factors remain what they have always been. In other words, national elections, balance of payments, company earnings and dividend, the business cycle, government monetary and fiscal policies are still the leading phenomena to affect a country's securities prices.

RENASCENCE AND RECOVERY

World War II did perform a backhanded service for Europe's economies. War damage and civil destruction often wiped out the oldest and least productive industrial plants. Power stations, port facilities, rail terminals, and steel plants occasionally dating from the childhood of the Industrial Revolution were destroyed. Plants built to withstand eternity might not prove terribly efficient by modern standards, but they worked. As long as they did work, they remained intact. British civil engineers, for instance, could never quite justify tearing down whole categories of ancient steam boilers. France too, was handicapped by antiquated equipment, some of it dating back to the 1880s. The steel industry was a prime example: in 1946, France had no blast furnaces of 500 tons capacity, whereas in the United States the average in 1927 was 500 tons.

Through their victories, the Western Allies managed to keep their industrial plants functioning, if not intact. With regard to the enemy, the Allied campaign was a success, destroying his working economy and leveling his industrial capacity. The Axis Powers—in a broad sense—had to start the Industrial Revolution all over again. But this time they had access (as the United States in the nineteenth century had access to Europe's experience) to the latest techniques, the most advanced industrial conceptions.

Wars may or may not be responsible for a high rate of invention and discovery, but they do favor their implementation. Defeated nations wisely took advantage of light steels, synthetic rubbers, plastics, alloys, and a variety of other industrial processes perfected during the war. Moreover, they reorganized, streamlined, and even automated their newly rebuilt industries.

Thanks to Allied efforts the defeated powers were forced to build the most advanced industrial systems, while the victors struggled along with their old plants. In fact, a fair case can be made for an inverse scale between destruction and postwar growth. Countries that bore the brunt of the devastation—assuming they had going industrial systems—did not initially make the fastest industrial recoveries, but did grow most rapidly through the 1950s. Austria, Germany, Greece, Italy, and the Netherlands were particularly hard hit; however, the gross national products of these countries (using 1950 as 100), show the sharpest rises: 73 per cent, 108 per cent, 84 per cent, 78 per cent, and 61 per cent increases respectively. The average increase for Western Europe was 58 per cent while by 1960, the United Kingdom's GNP had risen only 29 per cent.

Certainly without the European Recovery Program, commonly known as the Marshall Plan, Europe's growth rate would have been somewhat slower. The quinquennium, 1945–1950, proved to be an apt prologue to what has been called "one of the most remarkable periods of virtually uninterrupted economic growth in history."

Actually how remarkable was this period of growth? Whatever measures one uses, the transformation was prodigious and is continuing. Population rose by 10 per cent from 1950 through 1962. Farm output increased by over 50 per cent as farming population shrank. Wages generally increased faster than consumer prices. Per capita income approximately doubled in Western Europe from 1952 to 1962; presently, the average per capita income in Western Europe is $1000, though variations are great from nation to nation and area to area, compared to $2,500 in the United States. European gross national products rose by nearly 60 per cent. Never before has an era of expansion lasted for so long.

The reasons for this European vitality are, of course, many and complex and no explanation can be expected to be all-encompassing. Some elements in Europe's postwar expansion were solitary occurrences, by-products of the Second World War. They are not likely to be repeated. The war's deprivation set up strong consumer demand throughout the whole of European society. This pent-up demand was given yet greater impetus by the postwar baby boom. Once the restraints and the rationing were abolished, appetites increased with the eating. To satisfy consumer demands Europe's new managers released a "backlog of unexploited technology."

Both private business and government worked to expand fixed capital investment, preparing the economic groundwork. European businessmen ploughed money back into their enterprises at an unprecedented level. This capital formation, largely in the form of equipment and machinery, ran considerably ahead of the U.S. rate throughout the fifties. European governments control a higher proportion of investment activity than does the U.S. government. But in no two countries do governments follow parallel courses. In France and the Netherlands investments are regulated through voluntary government planning. In Germany and Sweden fiscal adjustments are liberally used whereas monetary manipulation of the bank rate is heavily relied upon to expand and contract credit in the United Kingdom. In Italy and Spain quasi-governmental agencies play a leading role in development. Naturally, variations and combinations exist within every state.

Another factor speeding Europe's growth was the cooperation of the trade unions. In the immediate postwar period and most of the 1950s, labor had to be satisfied with the balcony; today, however, it is insisting on orchestra seats. Toward the end of the 1950s, trade unions bent on a larger slice of the general prosperity pressed their demands. A series of sharp wage rises followed. As a political faction, they were out of power during this period, as in England, or at best one voice in a none-too-stable coalition, as in France and Italy. But perhaps most important in many countries there was now a new knight to joust: the government as the single largest employer.

Inevitably, by imposing wage stability in its own sector (a wage-push inflation would have jeopardized exports, making them expensive), the government set the pace for private industry. In some countries in fact, the state assumed the role of *pater familias,* creating minimum criteria for industry. In France, the government decreed the "incompressible human and social need" of the "minimum Frenchman." Its *Salaire Minimum Interprofessionnel Garanti,* SMIG, the rock bottom interprofessional wage based on a series of consumer prices indices, and itself the primary point of reference for other prices such as rents, soon became the butt of political cabarets. For weeks, comedians combed the professions and trades to find this minimal man. Finally they adjudged the street-sweeper of Paris the "Incompressible Frenchman." He was entitled to fifty baths per annum, not fifty-two—the two-week-vacation period was presumably excluded—and a new shaving-brush every five years. Indeed, the question of the day for the indexmakers became how many *biftecks* a worker should eat and how many suits he needed. ("Why two, when the good suit is only worn twice in one's life—once to get married and once to be buried in?")

THE EEC AND EFTA

While the 1950s were Europe's period of greatest expansion, they also provided a foretaste of future potential. But the renaissance was not confined to economic and financial realms, a profound political, social, and psychological realignment was taking place. First, there has been a startling move toward European unity.

The European Economic Community (EEC) and the European Free Trade Association (EFTA) hastened the possibility of European union, a concept traceable to Richelieu's first minister Sully and his Grand Design. Napoleon had similar thoughts and so did a number of European politicians up to and including Hitler. In fact, the Germans were probably the first nation to think of unity in terms of economic integration, for in 1834 seventeen German states formed a tariff union or *Zollverein*.

Although the concept of a political and economic union has a long ancestry, the first Pan-European movement began with the EEC. The Common Market first saw the light on January 1, 1958, when Belgium, France, West Germany, Italy, Luxembourg, and the Netherlands affixed their seals to the Treaty of Rome. These nations known as the Inner Six, agreed to a schedule which called for free trade among themselves and uniform external tariffs on goods from nonmembers. This external tariff schedule is to be in complete effect by 1967, possibly three years ahead of the original projected date. The new tariff wall will be an arithmetic average of the members' rates as of January 1, 1957. Generally speaking, German rates will remain almost the same, but French and Italian rates will be lowered while those of Belgium, Luxembourg, and the Netherlands will be raised. On the other hand, successive steps for a free internal market have gone so smoothly that the target date of 1967 should be easily met.

The two tariff conditions are the central and pragmatic functions of the European Economic Community. However, there are other important aspects of the union that will be part and parcel of a completed common market: the free circulation of labor, capital and services, common policies in the field of agriculture, transportation, foreign trade, monetary and fiscal planning. The 1957 Treaty of Rome containing 248 articles is, of course, the organic instrument. Mixed among the conditions are provisions establishing a Court of Justice, European Parliament, Council of Ministers, and an Executive Commission. The Court of Justice passes on a variety of complaints against countries, industries, companies, and individuals that are allegedly breaking EEC regulations. While the European Parliament is not empowered to pass laws, it does air and discuss proposals, submitting advisory resolutions to the Council and the Commission. The Parliament—made up of 142 solons from the national congresses of each member country—is a useful liaison in smoothing the way for new policy decisions that must be passed by the national legislators before they can become EEC regulations.

The two other bodies of the Common Market, the Council of Ministers and the Executive Commission, respectively represent the official government policy of individual countries and the completely nongovernmental point of view of the Community. Ministers are appointed by the government to make major decisions on the proposals of the Commission. It is the Commission which not only proposes, but disposes. Once policy is formulated, the Commission acting "in the interest of the Community" may make independent decisions that fall within the scope of the Rome Treaty. This Commission, a body that in the words of one observer has "far more power, and influence than any international 'secretariat' yet created" is assisted by eight departments that range from agriculture to transport.

The United Kingdom could never make up its mind as to whether or not to join the EEC. England's ambivalence toward a European union stemmed from several considerations. As a leading practitioner of balance-of-power politics in modern history, an economic or politically unified bloc on the Continent would displace and/or diminish British influence. Moreover, political federation might well compromise national sovereignty and the legal structure of the nation. Further, preferences for the Commonwealth complicated the picture. England wished to get her industrial goods under the Community's tariff barrier, but was reluctant to let in European agricultural produce and raw materials that would have competed with Commonwealth produce. While none of these factors was decisive in preventing England from joining, the great national debate that the question engendered led the Conservative government to negotiate with extreme cautiousness. In the end, the decision was taken away from them when General de Gaulle vetoed their application for membership in January 1963.

No sooner did the EEC begin than nations outside the Inner Six claimed economic discrimination. Since the EEC nations manifested a curious xenophobia in restricting admission (Greece is presently an associate member) most of the remaining European nations led by

Great Britain formed their own free trade club, the European Free Trade Association (EFTA). Under the provisions of the Stockholm Convention signed on November 20, 1959, Austria, Britain, Denmark, Norway, Portugal, Sweden, and Switzerland—with Finland as associate member—formed the EFTA as a countervailing force to the EEC. EFTA goals somewhat resemble the Common Market: internal tariff reductions and abolition of industrial quotas among member nations. However, there is no provision for a uniform tariff against nonmembers or a comprehensive agricultural policy.

As with the EEC, internal free trade is expected by 1967, but unlike the EEC, the EFTA has no control over the movement of capital or labor among members. Basically, the EEC regulates while the EFTA supervises. The latter has no plan for political unity. The Common Market nations on the other hand, look to political integration and sometimes picture themselves as a third force, "a new world power," interposed between the United States and Russia.

The European Economic Community at first seemed little more than a blueprint for a customs union, though its original advocates had larger and more grandiose ideas. It was hoped that the spirit and functioning agencies of the Community would knit Europe into a political as well as economic commonwealth. Historically, customs unions were the indispensable yeast in the rise of larger, viable political states. Political union without economic integration, in fact, usually proved ineffective or rebellious, usually both. The EEC's aim to achieve a perfect customs union may thus be the prelude to an historical pattern. Whether a United States of Europe is within the realm of the feasible, however, is another matter.

Within the last few years a series of economic difficulties and ideological differences have dampened the enthusiasm of the Community's supporters and well-wishers. The first few internal tariff reductions went smoothly, but as the tariff walls fall more and more cries of distress are raised and extensions of protections are sought. As the Common Market moves toward its *dénouement* competition will be fiercer and many of the *entreprises artisanales* of France and Italy will be pushed to the wall either to merge or modernize. One of the alleged advantages of the Common Market is the advent of a new spirit of competition in contrast to the past when markets, prices, techniques, and profits were tightly controlled. While it is obvious that consolidation has taken place, it is not clear as to whether the Community has indeed created more or less competitive soil.

A study group of the House Committee on Foreign Affairs reported to the Congress that Community officials "are convinced that restrictive practices exist. Indeed the air seems to be heavy with agreements, understandings, conversations and alliances of vast implications."* Europeans assume that consolidation is necessary if they are to successfully challenge U.S. businesses and finance their capital goods industries. Alfried Krupp in his company's annual report for 1963 remarked that "the German legal system does not forbid it [concentration]. Faced with tough international competition, German industry could not survive if it were split into innumerable small and medium size enterprises. . . . In the U.S., for example, there are about 50 companies each with a turnover exceeding $1,000 million, while Europe does not even have 15. The turnover of *Volkswagenwerk,* the largest in Germany, amounts to roughly 10% that of General Motors." The real difficulty may not be in challenging U.S. firms, but what such consolidation does to the structure of European industry. Though she may not have the highest standard of living on the Continent, assuredly Germany is the most industrialized country capable of out-producing France and Italy combined. This imbalance within a free trade area may yet prove a disadvantage to smaller member nations and nonmembers' trade.

Growing consolidation and lower internal tariffs in both trade groups might be expected to benefit the consumer. It is too early to be conclusive, but preliminary studies indicate that they do not. Internal tariff reductions at the half-way point have "not produced an equally substantial slashing of consumer prices. Businesses have taken a share of the savings, too, in higher profits."†

Consequently, it is not clear that freer trade is what industrialized and protection-oriented Europe really wants or is actually pursuing.

---

* House Committee on Foreign Affairs, *Special Study Mission to Europe* (Washington, D.C., January 25, 1960), p. 77.

† *New York Times,* June 15, 1964.

Trade is, of course, freer among the members, but tending to be less so with nonmembers. The Community's international trade balance has progressively worsened since 1961: imports continue to rise, but exports have grown expensive and are leveling off due to continuing inflation. Autarky or self-sufficiency in industrial and agricultural sectors appears to be one of the unexpressed goals of the EEC. The seriocomic chicken war of 1963 between the United States and the Common Market may be an indication of further things to come.* In December 1964, the Community surmounted the last stumbling block to further economic integration by agreeing on uniform grain prices. Though the agreement does not become effective until July 1, 1967, it may sharply reduce American farm exports to Europe by encouraging marginal land and the possible use of a variable tariff levy that would effectively close the door to the United States farmer.

In the ideological field, General de Gaulle's ascendancy has caused a significant shift. The EEC is being interpreted more narrowly than previously expected—in the words of many critics—more "inward looking." Whereas at one time there was some hope that the two trade blocs would affiliate or merge, any such prospects appear to have vanished. As policy decisions were shifted from the national states to the Community, no comparable supra-sovereign power was exercised by the EEC Commission. In brief, a decision-making vacuum has developed in the Community's apparatus. To a large degree this is a reflection of General de Gaulle's philosophy, his *Europe des patries,* though the General has denied using this phrase. The movement is seen as one away from a federated European power, toward a limited confederated authority of the member states. Even so eminent a statesman as Paul-Henri Spaak, Foreign Minister of Belgium, has admitted that this approach is apt to be the more successful one in a Gaullist-oriented France.

Perhaps this road will in the long run better serve European interests. The very term "European" is one heard more frequently among non-Europeans than Continentals. While there are many

* For a critical evaluation of the EEC, see Sidney Dell, *Trade Blocs and Common Markets* (New York: Alfred A. Knopf, 1963), particularly chapters III and IV.

similarities among Europeans, there are unquestionably many more dissimilar characteristics, habits, techniques, customs, religions, and mores. The president of the EEC commission, Dr. Walter Hallstein noted that the members "have no flag, no common language and no emblem, nothing to establish our identity except our common tariffs."

One thing they certainly don't have in common are uniform products, a fact which, of course, adds to Europe's charm and manufacturers' difficulties. Standardization, whether it be in the realm of law, the length of wallpaper or office stationery, has run into major and minor dilemmas. One of the more amusing problems was cited in the Twentieth Century Fund's *Europe's Needs and Resources:*

> The wool industry in each country makes eight to ten different sizes of blankets, which are not the same from one country to another. The German consumer is strict about maximum dimensions, for he does not want to tuck the blanket under the mattress; the French consumer is strict on the minimum size, for he does not want his feet or his hands to become uncovered while he sleeps. The Germans and the Italians prefer twin beds, which the French and the Belgians regard with horror. Sizes of sheets, pillows and beds themselves vary from one country to another; blanket sizes cannot be standardized without taking account of these differences. The specific weight demanded in each country is different. Design, absence of design, borders and colors are the subject of national fads. Six greens exist (German green, French green, Swiss green, etc.), each one of which is accepted only in one or two countries at any one time.*

In a more serious vein, there is no likelihood of unified, let alone standardized, monetary and fiscal policies for Europe within the immediate future. Within the Common Market there are no barriers to the free movement of capital, and equally important, no real controls as yet, though the Community sees the obvious need for them. National ministries are left to cope with the international monetary conditions that arise directly or indirectly from the Community's actions. For instance, the Community had no power to act as Germany's trade surplus reached staggering proportions in 1964, almost in direct proportion to the French and Italian deficits. It is in this field where cooperation and control may be most needed.

* J. Frederic Dewhurst, *et al.*, *Europe's Needs and Resources* (New York: Twentieth Century Fund, 1961), p. 838.

The financial communities of every European nation are also diversified and complex; assuredly, they will be among the last institutions to be subject to uniformity in an integrated Europe. Not only are Stock Exchange practices divergent, but so are national tax policies, corporate structures, accounting procedures, past history, current traditions, and the whole psychological *ambiance*. Nevertheless, there are forces working within and without Europe that are making for greater public understanding and participation, fuller disclosure of financial information, and easier international comparisons. An Association of European Bourses is a voluntary organization attempting to bring some uniformity into stock trading practices. For example, listing requirements are decided by committees having different ideas as to what sort of information should be divulged. Some demand an accountant's report, others are satisfied that the issue was sponsored by a respectable underwriter, still others require little more than a pro forma statement of intent. The association has thus far had limited success.

Another force, though perhaps a less formal one, has been exerted by security analysts and economists in the last decade. Though still an infant profession, analysts' societies have sprung up in most countries and every respectable bank will have several analysts on its staff. Many European analysts were trained in American banks and brokerage houses. Several Continental banks, often in collaboration with American or English banks, have established research organizations. Three are particularly well-known: Eurofinance, Eurosyndicat, and Eurounion. Their published studies—usually only available through a member bank or on a subscription fee basis—are considered to be among the most astute in Europe.

Finally, the Common Market's monetary committee has suggested steps to further the free flow of securities among member states. There are no longer any impediments to holding securities of companies within the Community. However, the EEC would like to see many more cross-listings in other Exchanges, which is not yet a common practice.

1. ENGLAND

In the City
They sell and buy
And nobody ever
Asks them why.

But since it contents them
To buy and sell
God forgive them!
They might as well.

—Anonymous

Between Fetter Lane and Aldgate, the Thames river, Charter House, and Houndsditch, you can indeed buy and sell almost anything. Every kind of mart is located within "the square mile" which constitutes the City, London's financial center. Its most important market, however, is the London Stock Exchange, largest and most diversified in Europe, perhaps in the world.

Does it rival Wall Street in size and importance? In terms of the number of securities listed, London is undoubtedly ahead; in dollar volume, it is not. London has well over 10,000 quotations though some are not actively traded. Approximately 4,500 companies list in London. Their various issues combined with 900 or so government and municipal bonds bring the total to 9,600. Then you must add the 760 shares listed on 21 provincial Exchanges which can be traded in London; in fact any stock listed on any other Stock Exchange in the world can be dealt in London—Rule 163(1)(e). Wall Street for comparison can claim about 3,700 stocks and bonds listed on the New York and American Exchanges. However, if the over-the-counter market is included, then Wall Street makes a market for some 40,000 more, actively traded, securities. What about the value of the paper traded? In 1963 the market value of all listed securities on the New York Stock Exchange was $529 billion; in London the figure was £55.3 billion ($155 billion) or about 29 per cent of the New York value. Great Britain, of course, is a much smaller country with 95,000 square miles and a population of 53 million.

Public information on the London Exchange has an Alice in Wonderland quality. The Royal Commissioners investigating the workings of the monetary system in 1959 gently chided the powers that be: "Such information as is available about the volume of business done on the Stock Exchange is inadequate; we hope that the Council of the Stock Exchange will examine the possibilities of publishing better data on the business transacted." No daily volume figures are available and the conscientious financial press can reveal only what the Stock Exchange itself discloses, "the total of 'bargains' marked." In 1964 the London Stock Exchange took another historic step toward fuller disclosure of financial information by revealing its monthly turnover figures. They indicated that stock transactions were only 35 per cent of the New York Stock Exchange's volume, but bond transactions were over four times as great.

A "bargain" is a deal, either a sale or a purchase and a "marking," the purely optional recording of the transaction. Humorists in the City have it that "only the bad bargains are marked," so that a broker called on the carpet by his client can substantiate his price with written proof. Actual practice, however, varies widely. Some brokerage houses make it a rule to record every transaction; others do not bother. It is estimated that roughly half the City's business is marked. The average bargain, according to an expert's guess, is £1,250 ($3,500) and a 15,000 bargain day is fairly typical. Thus in brisk trading £18,750,000 ($52.5 million) per day change hands in the City compared to the New York Stock Exchange's average $233,-000,000. For London, however, all figures are only approximate. Why then does the Exchange even bother to compile such inconclusive figures as "the bargains marked"? "Oh," one Exchange statistician replied, half tongue in cheek, "but we've always done it that way."

THE CITY

Greater London today sprawls and engulfs the City. It was not always so. Commercial London, "the Floure of Cities all," encircled by walls and bounded by fields was a short ride from Westminster, the political center. Seven gates and one on London Bridge led to the City, and to the bustle of commerce. The hills were long ago paved over, but the City of London is still an independent municipality; it has its own charter, its own cathedral, its Lord Mayor, and its distinct habits.

During World War II, German incendiaries and V-2s reduced an extensive section to rubble but, thanks to these bombs, the City now has a few tall structures. Otherwise, it is a horizontal area where buildings are no more than four or five stories high. So far, the canyons of Wall Street are absent, but an extensive redevelopment plan projected for the bomb-gutted area behind Guildhall promises to change this. Henceforth, steel and glass modernity will co-exist with cobblestones and masonry in the old part of the City.

There, the setting alone is impressive. The gilt signs of Lombard Street, which used to mark houses before the introduction of street numbers in 1766, now point the way to insurance companies and banks. From the outside, these massive and venerable buildings seem impervious to human behavior, if it were not for the milk and the tricorns of cream left on the outer steps to accompany afternoon tea.

Besides the signs, there are the omnipresent inscriptions. Britain's "merchant adventurers" with an appropriate sense of balance took pleasure in their dealings but did not glorify their calling. "Unto God only be honour and glory" is the motto facing the Stock Exchange. *"Domine Dirige Nos,"* ("God direct us") crowns Guildhall and is also inscribed on the menu of Lyons restaurant, where between 1 and 2:30 P.M. the traders go for a lunch of roast beef or lamb. Down the street is the Royal Exchange, a Corinthian temple reminiscent of Wall Street's Sub-Treasury building, on whose architrave is the biblical reminder: "The Earth is the Lord's and the Fulness Thereof." The Bank of England, across Threadneedle Street, would no doubt agree, for as secular custodian of the Lord's treasure, its basements are full of the fullness. Even the London Stock Exchange has a motto: *"Dictum Meum Pactum"* ("My Word is My Bond").

Some 400,000 people work in the City by day and the majority are men. Women have only recently come into the square mile to work as secretaries and tame the adding machines. They do not venture into the Dickensian pubs with signs like "Jellies, Invalids" in gold-rimmed letters. Even the oyster bars with their sawdust floors and leaded windows are exclusively male preserves.

"For a man choosing a career, the City affords one last stronghold of individualism," a partner in a brokerage firm asserted. Yet at rush hours the visitor has the uncanny impression of having stumbled into the midst of a deacons' convention. All City men, irrespective of age, dress with but little variation on a single theme: bowler, off-black suit, umbrella, drab tie—distinguished, but indistinguishable. In fact, should a broker appear on the floor of the Stock Exchange wearing a bright cravat, it might be unceremoniously snipped off. A member wearing objectionably bright clothes will be bounced around the floor of the Exchange by his confrères, like a basketball.

On the street, umbrellas lend an air of jauntiness to a City man and are habitually handled with a four-part wrist action: down, back, up, and forward. In any weather, the bone-handled umbrella serves as an accessory gearshift, taxi flag, and crowd disperser. The bowler and the bumbershoot are as much City symbols as the pound sterling. In fact, the City breeds the club-like atmosphere of men with a common background and a common purpose. With families that have been in the brokerage or banking business for centuries, the City presents a homogeneity and solidarity no other financial center can equal. Many City men bring to their work a series of interrelated acquaintances and relationships called "the old boy net." Brokers know a man's background, his schooling, his family. Many in the upper echelons of the City's financial institutions come from the same public schools and belong to the same social clubs. However, the world of finance has expanded beyond the confines of a private club, though the vestiges die hard. University men are not a rarity—the London School of Economics is well represented—but the influx of postgraduates in economics and law school men Wall Street has experienced is so far almost unknown in Throgmorton Street.

Close relationships have their advantages and disadvantages. They make possible raising considerable amounts of money with greater speed and ease than on Wall Street. On the other hand, continuity generates conservatism and extreme caution in undertaking new ventures or abandoning outmoded ways. Automation is a case in point. Though the Stock Exchange has installed some mechanization in its settlement department, only 150 stocks are cleared by this process. Clerks of the brokerage houses matching books the following morning check all trades. As for computers, only three brokerage houses in all of London have their own. The remainder either send out their accounts to be processed or do them manually.

THE STOCK EXCHANGE

The Stock Exchange, a wedge-shaped building, faces Throgmorton Street, with its back on Threadneedle. It is around the corner from the Bank of England, from all the major English and foreign banks, from those new investment giants—the insurance companies—and close to Mansion House, the residence of the Lord Mayor of London. It is, in fact, the center of the world of credit.

The Exchange has no charter and is an unincorporated group kept together by the cement of common function and a trust deed dating from 1802. (The agreement establishing the New York Stock Exchange dates from 1792.) As an institution it prohibits its members from advertising and until recently cloaked itself in anonymity. During 1962 it broke a precedent and started to advertise its function. However, even today the unaware tourist may walk past the building. The entrance barely identifies itself except by the stern warning "Subscribers Only Admitted." The only clue to the building's importance is a sign at the head of the street prohibiting vehicular traffic.

Between trading hours, 9:30 in the morning to 3:30 in the afternoon, over a thousand men may mill about the floor of the Exchange, congregating around twelve pillars or pitches which punctuate the space. Shouting across this three-quarters of an acre expanse, the waiters—a term harking back to the days when trading took place in coffee houses around Change Alley—page members from raised platforms. They are ruddy, barrel-chested types, sporting navy and red uniforms and gold-banded top hats. The acoustics are not bad but the waiters must bark like master sergeants to be heard over the din. Indicator boards and radio pocket beepers also summon members to the phone or alert them to messages.

Each pitch designates an area where particular markets are found, e.g., gold shares, oils, motors, and so forth. Bulletin boards hang from the pillars, and colored annotations are the key to price movements; blue for up, red for down, and black for the previous day's quotes. The seats are for the jobbers, specialists in groups of stocks. The London Exchange provides chairs for one-fifth its membership. This is a somewhat better showing than the New York Exchange where "seats" are chairless. As for the rest of the London members: "Each broker or jobber engaged in his labor/Must bear his own burden, or lean on his neighbor."

Four change boards announce the bank rate, the rate at which the Bank of England, fiscal agent for the government, will discount prime commercial paper. Exchange Telegraph, a business information service, flashes business and economic news onto the translux screens posted throughout the cavernous hall: two bells for important and detailed announcements, one bell for news of minor importance. London has no New York style translux tape and thus one cannot follow price movements or transactions except in the most general way. The Exchange Telegraph service reports only some of the prices, some of the time, and is moreover late by a few minutes to three-quarters of an hour. Wall Street's newest acquisition, the electronic console which at the tap of a company's ticker symbol instantaneously tells you all you want to know—last price, present dividends, past performance, and more—is nonexistent in London.

On the floor, decorum is now the rule, but before the war practical jokers had a freer rein. "Oh, yes, the boys have toned down a lot; the visitors' gallery put them on good behavior," one old-timer reminisced. To break the routine on slow days, a favorite sport was throwing a roll of ticker tape high up over the rafters, setting a match to the ends as they dangled down, and taking bets on the outcome. Paper birds sailed to the ceiling while enterprising brokers took odds on their descent. It was less lucrative than speculating on a favorite company, but it kept the sporting instinct keen. In 1953, the gallery put the Exchange on partial public display. It is glass enclosed and the visitor sees and hears rather little.

Thirty-five hundred men are members of the Exchange and they proudly boast that everyone knows everyone else. No outsider has ever been able to walk across the floor. A number have tried on a bet, but none has succeeded. The majority of men on the floor of the Exchange are members of brokerage firms, 293 in all, of varying size and importance. The balance are jobbers constituting 83 separate firms. A new rule now prohibits one-man firms, but there are still a dozen or so about. The broker, acting as agent for the public, may take care of all transactions himself or, if he chooses, never set foot on the floor, but leave the dealings to an authorized clerk.

To become a member, it takes a proposer and seconder, the purchase of a seat from a retiring member, approval of three-quarters of the Stock Exchange Council, and the ability to pay the £1,050 ($2,940) entrance fee and the £189 ($529) annual subscription. Some jobbers deal in memberships, purchasing them from retiring traders and holding them until interested applicants come along. For this they charge a fee. In any event, memberships are a good deal cheaper than Wall Street seats. In London, they have changed hands for as little as £1 ($2.80) or as much as £2,000 ($5,600), cost varying with supply and demand.

Jobbers

A jobber must be "intelligent, imaginative, ambitious, tactful, tolerant, fearless, patient, long-suffering and the possessor of a large amount of capital," according to the man who runs the largest firm of jobbers in London. Obviously, a tall order, it undoubtedly is the reason the number of jobbing firms continues to diminish. Besides possessing the above qualities, jobbers are expected to make a market for a variety of securities. To borrow a phrase from Oscar

Wilde, brokers have been accused of "knowing the price of everything and the value of nothing." The man who presumably knows value is the jobber. Like the specialist in New York, the jobber does not deal with the public but only with other brokers. He may deal in several hundred stocks; in fact, the largest firm makes a market for over 1,400 different stocks, but in competition with his confreres. In London, unlike New York, all business must first be offered the jobber. The British Exchange is not an auction market, but a bazaar.

While the jobbers keep store at Throgmorton Street between 9:30 A.M. and 3:30 P.M. they are not limited to dealing between these hours. Indeed, they are quite active after the Exchange closes, sometimes until the New York market closes at 8:30 P.M., their time. In the market the jobber is stationary, to be found at this post or that. The broker, like the peripatetic trader, makes his rounds. After the preliminary friendly chatter he asks a price. The jobber not knowing if he confronts a buyer or seller, quotes a spread—two prices one at which he'll take on stock, the other at which he will sell. The broker's query, "anything in between" may narrow the spread. The bargaining may continue; the broker may successfully carry out his transaction or he may approach another jobber and begin all over again.

The British are gentlemen in their trading. Seldom do they take advantage. A broker hearing a jobber quote a price obviously out of line with the market will seldom jump in and take a quick profit. Probably he will tell his man. On Wall Street, such courtesy is none too frequent. The broker lives by his commissions, the jobber by his "turn," the difference between the price at which he bought and the price at which he is prepared to sell. The jobber's turn rings an unpleasant note in his ears and he would prefer "margin of opportunity." A more venturesome breed, the jobber works purely as a principal for his own account. His risks are great but then so were the profits at one time. Two factors in particular have put the jobbing system under stress. First, the size of deals the jobber is required to handle. As institutions become larger and pension funds are more powerful, the jobber is required to deal in larger amounts. This involves a greater commitment of capital and the jobber consequently is faced with greater danger. Many deals today, especially the larger ones, are negotiated and simply go through the jobber as a matter of custom. The jobber takes a minimum turn on them. The second factor decimating the ranks of jobbers is the heavy death duties. Since they are not limited liability companies, their capital comes under increasing pressure as partners die off.

Jobbers make approximately d.3 (threepence) on a turn. However, their net profit varies between one-eighth and one-half per cent per share, hardly an exorbitant profit they claim, considering their services. Dr. Johnson's uncomplimentary definition, "A stock jobber is a low wretch who makes money by buying and selling shares in the funds," seems out of date. Members of the London Stock Exchange are quick to point out that the jobbing system, the only one in the world, makes London the freest of markets as jobbers always stand ready to buy and sell shares regardless of which way the market moves. Critics of the jobbing system insist that the price set by jobbers is somewhat arbitrary. They point to the May–June 1962 panic, when on one day prices fell in New York 5.8 per cent on great volume, but fell in London 6.4 per cent without any equivalent increase in "markings."

The jobber, of course, cannot wait for the consensus of public opinion. He is constantly trying to outguess the market. Is there a selling wave in the offing? If he sees indications of this, the jobber will lower his prices by whatever per cent he thinks adequate. Unlike the specialist, who jumps in once the result of the auction market has made public opinion known, the jobber does not act as a leveler. He does not buy or sell against the market, except for his own profit. The specialist is legally obligated to "maintain a fair and orderly market," keeping price fluctuations minimal. The jobber is under no such official obligation. The specialist, however, runs less risk, or at least his risk is intermittent rather than continuous. He is free to watch the market rise or fall without acting as a principal in each transaction. The jobber *is* the market, even though as many as 17 different jobbing firms will handle one stock, Imperial Chemical Industries, for instance.

English observers like to credit the stability of the London market to the jobbing system, and ascribe the roller-coaster quality of the New York market to the specialist and the auction system. Perhaps, but theoretically the opposite might as easily be valid. Probably closer to the truth would be the restrained character of the Englishman as opposed to the American. It was G. K. Chesterton who remarked that Americans "have a sort of permanent intoxication from within, a sort of invisible champagne."

The jobbing system, for the investor, has one distinct disadvantage. It is difficult if not impossible to put an effective stop-loss order on a stock. The jobber's book, is not the equivalent of the specialist's. It is merely his own record of his purchases or sales. Unlike the specialist's, it contains no future commitments, orders to be filled at such and such a price, or stock to be disposed of. In the English market, the most an investor can do is to tell his broker he would like to sell around a certain level. A stop-loss order is ineffective, as the price may never reach the specified level; it may—as is true in the United States —drop far below. Moreover, there is not one price but several, sometimes as many as there are jobbers. It is up to the broker to negotiate the best bargain.

English brokerage and jobbing firms take one of two forms, partnerships or unlimited liability companies. In either form, members or partners are personally liable to the fullest extent of their personal assets in case the firm fails. Such failures are infrequent, to be sure, but do occur. However, should a firm be unable to meet its obligations, the investor, British or foreign, is fully protected, and upon filing a claim will be fully compensated out of moneys in the Stock Exchange Compensation Fund.

A firm's failure is made public with much pomp and ceremony. The ritual is known as "hammering," and the firm's partners cease to be members of the Exchange. Heavy wooden mallets resound alternately from either side of the house, preceding the announcement. Two waiters standing at opposite ends of the floor call out: "Gentlemen, Mr. A and Mr. B," and here may follow a long list as each partner or each member of the firm is mentioned by name, "trading as X and Company beg to inform the house that they cannot comply with their bargains." Announcements in the press, of course, follow. Actually, the ominous sound of the hammer is seldom heard; since the war there have been less than a dozen failures and most were fairly small one- or two-man firms. A new Stock Exchange ruling now bars the formation of such firms.

In London, there is no equivalent of the Securities and Exchange Commission and no outside body ever looks over the shoulder of Exchange members. The London Stock Exchange is regulated only by its members, the council, composed of thirty-six elder statesmen. Naturally, they are assisted by a series of committees and departments to administer the daily details. One such department is Share and Loan, the watchdog of the London Exchange. It passes on a company's application for listing upon the Exchange, making sure that the company is legitimate. From time to time, the Share and Loan Department will suspend trading in a security if evidence should warrant it. There are no special laws for fraud since common law covers common theft. In any event, shady practices are few, and the foreign investor can feel as secure in London as he can at home.

The Account

Each civilization in the history of man has developed its characteristic calendar; the London Stock Exchange too parcels out time in its own fashion. The Stock Exchange year is split into 24 accounts, or trading periods, 20 of which are a fortnight long, and the remaining four of three weeks duration. A normal, two-week account begins on a Monday and lasts until the Friday of the following week. Account day, the day "all bargains must be settled," checks and transfers delivered, falls on Tuesday, eleven days after the account closed. This system allows the investor a period of grace between the purchase time and the due payment.

Thus, if a purchase is made on a Monday of a new account, the investor's check must be on his broker's desk three weeks and a day later. If he buys midway in the account the time lag will be shorter. Of course, for a sale the process is the same but reversed—it is the investor who waits for payment until the end of the account. Under English usage and if the broker consents, it is possible to deal for "new time" on the last two days of the old account. The investor thus has a further two-day extension. Two other techniques exist, though in practice they are rarely used in the British market. One is contango, the other its converse, backwardation.

Contango, known also as carry-over or continuation, is an arrangement to postpone payment for a stock in the case of a purchase or delivery in the case of a sale to the following account period. If the "giver," the investor who wishes to delay payment, finds a "taker," a seller who wishes to delay delivery, a contango can be arranged. The "giver" pays the "taker" a fee, interest depending on the availability of stock, usually ranging from 4 to 10 per cent. The average is 4 and one-half to 5 per cent. All contangos in any given security are generally effected at the same price. This is fixed by the contango market and is known as the "making up price." Contango is more a textbook technique than one used in practice. Facilities for contangoing exist if your broker is willing to extend them, but some houses exclude contango as a matter of principle. Others will make it available to a "principal," a man of independent means, or a person who is self-employed and obviously solvent, or a client whose stock is held by a brokerage house. Usually, contangos are arranged with jobbers, though sometimes a broker can accommodate his client without going into the market.

Backwardation is the opposite of contango. A seller, not wishing to deliver within the account, wants to borrow stocks to cover himself. Should there be heavy selling pressure in the market, he may have difficulty arranging this. Therefore, instead of receiving interest—as he normally would under contango arrangements—he may have to pay the interest. The speculator who sells but has no stock to deliver thus pays a fee to borrow. Some brokers, while they do not make contango or backwardation facilities available on their own, will refer interested clients to option houses which look on the element of risk with less jaundiced eyes. As with most things on the London Exchange these matters are private arrangements between the investor and his broker, available under special circumstances. There are no statistics available on how frequently these techniques are used, but the consensus among the large brokerage houses is generally negative. Nothing prevents the foreign investor from making use of contango or backwardation if he can find a house willing to put these facilities at his disposal.

Options also exist in the British market though until recently the practice was forbidden. The Socialists were against them, considering such techniques as evidence that the Stock Exchange was merely a den of gamblers. Now, dealing in options has been revived and they can be purchased for up to three months' duration. Many brokers will not deal in options, but there are firms specializing in them. Option dealing as well as contango facilities are courtesies which the British broker will extend sometimes, and to some clients, unless the house bars both techniques.

The Brokers

At the entrance of one of London's larger brokerage houses is a sign: "Partners here," then underneath, "Escape to roof and adjoining building is available at 3rd floor level." There is, of course, no connection between the two statements, yet the sign is symptomatic. The British broker's reticence is real compared with the American's.

Clients do not come and go freely or sit and watch the tapes in the board room, for two reasons. First, in London there is no translux tape which instantaneously records a transaction. There is no way of knowing the amount of a bargain or deal. All that the Exchange Telegraph ticker transmits are random prices and company news. There is no indication of either volume or activity in any one stock. Second, public display of the news ticker would be construed as advertising. The place to watch the ticker is in the smoke-filled privacy of one's club. The large, glass enclosed ground-floor offices so typical of American brokerage houses are nonexistent in London. No one casually wanders in during lunchtime and, when they do come, it is to consult one of the partners—always by appointment.

Most brokerage houses cluster around the Exchange. Offices are apt to be at the back of the busy but carless rabbit warren leading to Copthall Avenue, or hidden in the recesses of Austin Friars. Victorian and solid outside, the inside is often walnut paneled and lushly carpeted. A liveried guard, from the ranks of retired veterans, asks the visitor's business. If he is expected, he will be lead into a board room, dominated by the founder's portrait, furnished with comfortable leather chairs, and usually with a large buffet and a sideboard where liquor is stored. A red light above the door ensures privacy and indicates a conference in progress or a client waiting. The setting suggests solidity, tradition, and complete discretion.

In some respects, City ways have not changed much since the 1800s when James Mills, John Stewart Mills, and Charles Lamb clerked for the East India Company. The way to success for the City man is still through hard work. The two Millses came to head the office, but Lamb's philosophy of "making up for coming late by going away early" hindered his promotion. Today, partners as well as clerks often work long hours, and it is not uncommon to see lights shining well after 6 o'clock. Wall Street's 9:00 to 3:30 shift is a rarity in London.

The size of brokerage houses and the volume of business have increased greatly in the past decade. Ten years ago, 100 bargains a day was a feat while today's average is 250. Office space has often not kept pace, and the business part of a London brokerage house is usually at the back or on the upper floors. Rooms dating not only from a pre-electronic era but also from the pre-electric era have had to be adapted to office use. Electric wiring clings to walls like vines, branched here and there to feed a fan or a heater perched high up out of work's way. Outlets dangle from the ceiling to meet the airborne wiring of typewriters and calculators—lending an arboreal quality. A calendar of account periods hangs prominently on the wall next to a folio of defunct companies. Calculators and teleprinters clatter, half a dozen phones as well as telephone adapters broadcast conversations to the room. Three colors identify the uses of phones: two-tone green to the floor of the Exchange, red for internal communications, and black to the outside world.

However, the phone is not yet the *sine qua non* it has become in the United States. For the Englishman it is not uncommon to give instructions by letter despite the day's delay occasioned. English brokers will do both more and less for their clients than their U.S. counterparts will. The U.S. investor should not expect a regular statement outlining his position, dividends paid, or other investment data from his British brokers, as it is not their habit to send such a monthly reckoning. The firm will send a "valuation" on request, or between once and four times a year, depending on the size of the portfolio. This investment review is far more comprehensive than a mere statement. The firm will figure return on capital after taxes (taking into account United Kingdom, federal, and state levies) and will include a list of detailed suggestions and recommendations for the investor's consideration. Brokerage houses make a thorough job of it; their craftsmanship is apparently appreciated by British investors, who follow about 75 per cent of valuation recommendations.

Research, too, is handled very differently in Britain. First, in sharp contrast to the U.S. practice, research findings are "For Private Circulation Only." Printed in limited numbers, they are available only to the firm's clients, and to banks referring business to the house. Making them available to the general public would be considered advertising. Partners and research men stay on the phone calling dozens of clients a day before issuing the report. Usually, reports are timed, as are the British financial weeklies, to reach the firm's clients by Friday or Saturday morning for leisurely weekend perusal. However, personal contact is often the decisive factor. "No one pays any attention to written reports unless we call beforehand," the head of one of the research departments remarked. Sometimes a firm, sensing a good thing, will buy a line of stocks before it issues any research findings. The broker will then sell to his client at cost—member firms of the Stock Exchange never deal for their own account. "If you get too many requests and the price has gone up in the meantime, what happens then?" "Well, then you are up a gum tree aren't you?"

To complicate matters further, there are brokers who *always* deal for their own account. Moreover, they also advertise in a mild manner. Termed "outside brokers," they are not members of the Stock Exchange but are licensed to deal in stocks and shares by the Board of Trade. The category of licensed, nonmember dealers also includes institutions who for one reason or another wish to deal for their own account—insurance companies, banks, pension funds, the issuing houses, and others. The outside broker alone, however, sells to the public. Acting as a principal, he is essentially a retailer who buys in large lots and re-sells small parcels at a slight markup. He purchases a line of stock below market price from a regular broker, puts out a circular letter advertising his acquisition and re-sells it at a slightly higher price. Usually, outside brokers handle stock of small, less-known companies, securities that would be in the over-the-counter category in the United States.

For the investor, the bank and the broker are two aspects of the investing equation. Each performs a specific series of services. For British brokers, however, banks are their lifeline of contacts; they are the intermediaries who channel business and clients the broker's way.

Brokers, because of a Stock Exchange prohibition on individual company advertising, are by U.S. standards in a rather awkward position. A firm must remain anonymous—and this interdiction applies even to news articles. An article might say, for instance, that an excellent research study appeared for X company, but will never mention the brokerage house. A partner lecturing to a group or club interested in investments may not divulge his company's name or tender his card, except on request. If someone in the audience approaches him, that is all right, but he may not leave a stack of cards or literature with the firm's imprint where it will be freely available. That would constitute advertising. This distinction is a fine one, but it is real enough.

Without exception, the firms who co-operated so fully in making this chapter possible insisted, "You won't mention our name will you?" To respect their request, no member firm of the London Stock Exchange has been singled out by name.

How then do clients find brokers and vice versa? The Stock Exchange itself will on request supply a short rotating list of firms. It is supplied without qualification as to size, what the firms may specialize in (for instance, if they specialize in handling foreign accounts), or any other descriptive comment or qualification. Let the investor pick and choose! "A raw onion," a new investor, may thus be in somewhat of a quandary. Most people come through "channels" recommended by a solicitor or by the bank to the bank's broker. Banks are thus the normal conduit, the easiest means of access. Of course, an American has several choices: he may open an account with a branch of a U.S.

bank with a London office; work through a U.S. brokerage firm with or without a London office; deal with a British bank; acquire a British broker. Combinations and permutations are also possible.

THE BANKS

Obtaining reports on research conducted by brokerage houses other than one's own is difficult. If an investor wrote to a house he did not have an account with saying, "I've heard of your excellent study on company X and would appreciate a copy," he would most likely be refused politely but firmly. He might be able to obtain it from a British or American bank, assuming of course he had previous knowledge of the study's existence.

Banks make a practice of sending out brokerage materials only when a specific study is requested, never continuously or *en masse*. The five largest British joint stock banks—Barclays, Midlands, Lloyds, Westminster, and National Provincial—are huge national institutions with thousands of branches among them. They do not ordinarily tender investment advice. The banks that do advise, for a fee or a commission to be sure, are the small but influential and highly dynamic merchant banks: Rothschilds, Barings, Hambros, Samuel Montagu, M. Samuel, Lazards, Kleinwort Benson, Morgan Grenfell, Warburgs, and the like. Their investment services are highly regarded since many companies look to them for financial guidance. However, merchant banks will rarely accept an account if it is under $25,000.

Only 1 to 5 per cent of British stockholders leave their certificates with their brokers. Many investors leave securities in bank nominee accounts to enable the bank to take care of all technicalities such as dividend collection, transfers, and rights issues. For British as well as foreign investors, it is much simpler to handle transactions in this fashion. For these services, the banks charge a nominal fee. It should be noted that in order to register British government bonds in a nominee account the nominee must be a corporation and not a partnership.

Until recently, the English system of stock transfer defied description because of its complexity. Each share had a serial number and each number had to be duly accounted for in any trade. This archaic process occupied thousands of clerks armed with steel-stiletto pens for innumerable man-hours. Stock transfer is now somewhat simpler. Parenthetically, the price on the transfer note may differ from the price on the broker's contract note. If you bought shares that have been traded two or three times during the account period, there may well be differences between the first sale and your purchase. Once the transfer papers have been signed, witnessed, and delivered to the broker, sit back and relax. Legally you were the owner of the shares the moment the broker and jobber completed their deal. Delivery of stock certificates takes a month or two owing to the slow and stately business techniques in Britain. For foreigners, the banks also serve another function: they handle currency conversion and the purchase and sale of "blocked sterling." Technically, every time a British security is bought by a foreigner, it is purchased with "investment, blocked or switch sterling," a pool of funds which can be used for no other purpose.*

For instance, an investor settling in England could not merely sell his British securities and expect to live on the proceeds. He would dispose of his blocked sterling to another investor and would collect at a rate dependent on supply and demand. If foreigners wishing to purchase blocked sterling are too numerous for the moneys available, the cost of the currency rises until it reaches a maximum point which is the spot exchange rate. Conversely, if the pool of funds goes begging for interested takers, such sterling may sell at a discount. It is to the foreign investor's advantage to purchase blocked sterling which is usually slightly cheaper than normal currency, or "spot sterling." Thus, the American or other investor can enter the British market on favorable terms.

In effect, blocked sterling today is easily bought and sold. Conversion into pounds, dollars, or other currencies presents no difficulties whatever, and the foreigner has no difficulty repatriating his capital at the going blocked currency rate. However, blocked currency accounts do have some limitations. For instance, foreigners cannot buy foreign

* John Fountain, " 'Switch Currencies' and other 'Monetary Mysteries,' " *The Financial Analysts Journal* (January–February, 1961), pp. 3–7.

currency securities with blocked accounts or, to put it another way, an American resident cannot deal in dollar securities in the London market. Nor can the funds of a blocked account, sometimes referred to as "switch currency," be used for short-term bonds, those reaching maturity within five years. It should be recalled that the British government has in the past and, indeed, could in the future clamp further restrictions on its currency. Of course, the general European trend is in the opposite direction—toward greater liberalization—but the other possibility should be kept in mind. Conversely, Englishmen wishing to invest abroad either in businesses or in securities must buy "investment dollars." This rate too fluctuates with availability. Now and in the recent past, there has been a premium on investment dollars of between 5 and 15 per cent. Of course, should investment dollars become less scarce, the premium will shrink or disappear.

A related caveat is in order here. Should an American pick up the stock page of the London *Times* or the *Financial Times*, he would see U.S. securities selling at seemingly astronomical prices; General Motors for example quoted at $65 in New York would be $129 in London on the same day. The investor should not be tempted to buy in New York and sell in London in order to pocket the difference. The reason for the price discrepancy is simply that dollar securities are quoted at the fictitious rate of $5 to the pound. This mythical currency, termed "dummy dollars" or "London dollars" according to one banker, is "one of those pleasant British fictions in which no one sees any sense whatever, but it persists by force of habit." It harks back to the ego-bolstering days before the devaluation when the pound was worth $4.86.

To convert dummy dollars to real dollars the procedure goes like this:

$$\text{London dollars} = \text{U.S. price} \times \frac{5}{\text{exchange rate}} + \$ \text{ premium if any}$$

Thus, if G.M. sells for $65
the $ premium is 11%
and the exchange rate is $2.80 to the £,
then the London price is

$$(\$65 \times \frac{5}{\$2.80}) + 11\% \quad (\$12.76) = \$128.76$$

$$\text{or } \frac{\$128.76}{5} = \pounds \ 25 \ 15s. \text{ at the fictitious } \$5 \text{ rate}$$

It should be underlined that English equivalents quoted in the papers may or may not take the premium into account. For General Motors the English equivalent was thus quoted at $116 without premium, but $128.76 with premium. Under normal circumstances, an American would not be purchasing domestic securities on the London market, and therefore these quotations need not concern him. He should be aware of these quotation devices to avoid mistaken impressions. Incidentally, a foreigner cannot sell short on the London Exchange. This is not a rule of the Stock Exchange but a foreign exchange regulation. A short sale by a foreigner would maintain an open leak in the exchange dyke. "If we're on the way down, the rule prevents you from helping us along, doesn't it now?" Recent sterling crises when foreigners speculated heavily against the pound are always cited as examples. The rule operates much the same as the New York Stock Exchange's regulation against short sales in a falling market, except that it is a more comprehensive prohibition.

THE MECHANICS OF TRADING

There are two distinct ways an investor may purchase or sell British securities: he may channel his order through his American broker, or he may open an account in London. The easiest way, one obviously commonplace for domestic securities, is simply to instruct one's broker to make the purchase, leaving methods to his discretion. The broker may then be faced with a plethora of choices: if the stock in question is a listed security, he can buy it on one of the American Exchanges; if it has ADR's outstanding but is unlisted, the OTC market is the place to go; or, should there be no ADR's oustanding, the arbitrage houses will make a market.* Depending on which of these three techniques he utilizes, the purchaser or seller will be faced with different costs.

* See chapter on American Depositary Receipts, p. 284.

Listed foreign securities and some over-the-counter issues usually have sizeable markets and buying and selling them, at least in moderate amounts, presents no problem. The initial price paid would be roughly equivalent to what an Englishman would pay in London. It is the costs of the transactions which differ. An Englishman purchasing British Petroleum in London might pay s.52 per share; 100 shares, before the commission charges, would therefore cost £260 ($728). As noted previously, a direct purchase in London is fractionally cheaper since money, i.e., blocked sterling, sells at a small discount. Thus an American purchasing the same quantity at the same price need only pay—if the blocked sterling exchange rates is $2.7873— $724.70. The saving of $3.30 is the British government's incentive to invest in the United Kingdom, or an indication of foreign confidence in British investments.

For stocks that do not enjoy a transatlantic market, the above procedure becomes somewhat more complicated. The American broker, unable to purchase the stocks domestically, will have to go to a broker specializing in foreign securities. If he does not have it in his inventory, he will probably enter the original market to purchase it. Under the rules of the London Stock Exchange a broker cannot be a member of two Exchanges. Hence, the foreign securities house will have to pay its London colleague the standard London brokerage commission. The investor sustains two commission charges but one is invisible since it is included in the net price.

Besides the possibility of incurring two commissions, there are other costs one should be aware of before purchasing foreign securities on the London Exchange. Basically, there are three dealing expenses in the British market: the broker's commission; the contract stamp duty; the transfer stamp. The latter is always borne by the buyer, so sellers of English shares are faced with only two charges.

Brokerage Commissions

English brokerage rates are somewhat more flexible than American ones. Consequently, dealing can be simultaneously more and less expensive than dealing almost anywhere else. Basically, three commission rates apply to the three main categories of British securities. First and foremost are government securities—a broad group that in British parlance are called somewhat confusingly "stocks." These include not only government issues, issues of dominion and colonial governments, of local authorities, but all issues guaranteed by the British government such as nationalized industries and utilities. All such issues are traded on the floor of the London Stock Exchange and constitute approximately a third of the quoted value of the Exchange. They comprise the "gilt-edged" market and commission rates are the lowest, ⅜ of 1 per cent on the nominal amount of the bonds, not their current value. For purchases over £10,000 ($28,000), only ¼ of 1 per cent on the remainder is charged.

A broker's commission for nongovernment bonds and debentures, whether registered or bearer, is ¾ of 1 per cent on the current value of the bonds. The English refer to this price or value as the "consideration." On common or preferred stock, the commission rate is 1 and ¼ per cent of the consideration, equivalent to three-pence on the pound.

There are basic concessions London brokers are willing to make that act as incentives to investors. Two enticements are of particular interest: for a transaction in one security in which the cost is over £2,500 ($7,000), a full commission must be charged on money up to that amount, but the commission can be reduced by half on the balance.

The other concession, particularly appropriate to the speculator, the indecisive, or the profit taker, is the reduction by half of the commission rate if the same stock is bought and sold, or vice versa, within the same account period. This "free closing" is sometimes offered if the proceeds of a sale are used to re-invest in the next account period as well. If the purchase and sale of two different securities takes place within one or sometimes two accounts, a full commission is charged on the sale and half commission on the new investment. Commission differentials between round and odd lots characteristic of U.S. domestic dealings do not exist in the British market, though there is no end of odd-lot purchasing.

Contract Stamp Duty

The English government lost the American colonies over a stamp duty, but the American Revolution never deterred the government from imposing whole series of domestic stamp acts. English legal and financial documents are bound with enough revenue stamps to make a philatelist's heart jump. Nor is it any different in the securites business. Contract stamp duty is negligible, but the stamp must appear on the contract note which the broker sends the investor. The maximum duty is £2 ($5.60), regardless of the transaction's size.

Transfer Stamp Duty

More onerous than the above, the transfer tax is 1 per cent ad valorem of the purchase price on registered stock. This tax applies only to buying and not to selling shares. It does not apply to British gilt-edged securities or new issues of whatever category.

For an American interested in the British market, it is undoubtedly somewhat cheaper to work directly through a British broker, but not necessarily more convenient. To execute an order, the individual would have to absorb the cost of telephone calls, cables, or airmail. The latter is by far the cheapest alternative and not as inappropriate as would first appear.

A majority of individual British accounts are handled by mail rather than by phone. American brokers situated in London are constantly instructed not to call upon the completion of a trade. The mass of personalized correspondence that a British brokerage house produces would stagger the staff of a Wall Street concern. While timing is an important key to success in the stock market, English investors are less influenced by the daily momentary fluctuations of the market. Therefore, an American investing by mail is under no great handicap.

British and American commission charges are roughly equivalent. Up to August 1963, the ad valorem duty was 2 per cent, a fact that made trading in England more expensive. It is still fractionally more costly, even though sales do not attract the ad valorem charge. Deal-

ing costs, so long as the British government maintains its present 1
per cent ad valorem tax, will be somewhat cheaper in New York.

ENGLISH CORPORATE STRUCTURE

Perhaps the only way to understand the English market, is to try to
see it through the eyes of an Englishman, and the same applies to any
foreign market. English companies are organized in a fashion similar
to that of U.S. corporations. While there are technical differences
in law stemming from tradition, an American investor can feel perfectly at ease in the English corporate structure. His rights and prerogatives are similar, in fact as will be seen, he is even somewhat
better protected.

There is nothing to stop a foreigner establishing a British corporation and Americans investing in Britain are treated precisely as
British citizens—with but one exception. Neither a foreigner nor a
foreign corporation may own a British ship. In practice, this means
that Americans cannot own more than 25 per cent of the stock of
British shipping lines such as Cunard. This is a present-day anachro-
nism.

The earliest form of an English company with an independent legal
life was so endowed by the royal charter. The most famous so far
as Americans are concerned were the early colonial companies of
exploration and settlement. There were never many royal charters
granted, and with the advent of limited liability companies in the
middle of the nineteenth century this form of corporation has fallen
into disuse. Today there are only 20 or so such companies—mostly
banks and insurance companies—that have their origins in a royal
charter. The most prominent one is the Hudson's Bay Company, incorporated in 1670 as The Governor and Company of Adventurers of
England trading into Hudson's Bay. Though still largely English
owned, today the company is the largest department store chain in
Canada.

Close in character to the royal charter companies are the statutory
companies created by an act of Parliament. The Bank of England was
one such company and like most statutory companies has since been

nationalized. The only statutory companies whose shares enjoy a public market of any significance are in the field of waterworks. Future uses may be made of statutory companies for national purposes such as satellite corporations. The nationalized industries have of course ceased to be publicly traded; statutory companies run by the government manage them. The nationalized sector now includes: public transport (railways, railway hotels and properties, buses); gas; electricity; post offices and telephones; the British Broadcasting Corporation; coal; atomic development; the dock labor board, and others.

The limited liability company—known in the United States as the corporation—is the basis of British industrial society. These companies, registered under the 1948 Companies Act, are the chief conduit of private portfolio investments in the United Kingdom. As corporations that can issue stock against their capital—hence the name "joint stock companies"—they have the option to convert themselves to either private or public companies. Private companies, largely family organizations, usually do not offer their shares for sale to the public. However, a few private companies, though not traded on the London Stock Exchange, have shares held by the public. Since there is no public market, transactions take place only rarely. The company will then quote the last price at which stock was bought or sold as a basis for a new price. British brokers are justifiably somewhat skeptical about investing in such companies even though they may have excellent potentials.

The 4,500 companies listed—the English say "quoted"—on the London Stock Exchange, are public companies having issued prospectuses inviting the public to participate in their financing. These companies are restricted to doing business under their articles of association, to doing, in other words, what they originally set out to do, so that "an investor in a gold-mining company does not find himself holding shares in a fried-fish shop." As in the United States, the tendency in recent years is to draft objectives so broadly that companies are legally able to do just about anything, including running a fried-fish shop. Diversification has abetted this process, one not necessarily detrimental to the stockholder. Shares of all the listed companies are not actively traded, but that they are listed and passed upon by the Share and Loan Department of the Exchange gives them a token of soundness and "some evidence of respectability."

The British limited liability company has a capital structure almost identical with that of its U.S. counterpart. Though nomenclature may differ, function is pretty much the same. Loan capital, for instance, is termed "stock;" bonds are primarily foreign debt. Even though function is similar, there are idiosyncracies that will occasionally baffle foreign investors. The London bond market harbors as many varieties as New York, a dozen or so main ones. Until recently, the British government looked askance at bearer bonds, which could easily evade exchange control regulations. Consequently almost all English bonds are in registered form. The servicing of debt usually follows this order: first and second mortgage debentures, prior lien debentures, secured debentures, participating debentures, convertible debentures, unsecured loan stock, convertible loan stock, notes, convertible notes, ad infinitum. Debt funding has been a British specialty and one authority claims they have muddled through 72 different species. It is important therefore to know what other issues have prior claims or *pari passu,* that is, equal rank.

The most senior of British securities are, of course, government funds, the "gilt-edged" market or "consols" market. All but the shortest of government securities, Treasury bills, are quoted on the Stock Exchange. The oldest British bonds are consols 2½ per cent, an abbreviation for the Consolidated Fund of the United Kingdom, which have existed for over two centuries. They are "irredeemable," and pay £2, s.10 ($7.00) annually, though their yield is usually much higher. Whereas American bonds are sold in $1,000 units, English securities are sold in £100 ($280) units.

While all markets tend to act directly proportionately to the cost of money, or prevailing interest rates, the English Exchange is probably more conscious of it than most. Bonds are not only traded in the same room as equities, but when the government decides to change the Bank Rate—the official discount rate—the government broker strides into the center of the Exchange floor, stands on top of a chair and announces the new rate. Of course the association is more than geographic. The Bank of England sets the government interest rate, termed the Bank Rate. Since the Bank is "the creature" of the government, as one of the Chancellors of the Exchequer once remarked, the rate is adjusted to fit the prevailing government's wishes, though actual dictation of the rate is yet unknown.

By raising the Bank Rate say from 4 to 6 per cent the government is in effect making it more expensive to borrow money for expansion of industry, hoping thereby to stop inflationary tendencies in the economy. Alternatively, it might push up the Bank Rate to draw funds to London in aid of sterling or a weak balance of payments position. Conversely, a lower Bank Rate, say from 5½ to 3½ per cent, gives the economy a shot in the arm by making money and credit cheap. Whichever way the rate moves, yields are intimately affected, and so are prices. Other factors such as the economic forecast, government fiscal policy, the public confidence, all help to determine yield, but the Bank Rate is probably the chief factor.

The American equivalent of the Bank Rate is the Treasury discount rate, the rate that the Treasury sells non-interest-bearing, short-term bills to the market, at a discount below par. This discount is, of course, the interest rate that will be felt throughout the fixed interest market. The discount rate is somewhat less important than the Bank Rate since the American monetary system is less monolithic than the British system.

Other day-to-day differences between the British and American bond markets are not great but bear stating. English bonds are classified in four categories. "Longs" are over 15 years to maturity; "mediums" are 5 to 15 years; "shorts" are redeemable within 5 years; "undated" are bonds that have no final repayment date. Flat yields and yields to redemption are figured in much the same manner. However, interest on most English bonds is payable semiannually and yields to redemption are figured in that fashion. Domestically, interest is calculated annually even though payment is usually semiannual.

Another minor difference lies in the accrued interest. Domestically, bonds are traded at a price, plus the interest that is due since the last payment date. Bonds that are in default are traded "flat," that is, with no accumulated interest added since there is none. English bonds, except the "shorts," are always traded "flat," and the price includes the interest due. "Shorts" are traded in the American fashion, the buyer paying the additional interest.

The British government taxes all bonds at the "standard rate," presently 7 shillings 9 pence on the pound, before distributing dividends. However, there are a few government bonds that are paid "tax free" to residents abroad on application to the Inspector of Foreign Dividends, Kingston By-Pass Road, Surrey. The following list of bonds are "free of British taxes" to Americans, though of course are fair game for the federal and state revenue authorities.

Bond	Per Cent	Redemption Date
Funding Loan	5½	1982–1984
Funding Loan	4	1960–1990
Savings bonds	3	1960–1970
Savings bonds	3	1965–1975
Treasury stock	5½	2008–2012
Victory Bonds	4	By 1976
War Loan	3½	(No redemption date)
Savings bonds	3	1955–1965

It should be understood that War Loan 3½ per cent, besides being the largest government issue, is the only one of the above issues to pay interest without deduction of tax to nonresidents who need not make formal application to the Inland Revenue authorities.

There is one difficulty, a major one that should be underscored. Bonds are at the mercy of devaluation and inflation. Britishers and foreigners alike holding "loan stocks" in 1948 when the pound was devalued from $4.86 to $2.80 suffered a loss of 42⅖ per cent. While British credit is sound—after all, *"Dictum Meum Pactum"*—devaluation has been a constant threat to sterling, and a bond investor must keep a critical eye on the British economy and its balance of payments position. The obverse of this observation is that bonds prove to be a poor investment when the value of money is declining. Since the English economy has had one of the slowest growth rates in the postwar years, any attempt to induce higher rates through economic planning is likely to be inflationary and detrimental to bond holders in the long run.

Bonds are widely held, nevertheless, by the British investing public. "They are," one banker remarked half mockingly, "somewhat of a status symbol." Bond dealers are the only ones to sport silk top hats as part of their City uniform.

EQUITIES

Equity or risk capital has the greatest interest to British and foreigner alike, and probably nine-tenths of the financial information published deals with common stock. Again, the names differ slightly but the meaning is clear: common stocks are termed ordinary shares; preferred are preference; and in addition there is one class of stock without an American equivalent, the deferred ordinary. Though this deferred class is less and less used, it ranks after the ordinary shares for dividend distribution. Occasionally private companies going public hope to sweeten their issues by deferring their share of profits until all other equity has been dealt with. The portion of stock they keep for themselves is sometimes called founders shares.

Stocks and shares are interchangeable terms domestically, but to an Englishman they have nuances of meaning harking back to a previous period when the two were quite separate. Stocks were a fixed portion of a joint stock company, usually of large denominations, say £50, £100, or £500. Later, stocks were split into shares of smaller denominations, £1, s.10, s.5, s.2, or any small amount. The differences today are little more than technical and need not concern an investor.

Regardless of what they are called, all British securities have a nominal par value, thus for example British-American Tobacco (s.10) has the nominal value of half a pound. Where no figure is given, the nominal value is £1, such as for Imperial Tobacco.

Though nomenclature is similar, financial analysis is markedly different, standard ratios and guide lines undergoing a mathematical metamorphosis. Perhaps the easiest way to understand the British method is to take a typical quotation from the financial press. The press does not supply quotations on all the securities traded on the market, but only on the more active ones. Prices for a couple of hundred stocks are carried in the tabloids, while the London *Times* or the *Financial Times* run prices for 1,500 or 2,000 stocks.

Stocks are listed in two separate sections: dealings and closing prices. In the first section the previous day's markings are listed—bargains up to 2.15 P.M.—and in addition there are markings from the day before that, which were transacted after 2.15. This arbitrary afternoon break off gives the Stock Exchange time to prepare and collate the markings for the Stock Exchange Daily Official List. When the Exchange is further automated this may be prepared to include the whole day's activities. The second section is divided into a whole series of topical categories such as "hotels and caterers," "greyhound racing," "engineering and metal," etc.

Harveys, the wine merchant, will be found first under dealings where the following marks indicate that the stock was traded, (one can't tell if the trades are purchases or sales) at 25/1½, 24/10½, 5/. No trade is repeated twice though there may have been a dozen transactions at one price. The markings give the stock's price range and constitute a rough indicator as to the stock's activity. Professionals usually multiply by two, estimating that half the bargains go unmarked.

In the other section, closing prices, the following entries were made for Harveys:

High	Low	Stock	Closing Price		+ or −	Dividend or Amount	Times Cov- ered	Gross Yield %
25/4	20/9	Harveys (/5)	24/9	25/3	−/3	14	1.9	2.8

The highs and lows for the year are self-explanatory, but to Americans the rest is not. For the closing price there are two figures: the bid and asked at 3.30 the previous afternoon. The "middle" price an average between these two, is 25, threepence less than the closing price of the day before. Dividends are sometimes expressed as a percentage of nominal value or sometimes in monetary terms. Most often the percentage of nominal value is favored. In the United States, newspapers list the dollar value of the dividend. To determine the relationship of dividend to market or purchase price and express it as a percentage, divide price into dividend. In England, of course, it is basically the same but with the additional factor of nominal value to take into consideration. Usually, the dividend is expressed as a percentage of the nominal value. Hence:

$$\frac{\text{Nominal value} \times \text{Dividend \%}}{\text{Market value}} = \text{Yield \%}$$

For Harveys:

$$\frac{s.5 \times 14\%}{s.25} = 2.8\%$$

In money terms, the dividend would be:

$$0.14 \times s.5 = s.0.7 \text{ or } s.0.7 \times 12 = 8.4 = d.8.3^*$$

If the dividend were given in money terms, the yield would simply be dividend divided by price. As in American practice, the nominal value would not enter into the calculation. Dividends expressed in a percentage of nominal value tend to be deceptive; low par value means high percentages and high par value means low percentages. The important figures are basically the same as they are in the United States; market price, the dividend, and the consequent yield.

The next heading, times covered, is an attempt to gauge how many times a dividend is sheltered or "covered" by the net available earnings as stated in the company's last report. Assume company X earned a profit of £100,000 and distributed it in the following fashion:

Class of Security	Available After Prior Charges	Paid Out	Times Covered
Bond interest	£100,000	£20,000	5
First preference dividend	80,000	10,000	8
Second	70,000	35,000	2
Ordinary	35,000	17,500	2
Reserves	17,500	17,500	—

* Until England adopts a decimal system—they've been thinking about it since the mid-nineteenth century—it must be recalled that it is always necessary to convert percentages of the pound into shillings and fractions of shillings into pence. Since there are 20 shillings to the pound, one must multiply a fraction of the pound by twenty to obtain shillings. The same process must be applied to fractions of shillings. As there are 12 pence to the shilling, one must multiply a fraction of the shilling by 12 to obtain pence. Thus two distinct steps are needed to convert a percentage of the pound sterling to pounds, shillings, and pence.

At first glance, a dividend that is covered twice would seem very secure. If there were no prior charges it would be. This "simple" cover is somewhat deceptive in that a 20 per cent fall in profits would leave the ordinary shares "uncovered." Moreover, the first preference shares are covered eight times, apparently more secure than the bonds which were covered only five times. Obviously, this simple cover can make a mockery of logic. It should only be used as a rough guide.

Parenthetically, the previous example was that of a company with a high leverage factor, i.e., a good deal of debt stood before a relatively small proportion of common stock. Leverage is termed "gearing" in England and it has the same effect as it does in the United States: price fluctuations are more marked than for a comparable company without large debt. The English have put it in verse. "The higher the gearing, the faster the pace/ The lower the gearing, the less to face."

More informative to the investor is the "priority percentage" cover, giving the dividend in terms of per cent due to senior securities. This takes leverage into consideration. The financial press does not give priority percentage cover, but the statistical services do. The above example works out this way:

Class of Securities	Paid Out	Per Cent of £100,000	Priority Percentage
Bond interest	£20,000	20	0 – 20
First preference dividend	10,000	10	20 – 30
Second	35,000	35	30 – 65
Ordinary	17,500	17.5	65 – 82.5
Reserves	17,500	17.5	82.5–100

Though the ordinary shares were covered twice in the simple cover, the priority percentage method clearly shows that the common stock is in a dangerously exposed position: a fall of 20 per cent begins to strip the common of its dividend.

The last column in the financial press, gross yield per cent, was worked out above in the discussion on dividends. Since the British are probably more yield conscious than Americans, their press lists the yields as well.

TAXES: PERSONAL AND CORPORATE

Americans investing abroad should be familiar with the country's general scheme of taxation. Granting the intricacies of domestic taxation, foreign taxation can be doubtly infuriating and seemingly twice as complicated. Luckily, the U.S. government has negotiated a whole series of double taxation agreements with European countries which make life for the foreign investor simple. Such a treaty exists with the United Kingdom, and relief is assured. Rarely is an investor taxed twice.

As noted, Americans have no trouble in repatriating invested funds, dividends, or accrued interest. Capital gains are taxed at home and *not* in Great Britain. The short-term capital gains tax—the British call it a speculator's tax for political reasons—was introduced in 1962 for the first time and does not apply to Americans. Capital losses too are deducted at home. However, the American's dividends have already been taxed by the British government by the time he receives them, and he can claim relief on his federal tax return.

All residents and corporations of the United Kingdom are taxed at a "standard rate," presently s.7, d.9 on the pound. This standard rate might change at the discretion of the Chancellor of the Exchequer, but the principle seems constant.* In other words, for every s.12, d.3 the stockholder receives, the government has been paid an additional s.7, d.9 by the company. English companies act as tax agents for the government withholding the 38¾ per cent of the gross dividend accordingly. Since the British believe in the eminently sound proposition of taxing dividends only once, the shareholder pays no tax on his received dividends, unless he falls into a surtax bracket. Americans holding English shares can claim the 38¾ per cent dividend deduction against their federal taxes, though this is of real benefit only to the individual in a 38¾ per cent or higher tax bracket. For taxpayers in brackets below this "standard rate," the high with-

* The new Labor government elected in October 1964 has proposed to raise the standard rate to s.8, d.3. It will go into effect in April 1965 if Labor retains power.

holding tax works to their disadvantage; the English government will not refund the difference. For instance, a U.S. taxpayer in the 32 per cent federal bracket loses 6¾ per cent of tax credit. Mutual funds and closed-end investment trusts are not eligible for this tax credit since they do not pay taxes directly.

Dividends paid by the company arrive semiannually, often in two unequal portions since it is considered "good form" to end the year with an increased payout. The English fiscal year ends April 5 but this is no guide as to when companies will distribute dividends. The dividend check or warrant has a voucher attached indicating how much of the total dividend has been paid to the government. Some companies do not pay the standard rate of tax because of overseas operations and taxes imposed by foreign governments. Since the English Treasury receives something less than the standard rate, it will allow only what it receives as a tax credit. Consequently these companies have a rate of tax termed the "net U.K. tax rate" stated on the vouchers. The stockholder can only receive tax credits equivalent to this "net U.K. rate." If that rate is, say, s.5, d.9, then only that figure is retrievable credit and not the standard s.7, d.9. In other words, where the "net U.K. tax rate" applies, there is a danger that full tax relief under the double taxation agreement will not be forthcoming.

Occasionally, dividends are declared "free of tax." This is somewhat misleading, for the only sum paid gross is interest on the government bonds previously itemized—and then only upon application to the British tax officials except for War Loan 3½ per cent. "Free of tax" merely indicates that the company has already paid tax in the expected fashion and, all other things being equal, the shareholder can assume that he will not have to pay any further tax. Since taxpayers are informed by their banks or brokers about net dividend, plus how much the company pays the government, there is generally no need for him to "gross up," that is, calculate the company's gross dividend. Moreover, the financial press and the statistical card services supply the gross dividend figure. Once the gross dividend, expressed in percentage, is converted to money terms, it can then be multiplied by the difference between the standard rate of 38¾ per cent, and 100, that is, 61¼, to arrive at net dividend.

PRICE-EARNINGS RATIO

While grossing up is done by the investor at the dividend level, when it comes to earnings per share the given figure may or may not be grossed up, depending upon what one reads. Just as they express dividends as a percentage of par value, the English express profits as a percentage of issued capital. It is important, therefore, to know whether the profits are given before tax (grossed up) or after tax (net). By comparing the earnings to the dividends one can tell how many times the dividend is covered. This is simple cover and not priority percentage cover.

Finally, the sophisticated English investor and his American counterpart want to know the earnings yield or the price-earnings ratio. For Harveys, the earnings percentage is multiplied by the par value and divided by the price:

$$\frac{\text{Earnings \% } \times \text{ Par value}}{\text{Market price}} = \frac{26.6 \times \text{s.5}}{\text{s.25}} = \text{s.5.3 Earnings yield}$$

This earnings yield is simply the reciprocal of the price-earnings ratio:

$$\frac{\text{Price}}{\text{Earnings \% } \times \text{ Par value}} = \frac{\text{s.25}}{26.6 \times \text{s.5}} = 18.8 \text{ Price-earnings ratio}$$

British publications, unless specifically prepared for American readers, tend to calculate from gross earnings and dividends, instead of net, as U.S. statistical information is given. Gross figures as opposed to net statistics are no drawback provided one realizes that they tend to show basic investment ratios in a somewhat strange light; earnings and dividend percentages will be higher, yield will be higher, since it is expressed as a percentage of gross dividend, price-earnings ratio will be lower, and the earnings yield, higher. Therefore, English gross figures, though valid in themselves, are deceptive for comparison with American figures, and the unwary should convert all figures to net terms for common usage.

STOCK SPLITS, RIGHTS ISSUES, AND NEW ISSUES

British companies tend to finance growth from the outside and look to the market for new capital. Faced with the choice of setting aside reserves for expansion or distributing profits, most companies would choose the latter. Munificence pays off. In England, the higher the dividend paid out, the easier it is to obtain financing, and the more eagerly a rights issue will be taken up. In the United States, a growth company does not pay out much; if it does the investor is apt to feel that there is something wrong. The British seemingly reverse the process: often, the faster the growth, the higher the dividend. A company will skip a dividend payment with the greatest reluctance. It may not indicate that something is drastically amiss, but British investors do consider it a warning sign.

Stock splits are not uncommon in the United Kingdom, but are usually called by different names. To begin with, when the English change the capital structure of a company by freely issuing the company's own fully paid shares, such a distribution is called "free," "script," or "bonus" shares. The free or bonus factor is due to their origin—from the reserves of the company. No money changes hands during this capitalization issue. For the 100 shares held previously, a 3-for-2 (150 per cent) capitalization issue would leave the holder with 250 shares. If they were worth s.25 apiece before, they will be worth two-fifths as much after, or s.10.

Domestically, this type of operation is a stock split; the additional shares do not come from reserves but from a division of the nominal capital. The above procedure, a 3-for-2 (150 per cent) capitalization issued is termed a 5-for-2 stock split in the United States. In both cases, the value of the stock is two-fifths its original price and all statistical information will have to be so adjusted.

Rights issues are similar to those in the United States, with but one difference. A United Kingdom company making a rights issue notifies a stockholder or his custodian by "rights letter" or "provisional allotment letter," but may not call for the new issue money until some time later or in a series of installments. These new shares are then traded as "nil" paid or partially paid shares. Such rights are usually dealt on the Stock Exchange free of the 1 per cent stamp duty to the last day for exercising such rights. If an American investor holds ADR's on the company, the SEC prohibits his purchase of rights as the new stock is not registered with the SEC. The depositary is obliged to sell them. For investors with accounts in London, the question is a matter of personal decision. It is completely optional whether the rights are exercised or sold.

In the British market, new issues never had quite the vogue they enjoyed on Wall Street from 1959 to the market break in 1962. Possibly the American market is simply more bullish or the English less growth oriented. While it is not unknown for professionals to apply for new issues *in perpetuum,* ride the crest of initial enthusiasm, and get out quickly, such "stagging" is not as widespread as in the United States. Moreover, English underwriting techniques differ considerably from American practices and act more as a break.

Aside from a rights issue, there are four approaches to raising new capital: a prospectus, an offer for sale, a placing, or an introduction. In issuing a prospectus, the company petitions the public for funds directly, usually without the intermediary of a brokerage house. When an offer for sale is made, an issuing house (a member of the Issuing Houses Association, a merchant bank or broker) takes the distribution problem off the company's hands, buying the whole of the issue and selling it to the public. In both instances, a précis on the company and attached order forms are available, either in the financial press—usually the *Financial Times* or the London *Times*—or from the issuing house. A formidable spate of information and publicity will usually precede both issues.

This is less true of placings and introductions. A placing is made when a broker or issuing house distributes a new block of stock to their clients or places already existing stock at a fixed price. If shares are to be publicly quoted, the Stock Exchange requires information on the security, and a proportion of the placing must go to a jobber so that he may make a market. In the case of a private company the stock is "introduced" to the Stock Exchange and, assuming that Exchange requirements for information and public sale are met, dealing begins on a set date.

The "prospectus" and "offer for sale" generate the greatest interest in Britain. Distribution is completely at random and shares are parceled out purely on chance if the issue is heavily oversubscribed. Unless the company decides beforehand on how shares are to be apportioned, the issuing house will use a pro rata basis or some variant of drawing names from a hat. Thus, an American has as much chance of obtaining new shares as anyone else, provided a British bank or broker takes care of the details, since time is usually crucial.

The public has first call on new issues. However, to guarantee that all shares will be taken up in the case of public indifference or disinterest, the issuing house contracts with large institutions, such as insurance companies, trusts, banks, and pension funds, to take up the slack and "underwrite" the shares. The principle is analogous to the concept of risk in insurance underwriting. For their services, the underwriters are paid a fee, usually hovering around 2½ per cent. The commission rate, in fact, is roughly proportional to the risk. Thus a higher fee may be a danger signal, symptomatic of the underwriter's doubts concerning the security's intrinsic value. As such, a high commission should be regarded with suspicion; by law it may not exceed 10 per cent.

Occasionally, a new issue fires the British investor's imagination and a "queue" will wind around the issuing house, while people wait for application forms. Penguin books was a case in point. A few years ago, pocket books were regarded as a growth industry—after all, probably more books are published per capita in Britain than anywhere else in the world. Moreover, Penguin had just published a pocket-sized *Lady Chatterley's Lover*.

A court case with all the attendant publicity ushered the stock issue into the world, and orders poured in from both Britons and Americans. The issue was oversubscribed some 108 times! The offering was handled by the largest English brokerage firm, a house which sponsors 25 per cent of London's new equity issues, and even it was swamped by the paper work.

Penguin, watching the stampede for shares from the wings, complained that the s.12 issuing price was low. The stock jumped to s.16 the first day, and finally climbed to s.22.

A year later, however, the brokers' judgement on price was vindicated; Penguin was selling at only slightly over s.12. The distribution was handled purely mechanically with no one getting more than 100 shares and even the partners in the brokerage house going away empty handed. New issues are, of course, difficult to judge. There was great demand from both sides of the Atlantic when Wilkinson Sword, the rapidly expanding stainless steel razor blade manufacturer, went on the market. This led the issuing house to price the shares at an exaggerated figure. From the beginning the price of the stock slid and the underwriters had to step into the market.

CONCLUSION

During the 1950s, in the infancy of postwar U.S. investments in Europe, Americans at times miscalculated their moves. Tactical errors were threefold: they came into the market late after a stock had already seen a tremendous rise; they bought in volume without staggering purchases; and some analysts, taking British companies on the one hand and American ones on the other, made analogies between issues that were not strictly comparable. The same miscalculations are still made.

One famous example was that of Unilever, where American buying amounted to over 5½ million shares in the space of a fortnight, and 7½ million by the end of the month. U.S. purchases came *after* the stock had already had a considerable rise. Thus the further upswing was due almost solely to American buying. Once this ceased, without further support, the market dropped.

Many Americans bought without considering price; for instance, thinking in terms of U.S. dollars, many investors gave their brokers 25 to 50 cents discretion on the price of a British share. For U.S. blue chips which range from, say, $50 to several hundred dollars, this differential is negligible. For English equities which are priced much lower, a difference of 2 to 4 shillings is a sizable variation. That much of a jump between "bargains" is unusual.

To take Unilever again as an example, why such concentrated American buying? American analysts, comparing the price-earnings ratio of Unilever with that of Procter and Gamble, found Unilever cheap. However, taking that ratio in absolute terms proved misleading. Seen through British spectacles, the perspective was different. First, the two companies are not strictly comparable, Unilever being by far the more diversified of the two. Second, Americans are growth oriented while the British investor is much more yield conscious. Thus, once American buying pushed up the price, the Englishman looking at the stock objectively saw yield fall off dramatically. The higher the price went the lower the yield dropped. Of course, if a British investor already owned the stock, his *own* yield was not affected but, calculating from market prices, the drop in yield was considered a red flag. Thus Englishmen sold at the height of American buying. The English idea of a sound price-earnings ratio, moreover, falls well below what an American with the American market in mind would judge sound.

The Englishmen's yield consciousness has stood them in good stead on other occasions as well. Viewing the American market after May 1962, Englishmen calculating yields saw them rise significantly. Many Americans without such physical or psychological distance, hesitated, thinking that the market might drop further. Britons, satisfied that return on capital in various U.S. utilities and blue chips was higher than yields in their own pastures, happily bought. Of course, they were not locked in by losses and were free to do so. Distance lent enchantment. In this instance, it also lent a necessary detachment and a cushion from panic at fluctuations.

Another U.S. technique which is not always advantageous in Europe is buying a category, an epithet, a label. For instance, when Electric and Musical Industries stepped into the computer field, great interest developed in the United States. However, EMI owns Capitol Records, and what Americans were in effect buying was a participation in a domestic company, under the mistaken impression that here was a British IBM.

Another case in point is Associated British Foods. Americans picked up the stock because supermarkets were expected to do well in Britain. ABF does have a toehold in retailing—it prides itself on a large number of tea shops which also sell food—but essentially it is Britain's largest baker. "It's a nice solid business, making bread," ventured one broker, "but it's not what you might call 'exciting'." Americans bought for the "excitement."

Yet the American predictions were right in several instances: English Ford and Elliott-Automation did very well indeed. Engilshmen, on the other hand, were sometimes wrong in their own market. The most dramatic instance was perhaps the growth shares that never were. In the 1950s anything ending in "atomic" sold briskly for awhile. Then came the realization that atomic energy was still in the development stage, and electric power from atomic generators was not then and might not be for a decade competitive with power produced by conventional means.

Generally speaking, there is a time lag—between one and five years—between developments in the United States and parallel developments in Britain. After U.S. supermarkets had "peaked out," keeping competition keen only by offering incentives such as stamp plans and other selling gimmicks, self-service stores in Britain were still fairly uncommon. Woolworth and Marks and Spencer are thriving in England, while U.S. discount stores are no longer innovators.

The notion of this time lag is a sound one, but the concept should not be applied mechanically. Each industry must always be seen in the context of British manners and mores. Some, for instance, have no U.S. counterpart. Television and radio rental companies, to illustrate, are unknown in the United States. In England in the past few years, they proved a real growth industry. Of course, in the United States few would think of renting a radio or a television set. It hardly pays; transistors are cheap and TV sets are far from prohibitive. In Britain, luxury taxes on electrical goods, now at 25 per cent, were until recently, 40 percent. Moreover, with plans afoot to change the TV screen to make color transmission and European reception possible, few Englishmen felt like investing in a potentially obsolete set. Thus rental companies did very well indeed.

Even parallel institutions are seldom what they seem. For instance, the English development of property companies is far more sophisticated than the American counterpart of developing real estate. They were one of the more interesting growth situations in the late 1950s and early 1960s. The same might also be said of English mutual funds and closed-end trusts, known as "unit trusts" and "investment trusts," respectively.

Over 250 closed-end investment trusts are quoted on the London Exchange. They have a wide following, due in part to their long history but also in part to the high leverage factor inherent in some of their capitalizations. Some investment trusts derive half their funds from bonds. Parenthetically, many of the old Scottish trusts have a third or more of their investments in America. By law, investment trusts are not allowed to use capital profits for dividend distribution, but only for bonus issues. Some trusts have 300 to 500 companies in their portfolios and provide easy participation in the British economy.

Not as popular in the United Kingdom as they are in the United States, unit trusts–mutual funds—are growing rapidly owing to middle-class support. Shares are usually bought from and sold to the managers of the trust, the price depending on the market value of the underlying shares. There are approximately 63 unit trusts in existence in the United Kingdom. In the last few years a successful hybrid has grown up, as some unit trusts have developed portfolios of investment trust shares.

Just as the English have a long history of investing in the United States, the United States has an equally important stake in the British economy. Reportedly, direct American investments in England from 1950 through 1962 increased four and one-half times. Another study indicates that British investments in the United States are $6.3 billion, whereas American investments in Britain come to $5 billion. In fact, American holdings in the United Kingdom account for nearly half of American investments in Europe, as a whole. Undoubtedly future American commitments will be made even though Britain's recent growth rate is perhaps one of the slowest in Western Europe. Due to a relatively dear money policy imposed by the last Conservative government, gross domestic fixed capital formation as a per cent of the GNP is lower than in any country in Western Europe except Ireland.

In other words, capital investments are roughly 5 per cent lower than those of the Common Market countries. Nor do the projections by the Twentieth Century Fund seem to alter this picture in any great detail. Though Britain's GNP is relatively high per capita, there are still a dozen nations ranking ahead of the United Kingdom if measured on a world scale.

The perpetual difficulty in England's balance-of-payments position is to a large degree a reflection of her technical conservatism. The fastest growing technological areas which have spurred other nations' balance-of-trade positions are precisely those in which the English economy has shown the least response. For instance, scientific instruments, office machinery, electronic measuring devices, plastics, photographic supplies, organic chemicals, and synthetic fibers are among the fastest growing groups for modern industrial nations. In the older areas where British engineering seniority has carved a niche for itself —such as electrical equipment, shipbuilding, and locomotive construction—the British position continues strong. But it is these categories of trade which presently grow least rapidly. One economist summed it up: "There is thus, over the whole field of trade in manufactures, a systematic relationship: the faster world demand is expanding for a product group the more inferior is Britain's share in that market." Yet, the British economy will undoubtedly catch up with the most advanced nations in the West. She has the will, the technical skill, a strong and diversified economy, the world's largest merchant fleet, a growing relationship with the Continent and a sophisticated financial center. Besides, she makes her best showing in the face of adversity.

SOURCES OF INFORMATION

An investor wishing to delve more deeply for information can easily find more data than is given in the financial pages. The majority of English securities traded in London are recorded daily in the *Stock Exchange Daily Official List*. This list is supplemented monthly by a list of inactive shares. Two card services are widely used in the United Kingdom. While they are similar to American services, they tend to present only the pertinent facts and latest company statements; opinions as to whether the shares should be bought, sold, or held are not offered. The Exchange Telegraph Company Ltd. offers a wide combination of daily statistical cards and auxiliary cards of a more descriptive nature on United Kingdom, European, and Australian companies. Moodies Services Ltd., offers an equivalent service, but American investors are requested to ask Moodies' American affiliate to supply the United Kingdom cards. Some of the larger brokerage houses also have limited card services besides their market letters.

Newspapers and magazines provide commentary and criticism that is invigorating by American standards. The press acts as a public defender and tends to be far more outspoken and critical of company policies than their American counterparts. The *Wall Street Journal,* for instance, though highly articulate on political issues and government economic policy, tends to keep its opinions on company matters to itself. American journalism bows to facts and objectivity; its job is to present the information and let the reader interpret it as he will. British financial journalism is of a more crusading kind. English journalists put the cards on the table and have led many a battle on behalf of the investor when they felt management was mistreating him. The *Financial Times* is perhaps the best financial newspaper in Europe. It may advise investors not to accept a recapitalization plan or sanction a take-over bid. For the American 3,000 miles away, such militancy is a welcome eye opener.

For good balanced background information—often as extensive on American and European aspects as on the British—four weekly periodicals do a superior job: the *Economist,* the *Investors' Chronicle,* the *Stock Exchange Gazette,* and the *Statist.*

By assiduously reading the English financial press, Americans can be as well informed as the British investor, and such reading will go a long way toward tempering preconceptions and mistaken comparisons.

A company's annual report will also furnish a variety of insights. An American should experience little difficulty with English reports, since English and American accounting techniques are much the same though terminology may differ slightly. The first thing to note is that, as the English drive on the opposite side of the street, they also reverse their balance sheets with the assets on the right and the liabilities on the left. Almost everything else is self-explanatory; current assets are "fixed" assets, surpluses are "reserves," etc. For the financial analyst the only information English companies do not as yet reveal is turnover. However, even this is changing among the larger firms.

Perhaps as important as balance sheets and profit-and-loss statements is a technique to which English board chairmen are becoming addicted, the annual review. Discounting the public relations aspect of the review, occasional kernels of information appear that give a clue to the company's prospects. Such annual reviews are usually printed in the financial press as advertisements, often flanked by an editorial critique pointing out the strengths and weaknesses.

Most of the above-mentioned newspapers and magazines have their own stock indexes. Those published by the *Financial Times* are usually cited as the main market barometers. The *Financial Times'* Industrial Ordinary Share Index is made up of 30 "blue chips," a cross-section of the English economy at one time. It is not as representative as it might be, since the included companies are fairly staid and stable concerns. Moreover, some types of shares are not represented at all, such as property companies, entertainment, insurance, banks, and financial firms. The *Financial Times* notes that it's index is geometric, "the prices of the constituent stock are . . . multiplied together and the result is then expressed as a percentage of the answer which was obtained by the same process on the 'base date.' " The index base of 100 dates from July 1, 1935. A yield figure is also published daily for the index.

On April 10, 1962, parenthetically the start of the English short-term capital gains tax, the *Financial Times* began publishing the Actuaries Share Indexes. These are four separate indexes covering a much wider field than the Industrial Ordinary Index: a 500 industrial equity index; a financial group index of 94 companies; a commodity index; a fixed interest index. These indexes are calculated by using the "total market valuation—share price multiplied by number of shares in issue . . . at the base date is represented by an index number of 100."

SOURCES OF INFORMATION

There are a great number of books on English finance and on the British economy. Consequently, any brief bibliographical note is bound to be arbitrary and incomplete. For an introduction, the following should prove helpful:

ARMSTRONG, F. E. *The Book of the Stock Exchange.* 5th ed. London: Sir Isaac Pitman & Sons, Ltd., 1961. An old but useful guide to the London Stock Exchange.

FERRIS, PAUL. *The City.* London: Victor Gollancz, Ltd., 1960. A lively, journalistic view of the whole financial community.

THE FINANCIAL TIMES. *An Investors Guide.* London: 1961. Perhaps the most useful and authoritative book on English techniques.

GREAT BRITAIN. *Report of the Committee on the Working of the Monetary System.* Cmnd. 827. London: Her Majesty's Stationery Office, 1959.

HARROD, ROY. *The British Economy.* New York: McGraw-Hill, 1963.

MORGAN, VICTOR E., and THOMAS, W. A. *The Stock Exchange: Its History and Functions.* London: Elek, 1962. A new history of the London Stock Exchange.

PAISH, F. W. *Studies in an Inflationary Economy; the United Kingdom 1948–61.* New York: St. Martin's Press, 1962.

ROSE, HAROLD B. *Economic Background to Investment.* Cambridge: Institute of Actuaries and the Faculty of Actuaries, 1960. An excellent academic study that may tell the average investor more than he may care to know.

SAMPSON, ANTHONY. *Anatomy of Britain.* London: Hodder and Stoughton, 1962. An encyclopedic effort to sketch English society including England's financial establishment.

SAYERS, R. S. *Banking in Western Europe.* Oxford: Clarendon Press, 1962.

WALLACE, CARLTON, ed. *The Investor's Pocket Book.* London: Evans Brothers Ltd., 1960.

... les cours de la Bourse sont affaires d'opinion. Ils reflètent les idées, les imaginations sombres ou riantes. ... *

—Bainville, *Fortune de la France*

2. FRANCE

Entre le potage et le fromage, on fait du courtage.†
—Anonymous

Every weekday, at an hour when every other normal Frenchman is about to sit down to his leisurely two-hour lunch, groups of men emerge from the *bouche de métro, Bourse,* and from adjoining streets to converge on a newly cleaned Corinthian temple which dominates the Place de la Bourse. They are the *agents de change* and their clerks ready for the daily two-hour—12:30 to 2:30—trading session on the Paris Stock Market.

Surrounded by a huge colonnade and flanked on its four corners by colossal figures of "Fortune," "Abundance," "Justice," and "Prudence," the temple stands several feet above street level. It looks down on a *pissoir,* several banks, a number of cafés, and a building owned by the *Chambre Syndicale des Agents de Change,* the professional association of brokers. To be an agent de change is a governmental privilege and is restricted today to 86 individuals. They are the only legitimate intermediaries who may trade in stocks and shares, and orders are funneled through them by banks and various other institutions which dominate the French financial scene.

The Bourse itself does not radiate the sense of power and money which permeates Wall Street or the City in London. The neighborhood,

* ... trends on the Exchange are matters of opinion. They reflect ideas and intuitions that are somber or promising. ...
† Between soup and cheese, we trade.

63

in fact, houses textile wholesalers, newspaper offices and, on the noisy boulevard a few blocks up, movie houses and girlie shows as well as the large *brasseries* with their pin ball machines. The rue Vivienne facing the Bourse is lined with moneychangers displaying every variety and denomination of gold coin imaginable. The sign on the door reads in bold type, "For a Gift Give Gold" and assures, "Complete Anonymity Guaranteed in the Purchase of Money and Gold." A Paris streetsweeper with his broom of tied twigs leaning against the building makes a careful list: a ¼ Pahlevi, a very small Iranian coin is worth FF22, ($4.49); a Peruvian soles, FF410 ($83.67); Austrian ducats go for FF110 ($22.44), and gold Napoleons are worth FF440 ($89.58). Experts estimate that the amount of gold hidden away or buried in France is nearly equal to total banknotes in circulation. The moneychangers thus do as brisk a business as the boursiers across the street.

Before settling in its present location, the Paris Bourse had a peripatetic existence. Louis VII in 1141 centralized trading in *change,* letters of credit, moving the dealers from the great medieval fairs to the stately Grand Pont of Paris. The latter was renamed Pont-au-Change, but two or three centuries later the market moved to rue Quincampoix where John Law, a Scotsman, provided France with her first taste of wild speculation in the early eighteenth century. The government closed the Exchange as a result of Law's activities, a procedure it has favored every time speculation has become excessive. Repeatedly, however, the Bourse was reopened after such events; it was apparent that "not by breaking the thermometer can you cure the fever."

During the French Revolution all stock companies were outlawed and the Bourse consequently went out of business. When it reopened a few years later, it continued its peregrinations: the Louvre, Palais Royal, an abandoned church, a depot of the Paris Opera formerly used to store scenery. The final move was made in 1826 into the building it now occupies.

Built at Napoleon's order on the site of the former convent of the Daughters of St. Thomas, the Bourse has always been out of bounds for women. Anyone in "the full possession of their civil and political rights" may enter the Bourse. So ruled the early governors of the Paris Stock Exchange. Women were thus *personae non gratae,* along with bankrupts and criminals. Though their status was to change over the next century and a half, the distaff bar remains in force, though technically unenforceable. Today, French women have most of their civil rights, but not all. (Unless a woman insists on a division of property clause in the marriage contract, she may not open a savings bank account, own stock, or even acquire a library card without her husband's written permission.) But any Frenchman who wishes to talk to his broker or simply watch his order being executed, may wander in.

On an average day, a couple of thousand visiting citizens mingle with brokers, clerks, and officials of the Bourse, trying to "get the feel of the market." Before long, the heavy, pungent smoke of French cigarettes fills the trading rooms and noise levels become intolerable. Not only is the Exchange noisier than New York's or London's but it is also in constant motion. Whereas Anglo-Saxon custom forbids members to run on the floor, in France running, pushing, and shoving are the order of the day. Moreover, Mediterranean informality extends to the haberdashery as well, and bankers' blacks are rare.

THE BROKERS

Before January 1962, there were two separate though simultaneous markets: the *Parquet,* the official market of older and more thoroughly tested securities, domain of the agents de change, the official stock brokers; and the *Coulisse,* orginally a curb-like mart of newer growth issues held in the antechambers of the Bourse. The traders of the Coulisse, *courtiers en valeurs,* brokers by penchant rather than administrative fiat, were often more dynamic than the official brotherhood trading within.

With the Bourse reform of 1962, the agents de change absorbed their competitors and the two markets merged. Presently, 86 agents de change or brokerage firms, buy and sell the 4,000 securities listed on the French Bourse and on the *hors cote,* the over-the-counter market. Anyone wishing to transact business in stocks and bonds, whether an individual or a bank, must go through them. Appointed by the President of the Republic and approved by the Minister of Finance, the agents de change were heirs to a privilege handed down from father to son since 1639. Since the 1962 reform, however, they must pass a competitive examination. Brokers enjoy a privilege, a title, and a monopoly, but they are not in the government's employ; their income derives solely from commissions.

Privilege, however, carries with it certain limitations. An official broker must restrict himself to trading in gold and securities for clients' accounts. Like a physician or lawyer, an agent de change is sworn to professional secrecy and cannot be called upon to reveal his customers' identity, except by court subpoena. An agent de change may not participate in any other business, nor may he advertise his calling, not even to the extent of a name plate on the street. Most agents easily circumvent this ruling by hanging their plates in the omnipresent Parisian courtyard, a few steps from the street. Though they may advise clients in private or on request furnish detailed studies, agents de change may not publish advice. Most of them do not publish market letters, and those that do—about 25 per cent—publish little more than a synopsis of the week's financial press.

A broker's clients are secure in their dealings since the Chambre Syndicale assumes full responsibility in case of failure by one of their members; clients are reimbursed at current market prices. Moreover, brokers must meet certain governmental requirements; a minimum capital of FF200,000 ($40,816) of which the agent de change must personally control 25 per cent. Brokers cannot trade for their firm's account but, of course, do act as principals for their own private dealings.

Though the firm is always named after the ministerial appointee, associates termed *fondés de pouvoir* are common. They bring capital into the firm and get a share of the profit but, unlike the agent de change himself, enjoy a liability limited to their share in the business. "It is really the only sane way to be a broker," remarked one of the more aggressive fondés de pouvoir.

THE MARKET

There are two ways of dealing in France. The investor can put francs on the table and purchase stock in the cash market, the *Marché au Comptant,* or he can deal for settlement at the end of the month in the forward market, the *Marché à Terme.* The cash market is used primarily by two types of investors: purchasers of government bonds, all but four of which are dealt exclusively on this market, or of certain industrial debentures; and those who would purchase small quantities of equity, less than a round lot of 25 shares. Trading in odd lots is always more costly and thus it is slightly more expensive to pay cash, as commission rates on this market are somewhat higher. All listed securities may be bought on the cash market. However, all the blue chips and many other securities can be purchased on either the cash or the forward market.

Today, the normal way of dealing is on the forward market but, historically speaking, precedent is recent. First outlawed in 1724, the Marché à Terme was also considered immoral by Napoleon, at least, history has it, till a conversation with a contemporary boursier, Boscary de Villeplaine:

Sire, when my water carrier comes to my door, does he commit a crime if he sells me two barrels when he has but one on hand?
Certainly not. He is always certain of finding more in the river.
Well Sire, consider the Bourse; it is like a river of stock!

The Emperor was evidently convinced but the law was changed only in 1885. The forward market now comprises several subdivisions: the "firm" forward market, or *Grand Terme,* with stock purchased for settlement at the end of the month; and the option market, for settlement sometime within a three-month period, the maximum for French options. There is also a *Petit Terme,* or little forward market, but this is merely used to designate a group of securities on which no options are available. These comprise secondary companies and transactions must be completed at the end of the terme, usually around the 25th of the month.

There are several distinct methods of arriving at prices in the

Bourse; *à la criée,* used in the forward market; *cotation par opposi-tions* and *cotation par casiers* used in the cash market.

The central hall of the Exchange, a vast room rising to the roof, contains a series of round clusters around a central circle where the blue chips are traded on a term basis. Termed the *Corbeille,* or basket, it is the focus of the Bourse. Here prices are arrived at by yelling, screaming, stamping, and caterwauling: in brief, it is an auc-tion market, termed à la criée. By each major grouping, a signboard is prominently displayed with a list of the thirty or so stocks being traded. As the session opens, a clerk tries to match most buy and sell orders to arrive at a first price that will satisfy the greatest number of orders. When such a price is reached, it is underlined on the board and all trades are then completed at that price. If Rhône-Poulenc, a leading chemical producer, opened at FF335, those who wanted to buy at a limit of 330 will not have their orders executed, nor will those who wanted to sell at 340. In other words, limit orders can be used, though most French investors deal at the opening price when the market is usually broadest, or at the best price, i.e., the prevailing one. "Stop-loss orders," though not a favored technique, can be used.

Generally, market orders should specify not only the usual details, i.e., purchase or sale and the number of shares involved, but several other details as well: execution on the cash or the forward market, at the opening price, at "best" or at a limited price of X, and how long the order should be considered valid. Orders can be good for one Bourse session, until a given date, or until the end of the Bourse settlement month, but they automatically terminate at the end of the monthly account.

This auction system is extraordinarily fair to investors; they can be sure they are paying or receiving no more than any other investor in the market at the same time. If there is not enough stock to go around, everyone receives the same proportion of stock. However, it is slow and cumbersome and only one stock is traded at a time.

Each of the thirty blue chips has its opening price set in turn. When the process is finished—usually it takes a half hour—the list is begun all over again. On a typical day, the list is run through three or four times.

On the cash market, another method is used: la cotation par opposition, or matching orders. Brokers write their orders on slips, a clerk collects them and determines the extreme limits of the market. An official then designates a price at which most orders can be met. It is essentially the same as the à la criée method, but faster and less noisy.

A third variation of arriving at a price is also used in the Comptant, the cash market: cotation par casiers, in which order slips are collected, and deposited in pigeonholes. At the end of the day a broker matches them. Stocks on the cash market are usually dealt in odd lots, that is units of less than 25 shares, though they may be either blue chips or smaller companies. As this is a somewhat more volatile market—especially in the stocks of smaller companies—foreign orders or large orders are rarely executed on it. Dealings in the cash market are for immediate settlement.

On the forward market, firm commitments, that is, purchases or sales that will be concluded at the end of the month, must be covered by a deposit of securities or cash with the broker or bank. Though subject to change, the present requirements call for 70 per cent of the value of the transaction in listed stocks or 45 percent of the transaction entirely in cash. In brief, a purchase through a French broker requires collateral, a rate set by the two official bodies of the Bourse.

Should one desire to carry forward an open position through the following account period, it is possible to do so. This is similar to carrying over, or contango techniques in the United Kingdom. If you are a purchaser who does not wish to pick up the stock and you find a seller who does not wish to deliver within the month, a *report,* a carrying forward can be arranged. No extra costs are involved if buyers match sellers. If this is not the case, interest will have to be paid—usually between 1¼ and 5 per cent a year. In addition, since the report is technically a sale and an immediate repurchase in the new account, or vice versa, there are brokerage and tax fees to be paid by the purchaser although fractionally less than ordinary brokerage. For bookkeeping purposes, the stock sale and repurchase is at a fixed price set by the Bourse, termed the *compensation rate.* It is close to the market price but not identical with it. Depending on whether the stock has risen or not, your account is then credited or debited accordingly. Monthly figures are published on carry-over rates. Under this setup, no difference exists between long and short sales for carrying over; one is as easy as the other.

OPTIONS

An active option market exists in Paris, one that is often used by Frenchmen for current speculation. Reportedly, some Frenchmen have two accounts: one in Paris for the broad market in options, and one in Switzerland for long-term investments. The Paris option market is geared to sell only "call" options. "Calls" are sold for a day or for a maximum of three months. There are no special option houses. Instead, clients arrange with their respective agent de change or bank to sell options on stocks they own. "This appears to be the most profitable side of the option business," one French banker remarked. The seller is guaranteed a profit on his stock, plus the additional incentive of the contract money. There are more Frenchmen wishing to purchase call options than to sell them.

Options have only one settlement date, the *jour de la réponse des primes,* when one must either pick up the option or let it pass. Different costs, reflecting tax and brokerage, are charged depending whether an option is picked up or abandoned. Though costs differ, they are usually much cheaper than American rates. This has led to the buying and selling of call options on the four listed American securities on the option market: American Telephone and Telegraph, du Pont, Franco Wyoming Oil, and IBM.

CLEARING OPERATIONS

French securities, with the sole exception of insurance shares are in bearer form and must be safely tucked away. The difficulty here is that coupon clipping and rights issues that fall due on specific dates can be easily missed. To avoid these problems and facilitate clearing operations, a central clearing device was devised in 1949, called SICOVAM, Société Interprofessionnelle pour la Compensation des Valeurs Mobilières. Each agent de change or bank has an account with this central nominee, a semigovernmental agency, and transactions are simply credited and debited to his account. This makes purchases or sales a simple bookkeeping matter, and shares do not physically change hands. While it is not compulsory to hold one's shares in a SICOVAM account, most Frenchmen find it convenient and cheaper. Thus they need not be concerned with dividend collection, coupon clipping or other details for either French or foreign securities. Foreigners can also leave their shares in SICOVAM. However, for institutions and funds that are obliged under American law to have their shares held by an American depositary, removing the securities from SICOVAM presents no problems. Of course, the investor always retains beneficial ownership of the shares deposited with SICOVAM.

OPERATIONS OF THE BOURSE

The Paris Bourse is under the immediate jurisdiction of two official bodies: the Chambre Syndicale de la Compagnie des Agents de Change, the professional organization of brokers; and the Comité des Bourses de Valeurs, an outside body appointed by the Finance Minister and presided over by the Governor of the Banque de France. This latter group decides on what stocks will be admitted to quotation on the Bourse, what foreign stocks should be listed, collateral rates for dealing in the forward market, and, jointly with the Chambre Syndicale, decides on brokerage rates.

The Chambre Syndicale is more immediately concerned with the market. It can and does stop trading if price differentials become excessive in a selling wave—more than an 8 per cent drop in the forward market, or 3 per cent for bonds, 4 per cent for stocks in the cash market. They publish a daily official list, the *Bulletin de la Cote, Cours Authentique et Officiel,* which groups stocks by industrial categories and gives all other relevant technical information: a calendar of settlement days; the carrying forward rate, or *taux des reports;* and on the back page, a list of the agents de change and the prevailing brokerage rates. Transactions on the regional bourses—Lyon, Marseille, Lille, Bordeaux, Nancy, Nantes, and Toulouse—are also given in the back pages of the *Bulletin*. The Chambre Syndicale also sponsors a daily recorded telephone information service as well as radio and television broadcasts of the day's prices. However, the Chambre has not adopted any public relations program nor does it publish any material for the general public.

Without doubt, the French Bourse is highly supervised and controlled, and an investor of any nationality can rely on the correctness of Bourse transactions. This is the function of the agents de change as ministerial officials, in fact, their only function. Indeed, the banks have limited the brokers' role, making sure they do not tresspass on any bank functions, such as investment advice.

Commission Rates

In the cash market the rate for government bonds is either 3 or 4.5 per mill depending upon the type of bond. Industrial bonds are 5 per mill. Common stock and foreign shares are 7 per mill. There is a stamp duty of 3 per mill on bonds and 6 per mill on stock.

On the term or forward market the rate for French government bonds is 2 per mill whereas industrial bonds are 4 per mill. Common stock has a commission fee of 5 per mill. The stamp duty is 1.5 per mill for bonds and 3 per mill for stock. All commission rates are on the market value of the securities.

FRENCH CORPORATE STRUCTURE

According to the French Commercial Code, only two types of companies may issue shares: the *société anonyme,* the corporation, the most common garden variety of business organization in France; and the *société en commandite par actions,* a hybrid form which, though technically a partnership, has some of the characteristics of a corporation. For instance, Compagnie Générale des Etablissements Michelin, long known to tourists for its excellent guidebooks, is organized as a société en commandite par actions. The company accounts for 55 per cent of French tire production and 30 per cent of Europe's as a whole. For a company of this magnitude to be organized as a partnership is rare, but it does happen, even among France's largest industrials.

The stock of both types of companies is negotiated on the Bourse and, as far as the stockholders are concerned, confer identical rights. However, a company's charter may differentiate among diverse categories of shares. The most common types of shares are *les actions de capital,* or common stock, and *les actions privilégiées,* or a type of preferred shares. However, a charter may also include others. Founders' shares, *parts de fondateurs,* created without any incease in capital, but given to reward loyal service, may also exist. They share in a portion of the profits, the percentage varying from company to company. In one company, for example, 75 per cent of the profits might go to stockholders, 25 per cent to the fondateurs—but sometimes the founders' cut is much less. Needless to say, the fondateurs' percentage must be subtracted from the company's total profits to get the dividend of the shares.

L'action de jouissance, a share similar to common stock, also exists, but is a vanishing form. Sometimes a company uses its reserves to reimburse shareholders for the par value of their stock, without divesting them of voting rights. For the tax collector, the actions de jouissance are considered to derive from a distribution of profits, rather than from capital.

In France, the general rule is one share, one vote. However, there are exceptions. Compagnie Générale des Etablissements Michelin, the holding company which manages manufacturing and distribution in metropolitan France, for example, has A and B shares, the A shares carrying a double vote and preferential rights. There is also a prewar law, destined to prevent control of French companies from falling into German hands, which grants French owners a double vote as against non-French owners. This clause, though seldom used, continues on the books.

French corporations, though roughly equivalent to their American counterparts, do have characteristic differences. For instance, a French corporation's capital equals the par value of the stock outstanding; no-par value stock is an unknown concept. All shares must be fully paid for within five years, or sooner if there is to be an increase in capital. Fixed by the charter, the company's capital can be increased only by a shareholders' meeting and a vote to amend that document. Before this is possible, all existing shares must be fully paid up. New shares once subscribed to, must be paid for according to a pre-arranged timetable respecting the terms of the issue. A subscriber, for example, may put up 25 per cent of the market price of a new share by a fixed date. Six months later, he may be called on for further outlays. In the meantime, of course, the partially paid new stock is negotiable. But unlike most French stock which is in bearer form, it remains in registered form until fully paid.

Partially paid shares are characteristic of French insurance companies and are symptomatic of European insurance shares generally. Such shares are always in registered form for, in case of need, the company can call on its shareholders for further outlays of moneys. In practice, of course, this is rarely necessary and would normally mean that a company is doing badly or is on the verge of bankruptcy. Nevertheless, for this reason, many insurance companies restrict the sale of their shares to residents and sometimes to nationals of the country. In France, insurance companies comprise the only category of companies to be thus out of bounds to foreigners, and even here the statutes must be consulted, as the exclusion is not universal.

Much as in the United States, French companies utilize two methods of increasing their capital. The first technique is a distribution of free, or bonus shares, through *droits d'attribution,* which resembles a stock split or stock dividend. For the company, this distribution of shares is a bookkeeping operation, the new shares having been created out of earned surplus, *réserves.* It does not bring the company any more money, but gives shareholders an increased amount of stock. As French stocks hover at fairly high price levels, the effect is a welcome one; usually the price per share drops, often bringing more within the range of the smaller, nonprofessional investor. Distributions of free shares are thus encouraged as a means of increasing public participation.

The second device is a rights offering, a shareholder being offered a new share for so many old shares. These rights to subscribe to the new shares are negotiable and are quoted in the Official List under the category of *droits de souscription*. Technically speaking, the company's increase of capital is considered an accomplished fact only at the end of the 20- or 30-day subscription period. However, before that time has elapsed, the new shares can be traded as *promesses d'actions*. These too, are listed in the daily Official List.

THE BOND MARKET

"Can it be more difficult to govern this little corner of Paris called la Bourse than to govern France?"—Napoleon

The future Emperor of France decided that the price of government paper should reflect the glory and prestige of France, and thus appointed himself sole arbiter of the bond market. But the task proved more difficult than he had forseen. Napoleon was confronted with a selling wave; the bears were speculating against the government. No sooner had the peace with England been signed at Amiens in 1802 than, barely a year later, England broke the agreement. Moreover, the Germanic princes were at odds, the Dutch restive, the Swiss in difficulty, and there was a Bourbon plot to assassinate Napoleon.

To stem the tide at the Bourse, the Treasury poured in 50,481,531 francs. Slowly the market climbed; a French government loan worth 51 francs in 1803 soared to 80 francs by 1808. The Emperor was jubilant. Apparently, he considered this victory over the marketplace as important as any over the Russians or Austrians.

The modern bond market today is a far cry from Bonaparte's. However, two factors remain the same: a sensitivity to assassination attempts against the head of state, and a public reluctance to buy bonds. Of course, since 1958, France has been favored by unparalleled prosperity and a strong currency. The inflationary whorl has declined. Nevertheless, the experience of previous generations which had two or three times seen inflation dissolve the benefits of long-term investments dies hard. A folk witticism has it that *"les salaires montent par l'escalier, et les prix par l'ascenseur"* (wages go up by the stairs, while prices take the elevator), and statistics bear it out. Indeed, statisticians have calculated that the purchasing power of

1,000 francs was so drastically reduced that, in 1959, 1,000 francs could just about buy what 5 francs bought in 1914.

Thus public reticence continues and unless bonds offer some incentives, such as premiums at maturity, bonuses, and other special benefits, they are difficult to sell. For this reason the financial pages display a perplexing plethora of bonds. Besides classical corporate debentures, there are also indexed bonds, participating bonds, convertible bonds—which though well known in the U.S. have only recently made their appearance in France—and a multitude of government obligations. A partial list would include the following government obligations:

1. *Rentes perpétuelles,* bonds without a redemption date, such as the 3 per cent and 5 per cent of 1949

2. *Rentes amortissables,* bonds which have a sinking fund arrangement and can be repaid before their maturity

3. *Fonds garantis,* government guaranteed loans.

To encourage the sale of government bonds to the public, many rentes, government paper, are exempt from the purchase tax imposed on other securities, and are often free from inheritance tax, income or surtax, and sometimes both.

Until 1958 runaway inflation was a constant threat, therefore many bond issues floated before that date are tied to various indexes. If the index goes up, interest and sometimes the bond's redemption value go up proportionately. The 3.5 per cent 1952–1958 loan, for instance, is tied to the price of a gold Napoleon in the Paris gold market; others are tied to the cost-of-living index; and the 5 per cent national loan of 1956 is tied to a stock price index, and so forth. Bonds issued by the nationalized industries are often tied to that industry's service or product, that is, the price to the harassed consumer of such sundries as a kilowatt-hour of electricity, a cubic meter of gas, a ton of coal, and railroad tickets.

Indexation sometimes pays off handsomely. A case in point were some 3 per cent bonds of the Caisse Nationale de l'Énergie. Interest rates and value at maturity were both tied to the cost of gas and electricity to the consumer. These bonds got a 1 per cent cut of the gross receipts of Électricité de France and of Gaz de France. Thus in 1958, the 3 per cent interest cum bonus came to FF555 and repayment of the FF10,000 nominal bonds was fixed at FF19,454. However, General de Gaulle in 1958 decreed that in the future indexation would be legal only under very limited circumstances and subject to Ministry of Finance approval. No new loans with such index arrangements have been floated since, as indexing was itself considered a factor in the inflationary spiral.

The old indexed bonds are, of course, still sold and would at first glance seem privileged and most profitable. However, the market tends to neutralize their advantage. Sometimes, these issues will simply be more expensive, selling at a premium above par, but most frequently there is a difference in interest. Indexed bonds pay around 3 per cent, while nonindexed issues will return 5 or 6 per cent. It is then a matter of calculating probabilities: will the index rise faster and thus afford more than a 5 or 6 per cent return, or is it better to opt for a straight percentage now rather than a possible bonus later?

Another interesting category of bonds are the *obligations à lots,* bonds issued by Crédit Foncier, Crédit National, the municipality of Paris, and sometimes by the railroads, which are retired each year by a chance drawing of lots. Besides repayment of the face value of the bond, the winner is also entitled to a reward. By introducing this sporting element into the market, these institutions have enjoyed great public success. After all, aren't these merely more costly tickets than those sold by the Loterie Nationale? In fact, there is a marked tendency for people to enter the contest by buying these obligations à lots before the drawing and selling them immediately afterwards. However, the investor must purchase his bonds 13 Bourse days before the drawing to be able to participate. A foreign investor too can mathematically calculate his odds of winning, or if he wishes to buy cheaply, go against the crowd.

Another technique unknown in the United States, but utilized increasingly in France is the issuance of industry-wide bonds. The synthetic chemical industry, for instance, floated a $15 million, 18-year debenture in 1961. The bonds pay 5 per cent and in addition a premium of 14.6 per cent over the issue price will be paid at maturity. The advantage of these bonds is that both the interest and the repayment of the principal are tax-free. However, the sizable premium to be paid at maturity is typical of the more classical corporate debentures, *les obligations industrielles,* and will be evident even among the blue chips. Finally, for the internationally minded investor, the Paris Bourse offers a whole series of loans floated by international bodies and foreign countries.

THE ROLE OF THE GOVERNMENT

Probably no European country, unless it be Sweden, has as direct control over the national economy as the French administration does. France has had a long tradition of state participation in the economy dating back to the seventeenth century and to the reign of Colbert, Louis the XIV's Finance Minister. During the seventeenth century, certain French industries were given charters or otherwise initiated by the government, particularly tapestries, armaments, and coal mining. Consequently, some government monopolies are of long standing. Others, by far the more important ones economically speaking, date from the postwar nationalizations of 1945. Some of the French business élite emerged from the war a discredited group since they cooperated with the régime of Maréchal Petain. A few were tried as collaborators after the war and their industrial plants were taken over by the state. Régie Renault was one, and is still government run and the largest auto works in France. Other sectors of the economy are also nationalized, including many utilities, the railroads, Air France, some large insurance companies, and of course, the four largest banks. The government became thus the largest employer in France, paying the salaries of 11 per cent of the country's working population, and controlling well over 25 per cent of the GNP. Since France is the largest nation in Western Europe—213,000 square miles and a population of 47 million—these figures are substantial.

Government ownership has meant different things in different European countries. In France, with its tradition of a highly responsible and highly trained civil service, many sectors are run as independent entities. In fact, they have given the professional manager and planner free rein. France, perhaps more than any other European country, has adopted *dirigisme* on a rational scale. The prime example is *le Plan,* an extensive blueprint for French growth and the development of industry. Le Plan is really a projection, an estimate of future trends. However, because of its multiple functions, including making available funds for long-term expansion, the government is in a position to favor certain sectors, whose growth it believes is in the national interest.

Le Plan is one of the chief factors responsible for a long overdue revamping and modernization of French industry. Though the government's influence is pervasive, le Plan is essentially voluntary and the government issues no *dicta.* In many areas, the government entered by default, filling a void which no private institution or group was willing or able to fill. In the realm of long-term credit to finance industrial expansion, the government stepped in where others feared to tread. No private agency was willing to extend such credit or face the risks. French institutions as well as individual Frenchmen are cautious when it comes to long-range commitments, for the threat of inflation was always, in the past at least, just over the horizon.

In the last fifteen years, or since the war, it has been preferable to be a debtor in France than a creditor. Thus insurance companies had shied away from bonds, as have private banks, pension funds, and other obvious purchasers of long-term debt. The government then created a whole series of semipublic and public institutions to facilitate extension of credit. Among the major ones are: Crédit Foncier (long-term loans to property owners, local authorities and the merchant marine), Crédit National (a post-war agency which mobilized funds for reconstruction and now specializes in medium-term industrial loans), Crédit Agricole (credit to local and regional agricultural societies), and Crédit Populaire (a network of cooperative banks destined to help small business). Of these agencies, both Crédit Foncier and Crédit National look to the capital market for funds and the list of their bonds occupies one and a half columns in the daily Official List.

Another key institution must be mentioned in discussing the role of the state: the Caisse des Dépôts et Consignations, a sort of savings banks' banker which manages the funds flowing into the state and municipal savings banks, affectionately called the *"bas de laine de la France,"* the wool stockings of France. Together with moneys from the social security system and several other insurance schemes, the Caisse des Dépôts purchases government securities and grants loans to local authorities. The largest bondholder in France, and obviously a factor to be reckoned with in the bond market, the Caisse in fact constitutes the largest single fund of moneys in France. It provides the government with a mighty financial lever. Depending on the rate at which moneys are funneled into the economy, the state can accelerate or slow down growth. Moreover, these moneys were reputedly used to support the stock market, when in 1956 oil speculation threatened to carry the Bourse into a real *"crac!"*

When Egypt closed the Suez Canal to European tankers in 1956, Europe was caught off guard. Fuel reserves, nowhere near requirements were soon exhausted and the results were severe midwinter shortages. At this point the French government accelerated its search for oil in the Sahara, subsidized some of the companies and, to further help finance this expensive undertaking, promoted the sale of stock to the public. Progress was sporadic, the pace hindered, some jokingly asserted, by the camel who "refused to accommodate its habits to administrative regulations made in Paris." But far from the sun, the sand, and the soil samples, the public's enthusiasm was great. Overspeculation led to a panic and since many investors had used their other securities as collateral for the purchase of oil shares, the house of cards eventually came tumbling down as prices fell. In order to protect the *petit épargnant*—the small saver—innocently led to slaughter by the government, government agencies reportedly stepped into the market directly through the Caisse des Dépôts et Consignations. The government also made funds available to the banks for the same purpose. This operation to firm up the market was repeated, or so some believe, every time the government floated a bond issue, but preceding the issue by several weeks, to prepare the ground. Opinions differ as to the precise, direct role of the government and the government is not about to say. Most bankers, however, dismiss the Ministry of Finance as an active day-to-day market force.

The Paris market does, on the other hand, respond sharply if temporarily to political events. In the days which preceded the Algerian settlement, there were wild fluctuations in prices, sometimes as much as 15 per cent. These usually redressed themselves within 48 hours and some knowledgeable people suggest that the government stepped in via the Caisse and bought. "Does the government ever sell to lower prices?" "Oh, I believe that all the Premier has to do is say that the market is too high. That is enough, it will go down."

THE BANKS AND THE FINANCIAL COMMUNITY

The private banks in Paris are located in some of the most beautiful settings in the historical heart of the city. Many have offices around the Place Vendome, in apartments with gilded woodwork, painted ceilings, and antique furniture. Often rooms or whole floors have been declared part of the historical treasure of France and nothing may be changed or moved.

Others have buildings around the Madeleine area, or near the Opera. From the outside, the buildings are seldom made of marble, but have a guard at every door, plus inside courtyards, formal gardens, and lavish offices. Moreover, all offices have double doors; the inner, usually with surfaces padded and doubly convex, while the outer, of massive hardwood, assures privacy and silence. In fact, these settings recall old France and, along with it, a fast disappearing era which held bankers in awe, a period which vanished in the United States with the death of J. P. Morgan.

Once past the double door, the atmosphere still has a touch of courtliness and ceremony. Confronted with a query, the head of a private bank will weigh his answer judiciously. It is usually a pleasure to listen to. Fifty-five to sixty-five, the gentleman is often the scion of the *haute bourgeoisie* of France, accustomed not merely to wealth but also to style and steeped in the dye of classic rhetoric. He may speak at length on the philosophy of the question, the underlying problems posed, then point to reasons—often fossils of concepts embedded in Roman law—which make the proposition impossible. However, *"peut-être,"* something might be arranged. In France, *"C'est parfois possible d'arranger les choses; parfois . . ."*

A younger executive in the same bank will have a different approach, though the results come to the same. Trained at the Sorbonne's faculty of law, or the École des Hautes Études Commerciales or École des Sciences Politiques, his analysis is precise and pragmatic. To the same query, "Is this possible?" or "How is this done in France?" one junior man stated candidly, "I will answer you in three parts: this is the law; this is how things are usually done; this is what *we* do."

To the foreigner, these answers may seem rather puzzling, evidence perhaps of Gallic abandon, loose legal enforcement, or a total lack of it. Nothing could be further from the truth. This *modus operandi* derives, in fact, not from too little regulation but rather from too much. French law, like Janus seems to look both fore and aft, casting a side-long glance in between and missing very little. In France, the code, the edict penetrates everywhere: official authority permits or prohibits a Frenchman from opening a travel agency, theater, movie studio, from engaging in commerce or banking, not to mention posting notices on public buildings (the law of July 29, 1881), or the transport of a few bottles of wine past the time calculated as necessary to traverse the distance between store and home. Few aspects of French life have escaped the legislator's *loi cadre*, or basic law, which is then left to the particular ministry to implement by specific decrees.

Financial institutions are most strictly regulated and their functions and privileges precisely demarcated. Each institution has its specific sphere and may not trespass on an other's domain. However, most decrees are negative in nature; the law merely defines limits but says nothing of possibilities. Paradoxically, thus, once the negative is adhered to, certain categories of banks have far greater freedom in their dealings than what might be considered their U.S. counterparts. The French banking structure, though more tightly compartmentalized than most, allows great leeway to "arrange things."

French banking is divided into three parts: the *banques de dépôts,* or deposit banks, the four largest of which, Crédit Lyonnais, Société

Générale, Banque Nationale pour le Commerce et l'Industrie (BNCI), and Comptoir National d'Escompte de Paris, were nationalized in 1945; medium- and long-term credit banks; and the *banques d'affaires,* or investment banks. The whole is supervised by the National Credit Council, Conseil National de Crédit, and more directly administered by the Commission de Contrôle des Banques, a banking commission headed by the governor of the Banque de France, or the Minister of Finance.

The Deposit Banks

There are over 300 banques de dépôts which together claim about 85 per cent of the assets in French banks. The four big nationalized banks which have branches in every corner of France account for about half of this 85 per cent. By law, these banks may accept call and fixed deposits and may extend short- and medium-term credit. However, their participation in businesses is limited; they may not hold stock exceeding 10 per cent of a company's total capital. Both the large nationalized banks and the smaller private ones are important factors in Bourse transactions, as French depositors usually prefer to have their stock accounts in the same institution which caters to their general banking needs. Thus these banks will transmit clients' orders to their agents de change, hold the securities, and collect dividends. However, by and large, the nationalized institutions, though they provide various services for the investor, are not research oriented and prefer not to manage portfolios. Their general economic publications are often excellent; frequently, English translations are available. Among the private banques de dépôts, on the other hand, there are several that specialize in portfolio investment and will advise clients.

The Investment Banks

A specifically French creation, the banques d'affaires, literally, "business banks," have a prime role among the *dramatis personae* of the French financial community. A combination of commercial bank, savings bank, holding company, and investment bank, they assumed their present form in 1945, under terms of the same law which nationalized the four giant deposit banks. Their chief function, however, is to take up participation in various businesses, nurture and extend credit to such firms, bring them to the market, and float their issues.

The role of the business banker is somewhat akin to that of the merchant banker in England, though of course in France it is of more recent vintage. The merchant banks on one side of the channel and the banques d'affaires on the other are extremely dynamic institutions, interested in arranging mergers, bringing out new issues, and backing the newest and fastest growing sectors of their respective economies. In France, the banques d'affaires played an essential role in the expansion and overhauling of French business. Besides the large, publicly held institutions, such as the Banque de Paris et des Pays-Bas (Paribas, a subsidiary is active on Wall Street), Banque de l'Indochine, Banque de l'Union Parisienne (BUP), Union Européene, and Banque Générale la Hénin (with its deposit bank subsidiary, Banque Monod-la Hénin), there are also private banques d'affaires, which number in their ranks some of the largest family fortunes in France. Sometimes called "*la haute banque*," such an institution is part and parcel and often the focus of financial empires such as that of the Rothschilds and the Schneiders. Among the private banques d'affaires are: Lazard Frères et Cie., de Rothschild Frères, Rivaud et Cie., Hottinguer et Cie., de Neuflize, Schlumberger et Cie., Mallet Frères et Cie., Vernes et Cie., and Worms et Cie.

A company will often look for a banque d'affaires to back its expansion program. In turn, the bank may take up a good block of the stock for itself, sometimes as much as 50 per cent. After a period of time, the bank will present an issue of the stock to the Bourse, frequently at a price double what it paid. All this is legal and within the province and function of a banque d'affaires. It is how they make much of their money.

A banque d'affaires can hold any amount of a company's stock. Indeed, if the company is saddled with inefficient management, the bank can often bring about changes. French businessmen, dependent on their bankers for financing and credit, have sometimes felt that they are "*trop gourmands*," which means that they are too greedy, too demanding, or simply want too much. Whatever the case, the banques d'affaires have been in the forefront of industrial financing since the war.

Since the banque d'affaires often holds a plurality of a company's shares, aside from the fact that it takes care of a company's financing and banking, it is in a unique position to know that company's prospects. The bank, moreover, will often make a market in that company's shares. Thus, but for a few of the very largest companies in France, the voice and influence of the banks play a decisive role in determining the daily market price.

Do they manipulate the market? It depends on one's definition, and undoubtedly, by SEC standards, many a banker would long ago have been called on the carpet. But France is not the United States and American criteria are inapplicable. Bankers and brokers do not agree on the number of companies whose stock is thus "protected," but guesses run between 50 and 200. Banks, on the other hand, claim with a good deal of truth that they are stabilizing the market in the shares of their companies. On any given day the market price will reflect the bank's thinking and position in the stock. However, it is doubtful whether the banks have any say about the final price of securities in the long run. Much as the specialist in the U.S. does, they are making a market in these stocks. As specialists, they stand ready to buy and sell in any kind of market weather, though they have no public obligation to do this and the French investing public is often unaware of their function.

The banks provide the French Bourse with specialists in stocks that might otherwise fluctuate more violently, because the Exchange works on an auction system. In America there are complaints that the specialists do not always act as specialists; in France some observers claim that the banks act too much as specialists.

The banques d'affaires have a rather limited relationship with the general public, from whom they may accept only two-year time deposits, leaving other banking and advisory functions to the banques de dépôts. In theory and according to the letter of the law, the banques d'affaires may deal only with clients connected with the companies in which the bank holds an interest. Today, this law is observed more in the breach than in the enforcement. However, when it was first implemented, no institution could be certain of this. One small bank, rumor has it, got around this stricture by selling every depositor two shares in a company in which the institution held a beneficial interest. Once a stockholder, the client was free to continue his deposits and other dealings, no matter how small. Today, the law is more or less ignored, but some institutions draw the line more closely than others. As some banques d'affaires are not interested in small accounts, whether French or foreign, this law is often cited.

Because they are not supposed to handle small deposits, the banques d'affaires do not publish any material intended for the general public. They will, however, send their studies, economic reviews, and market letters to institutions and professionals. In general, research material of French banks is available to brokers and banks. Though private investors may not subscribe to these studies, they can thus have indirect access to them. This material ranks among the best available on French securities.

SECURITY ANALYSIS

Often, one French research man relates, American analysts arrive in France *"avec le sourire gros come la lune"* (with a smile big as the new moon) *"et pleins d'illusions"* (full of illusions). Being a security analyst, a profession which is barely a decade old in Europe, is much like being a detective. Thus French financial sleuths often have to make up an earnings picture from "any clues the company may carelessly have left around."

A classic example of such detective work is the analysis of Michelin, the tire and rubber company, a supreme challenge because of the firm's taciturnity. Here traditional French secrecy reigns supreme. The company, a family-controlled partnership with shares outstanding, a société en commandite par actions, gives out next to no information. Of course, this is the height of irony, for Michelin inspectors ceaselessly roam anonymously through France, snooping into everyone else's kitchens and hotel rooms. Their ratings can make or break these establishments.

A variety of ways are employed to determine sales, profit margins, earnings, and other vital data of this company. To cite but two examples: In a rash moment in 1948 Michelin revealed sales figures for its complete operations. It was never to do so again, but does annually reveal whether sales are up or down by X percentage. Through a series of calculations in reverse, one imaginative broker has come up with what he believes to be reasonably accurate sales figures. A bank goes about it quite differently. From the published figures on total tire production of the National Statistical Institute, the bank can estimate Michelin's portion of the market since all the other rubber producers do publish production figures. A comparison of probable profit margins of the other companies gives a rough idea as to the firm's earnings.

To be sure, Michelin is more secretive than most French companies. Reporting by other French industrial giants is considerably better; in Saint-Gobain, Péchiney, or Rhône-Poulenc investors have a much better idea of company prospects. Even in the medium- and smaller-size companies, the classic game of three sets of books—one for the management, one for the government, and one for the family—is a vanishing sport. Today the French government has an excellent idea of the earning capacities and tax liabilities of large- and medium-size corporations, as good an idea at least as their banks have.

The size of French companies goes a long way toward compounding the secrecy which surrounds them. Very small firms frequently will merge in order to launch a new product. This helps explain the often puzzling phenomenon of competitors' joining hands to form new companies. In France, there are almost no monopoly restrictions on mergers. Thus, it is easier to raise money and talent for a new enterprise by starting a joint subsidiary with one's immediate competitors. As a secondary consideration, it might also be easier to confound the *fisc* through interlocking holdings. Joint subsidiaries spread until a few years ago when credit became easier. Though the labyrinth-like maze might confuse and confound the Treasury, it was doing the very same thing for the management. Corporations expanded till it became harder and harder to arrive at any sound idea of a company's assets or earnings.

Analysis, though extremely difficult, is not impossible, but the crucial ingredient is often confidential or accurate information. If the parent company represents only a fraction of the group's total activity, to gauge its earnings without such information is very tricky. Only rarely do French companies consolidate either balance sheets or income accounts. But firms worth over FF10,000,000 ($2,040,816) are required by law to divulge annually their holdings in affiliates and subsidiaries where these exceed FF100,000 ($20,408) in book value. Thus a list of subsidiaries and the extent of the parent company's participation are available, but little more. The subsidiaries themselves seldom publish accounts, unless they in turn are publicly held. This is rare.

The rich diversity of subsidiaries, many of which are in related businesses, but some in totally unrelated areas, acts as a convenient screen. There are thus no grumbles from stockholders when large slices of profits are plowed back into one or another supplementary firm; research and development for a new product can be written off quickly and the parent company retains the mastery of the ship. Though itself publicly owned and responsive to its stockholders, the subsidiaries usually account to no one but the holding company. This, of course, grants the ultimate owners a great deal of latitude.

Analysts often resort to devious methods of arriving at a picture of total activity. Dividends received by the holding company, capital invested in subsidiaries, turnover or sales figures if such are available and, perhaps most important, learned estimates of subsidiaries' profit margins based on information gleaned from competition, government statistics, and export figures all contribute to solving the puzzle.

Confronted with a French balance sheet and profit and loss statement, the investor must think like a Frenchman. Only then is it possible to interpret published information. To ask a Frenchman how much he earns is a social *faux pas*. Much the same applies to companies. They will chronically underestimate earnings, for as a rule, reported earnings correspond not to true profits but to the sum the company intends to distribute to shareholders. French companies like to keep things on an even keel, reporting roughly the same earnings from year to year, smoothing out the ups and downs by funneling moneys into various categories of reserves. Thus the published net earnings do not necessarily constitute a true or accurate figure. This has the inconvenience of making impossible comparisons based on earnings such as price-earnings and earnings per share.

Consequently, European analysts and American analysts working on European companies have devised various ways of attacking intransigent accounts. One of the most common is to restore to the picture any of the earnings that might have been sidetracked into the reserve accounts, i.e., contingency reserves, reserves for accelerated amortization, reserves to renew inventories, plus any other special reserve provisions. These reserves, along with depreciation and distributed earnings, make up the cash flow. It is this figure that "is the only valid measure of the earnings capacity of French companies," claimed an American-trained French analyst. The cash flow divided into the total market value of all the common stock (MV/Cash Flow) then becomes a key tool. Another important ratio is sales divided into market value (MV/Sales). These figures can then be used for industry-wide comparisons and, if American figures are available or recast, for comparisons with American companies.

It should be stressed that though this is a highly regarded technique in Europe, some American banks and investment funds are skeptical of these estimates—not because they are wrong, but because they are not quite right. If a company will not declare its income in a fashion to satisfy orthodox American criteria, then these institutions are reluctant to invest or advise their clients to invest in them, regardless of their size or reputation.

The consequences of this very conservative approach would place many French securities beyond the pale for investors. Needless to say, many Americans have purchased French securities with less than perfect information. The more cautious, however, have turned to mutual funds as a way of participating in the French economy which obviates the risks of little French and less accounting.

Until recently open-end or mutual funds were illegal in France. The concept of a corporation, stemming from Roman law, defined it as an entity with fixed capital. The notion of one with variable capital did not exist. The French Parliament in 1957 modified this concept by passing a *loi cadre* which made it possible to set up such funds. However, the Ministry of Finance on whom the specific edict to implement the law depended, published its decrees only in September 1963.

So far eight mutual funds—*sociétés d'investissement à capital variable*—have been established. Four of these are offspring of the four nationalized banks. Briefly stated, their capital must be greater than FF20 million ($4.08 million); shares must be fully paid at the time of issue; if the capital falls to less than FF10 million ($2.04 million), they are forbidden to repurchase their shares; 90 per cent of their assets must be in listed securities and 30 per cent must be in government obligations. The tax status of these mutual funds was not decreed—apparently it will be subject to negotiations.

There exist in France approximately forty closed-end investment trusts, most of which are managed and directed by the banques d'affaires. Closed-end investment companies came into being in France only after the last war. They are not yet well known among the general public and consequently most of them are selling below their net asset value. The discount in the past few years has been as much as 30 per cent. Most of these investment companies are fairly small and quite diversified. The law provides that their holdings in any one company cannot exceed 5 per cent of their own capital, and furthermore their holdings cannot exceed more than 10 per cent of the outstanding capital of that company.

While the income in capital gains of an investment company are free of corporate income tax, there have so far been no capital gains distributions. Under present law, such distributions would have to wait until reserves realized from capital gains have become larger than the capital. Observers expect that such distributions will be made shortly and will undoubtedly be facilitated by the growth of open-end companies. Dividend distributions are free of the 18 per cent withholding tax. Parenthetically, a double taxation agreement has lowered dividend withholding to 15 per cent in the case of U.S. residents.

Though there are exchange regulations which prohibit foreigners from purchasing unlisted foreign securities in France, there are no problems in purchasing French mutual funds that are wholly invested in other countries, say in Spanish equity. Such funds would be considered French companies even though their entire holdings may lie outside of territorial France.

One final point is worth mentioning: French closed-end trusts are run on a much cheaper managerial basis than American ones are. This is possible because most of the funds are run as subsidiaries by banks.

CHARACTERISTICS OF THE BOURSE

Language is often an interesting guide to foreign institutions. In French one says, with no opprobrium attached, *"jouer à la Bourse,"* to play the market. There are two words to describe one who plays this game: *capitaliste* and *spéculateur*. Interestingly, the word *investisseur,* investor, was borrowed from English since the French had no equivalent concept.

Facts and figures on share ownership in France are most elusive—to be precise—nonexistent. Bearer shares give no clue to the owner's identity and SICOVAM accounts, the clearing corporation, are only with banks and brokers. One thing appears certain: share ownership is widespread with perhaps greater public involvement in the market than any other European country outside of England. Some years ago when the coal industry was nationalized, the financial world was surprised to find that most every *concierge* had a few coal shares.

A composite picture of the French investor reveals that he is likely to be over fifty and looking to safeguard his retirement. He buys to hold and speculates little if at all. Younger people, who in the United States actively follow the market, are the exception. Professionals and younger businessmen have all their savings tied up in offices or plants: even industrial fortunes are thus tied up. Since long-term capital is hard to come by, the mainstay of expansion is often the family fortune.

In the rush of the postwar reconstruction, the stockholder was perhaps the forgotten man. Expansion of the enterprise came first and foremost. In the United States, "growth" industries are forgiven their dividends; in Britain they pay out handsomely. "In France," however, one banker noted, "no industry pays serious dividends." The investor looks to capital appreciation and industry pays out only 1 per cent to 3 per cent in dividends in relation to its *chiffre d'affaires*, its total sales or turnover.

A typical yield in France is 2 per cent net; the government's 18 per cent withholding tax is already deducted when dividends are distributed and yields calculated. A tax credit actually improves the yield for Frenchmen. Managements generally want to lay aside money so that in a bad year they can equalize things quietly. "Companies in France let their stockholders sleep well at night." They neither alarm them with pessimistic pronouncements, nor let their blood pressure rise at good tidings.

There is no capital gains tax in France, though there is the 18 per cent levy on dividends. Therefore companies prefer to reward their stockholders, not with high dividends, but with frequent rights issues, bonus shares, and stock splits. These issues are handled very differently than in Anglo-American practice. New stock in France is usually issued at par or near par value, unlike the method at home of pricing issues near the current market price. For instance, assuming the par value to be FF100, and the stock is being quoted at FF500, the company might decide to issue one new share for every two old ones held. The price of the new share would probably hover around FF150, far from the market price of FF500. Thus two old shares plus one new one will be worth FF1,150. Dividing this by 3, each share is now valued at FF383. Subtracting 383 from 500, the stockholder can sell the right, should he so desire, at FF117, a healthy price. Therefore, what he loses in dividends, he makes up in rights.

Rights, naturally, are also negotiable for specific periods of time. To take a concrete case: The Banque de Paris et des Pays-Bas, the largest banque d'affaires in France, increased its capital in May 1963 by issuing 800,080 new shares. Two new shares were offered for three old ones. The new shares were to forego the 1963 dividend but would thereafter rank on par with the old.

For a month, April 29 to May 29, the subscription rights could be exercised. On the cash market, or *comptant,* the right was detached from the share on April 29 and traded separately. However, on the forward market, *marché à terme,* the share continued to be traded cum right until May 22. During most of the month-long subscription period, the interested investor had three alternatives: to purchase shares cum rights, buy shares ex rights, or simply acquire the rights for trading. It should be emphasized that the foreign investor can only take advantage of these frequent rights issues if he is willing to wet his feet and step into the original market. If he buys ADRs, he must sell the rights, as the new stock is considered unseasoned by the SEC.

For the company raising funds, pricing their new shares so near par usually means issuing many shares. This apparently meets with enthusiastic approval of French investors. "People want lots of shares, since they think it may mean higher prices even though it may mean watering the stock," remarked a banker. The compensating factor is that in France there is a general shortage of stock. The shortage is due, however, not to a demand which is too big but rather a supply which is too small. Such a situation is bound to arise in a country where the majority of industry is small and there is a marked tendency to self-financing.

For banks and institutions, this shortage of stock means that they must move with caution. Often a bank wanting a large block of desirable stock, either for its own account or on instructions from a client, will buy, say, 500 shares and on the same day sell 100 through one agent de change and 200 through another. This seesaw process to hide its hand may go on for a number of days or weeks in order not to push up prices inordinately. Sometimes, however, when even the most fastidious investment trust or bank moves from one stock into another, what they sell goes down and what they buy goes up. The differential may be as much as 20 per cent. Many companies, moreover, have their stock held firmly in a few hands. The family and its banque d'affaires may control 75 per cent to 90 per cent of the equity and will often step in to support the market. "Often, it is more informative to know who controls a company than to know what it produces." "And how do you get at this information?" "Oh, the socialist and communist press often does a good job of telling you. Very informative at times!"

CONCLUSION

The French market, no doubt, is tricky for the uninitiated or one whose access to information is limited to published matter. Printed data, incontestably, is inadequate or tardy if not both. Company reports are not consolidated and are issued six months or sometimes a year late. By the time the statistical or analytic services finish digesting them, twelve or eighteen months may have elapsed. The facts and the statistics in the American sense of the term often do not exist or, if they do exist, are not in published form.

In France, this has led to divergent results: on the one hand, because of the meagerness of published information, the grapevine has often accentuated and aggravated market trends; on the other, many made a good deal of money thanks to astute counseling. It should be emphasized, however, that things are changing in the country, company reporting is getting better, and analysts predict more improvements to come.

Another of the realities of French financial life is that the Bourse, the largest Stock Exchange in the Common Market, is nevertheless a thin market. This fact, the constant headache of institutions who eat up stock by Gargantuan mouthfuls, is usually no major obstacle for the individual investor. Yet, in view of all these difficulties, why invest in France? "Why, to make money, of course!" the man from Morgan said simply.

France, the largest country in the Common Market complex, is by far the most richly endowed geographically. Her soil and natural resources are her dowry. She now enjoys both political stability and an adamantine currency. By U.S. standards, inflation would still seem a problem, but by European ones it has been halted. The price index no longer rises 20 per cent a year but around 5 per cent. The years 1956, 1957, 1958 were years of economic delirium with prices and wages racing each other upwards. Inflation to a large extent was also due to the enormous drain of financing the Algerian conflict. A large cash deficit during that period led to a crisis in the French balance of payments. In recent years, France has achieved a surplus in her international trade accounts.

Contrary to Germany's or Holland's postwar paths, France's consumer boom is far from the prosperous pinnacle. The saturation point is far away; France, in fact, is just coming into her own and succumbing to the lure of modern housing, modern appliances, and such mass distribution techniques as instalment buying, mail ordering, and the like. Chain stores, supermarkets, and department stores are thriving and INNO, the French equivalent of a fancy discount chain, is opening new stores at a great rate. (The INNO stores in France are subsidiaries of the Belgian department store, Innovation.)

The country's productive capacity had to be rebuilt after World War II, not only because of German destruction but also because much was antiquated in the capital goods sector in particular. Today, the expansion of French industry continues at a steady pace. Faith in the country's future takes tangible form in le Plan. The Plan is not merely a blueprint or projection. It is in a sense a unique investment guide—in a general way, to be sure. Undoubtedly, the industries and areas favored by the planners will do well; they will probably do well by their stockholders too.

Technocrats cite an urgent need for more public works to keep pace with the demands of a growing population. (The large private French construction firms in this sector work not only in metropolitan France but are experts also in meeting the requirements of underdeveloped areas and have undertaken extensive projects in Africa and Asia.) There has been great delay in building enough schools, hospitals, and other public facilities, as well. Ironically, the French built these institutions *en masse* to meet the most modern specifications—in Algeria. The mother country is now the underprivileged one.

Waterworks companies, like the giant Générale des Eaux, are pushing accelerated projects, and heating companies have a hard time keeping up with demand.

In other areas, of course, the French have a long-acknowledged expertise. Precision machinery, glass, chemicals have long been their forte. Rhône-Poulenc in chemicals and St. Gobain in glass and chemicals lead in their fields, as does Péchiney in aluminum and Hachette in publishing. France, of course, is famous for her wine, cheeses, and mineral water. When Source Perrier went public a few years ago, the stock shot up. Machines Bull, one of France's leading companies in electronics and data processing, ran into trouble after a meteoric rise in prestige and price. Suffering from a shortage of money, the company came to an agreement with General Electric though the government was not happy with this extranational solution. The price of salvation, however, meant that the company was divided into three parts: one solely French to secure military secrets; the other divisions are assisted by the American firm.

How has the French Bourse been behaving in the past decade? From 1952 to 1954 it was extremely dormant. With the discovery of oil in France in 1954 and in the Sahara in 1955, lively interest in the market developed. A law passed to support drilling and research brought not only the general French public into the Exchange, but foreigners began to show interest as well. In 1958, with the stabilization of the franc, foreign interests entered in all seriousness. Americans, however, more wary than Europeans, waited until 1960 and bought near the highs; Americans looked too much for proven growth, for the société en expansion. "*Ils ont payé trop cher l'espoir*," they paid too much for hope, one banker commented.

Judged by a 1962 point of view the Bourse did not perform so badly. Alone among European Exchanges, prices on the Paris Bourse did not plummet after Wall Street's fateful Black Tuesday, in May 1962. The reason? There was less American participation in French securities, and stock holdings were smaller than in other Continental centers. Consequently, there was less panic selling. The market was stagnant in 1963, but in 1964 prices revived as stabilization measures took hold.

For Frenchman and foreigner alike, to tame the French Bourse, one connoisseur advised: "... *en principe, le moyen le plus sûr de gagner est de tourner le dos à la multitude comme les sages antiques le recommandaient pour la recherche de la vérité*" (In principle, the surest way to win [on the Bourse] is to turn your back to the multitudes, as the sages of antiquity recommended for those searching for Truth).*

* Bainville, *Fortune de la France*, p. 158.

SOURCES OF INFORMATION

There is no dearth of general economic literature in French and numerous books dealing with the Bourse and related subjects are on the market. Two excellent volumes are:

GASCUEL, JACQUES, *et* SÉDILLOT, RENÉ (ed.). *Comment Lire un Journal Economique et Financier.* 2nd ed. Paris: Dunod, 1960.

A perusal of this book is a *sine qua non* for the foreigner planning further reading of French economic literature. It does far more than the title implies, affording a comprehensive and basic guide to every aspect of French economic life.

HAOUR, PIERRE. *La Bourse.* (No. 365, *Section de Droit.*) Paris: Collection Armand Collin, 1962.

Other books include:

DÉFOSSÉ, GASTON. *La Bourse des Valeurs.* (No. 825, *Que Sais-Je?*) Paris: Presses Universitaires de France, 1962.

KNABEL, LUCIEN *et* TIXIER, JEAN. *Technique et Pratique de la Bourse.* Paris: Guy Le Prat, Éditeur, 1963.

PERQUEL, RAYMOND, *et al. Manuel des Opérations de Bourse.* (*Manuels Dalloz de Droit Usuel.*) Paris: Librairie Dalloz, 1963.

Compiled by three lawyers, this volume deals with all legal questions related to Bourse operations.

Books dealing with analysis or information on companies, or both, include:

ROSENFELD, FELIX. *Analyse des Valeurs Mobilières.* Vol. 2, *Collection Statistique et Programmes Économiques.* Paris: Dunod, 1963.

L'annuaire Desfossés. Paris: Cote Desfossés et S.E.F.

This is a yearly publication which gives a short run-down on all companies quoted in Paris or on provincial Exchanges. A newer and more comprehensive survey is now published by Société de Documentation et d'Analyse Financière, DAFSA, an organization dedicated to bringing sophisticated analytic techniques to French financial matters. DAFSA's investment service is geared mainly to banks and is rather costly. This two-volume reference book, however, is not part of the regular DAFSA kit and is inexpensive.

DAFSA. *Analyse de Portefeuilles. Tome* I, *Les Actionnaires des Sociétés Françaises. Tome* II.

Tome I includes: an evaluation of 7,000 stocks by categories, i.e., insurance, banking, agriculture, construction, etc.; Bourse capitalization; Exchange quoted; an evaluation of the stock based on latest balance sheets;

information on subsidiaries and company holdings; and for investment trusts, the volume gives portfolios, though obviously this is a list as of one particular day of the year.

Tome II gives a modified French version of *Who Owns Whom,* affording some information on who holds stock in which companies and how much, e.g., *les sociétés mères.* Some details on main subscribers to rights issues on new stock is given for industrials and the same information is available on nationalized companies. These two volumes are the most complete and handy reference works available on French companies to date.

Société d'Éditions Économiques et Financières (S.E.F.), is joint publisher with Verlag Hoppenstedt of an extremely useful series of fact sheets on companies. *Informations Internationales* appears in French, German, and English and affords valuable background on French firms, as well as on other European companies.

The main financial dailies are *Cote Desfossés,* which appears shortly after Bourse hours, and two morning editions: *L'Agence Économique et Financière* and *Les Echos.* The latter afford comprehensive coverage of the general European scene besides the day's financial doings in France. Weeklies are numerous, but nothing quite compares with England's *Economist.* The closest is *La Vie Française,* which is good for general information on business conditions in France, and will often conduct special surveys on particular aspects of the economy or specific economic problems. There are any number of other financial weeklies and monthlies on the newspaper *kiosques* but, since many do not distinguish between editorial matters and company publicity, their recommendations are to be taken with healthy skepticism.

For statistics, the *Institut National de la Statistique et des Études Économiques* (INSEE), is the source. It publishes a daily stock index based on 50 French and 20 foreign stocks, as well as a far more complete weekly index. The latter includes some 282 French stocks, 28 foreign stocks, 72 fixed income or indexed securities, 2 government *rentes perpétuelles,* 16 *rentes amortissables,* 17 bonds of the nationalized sector, 11 indexed industrials, and 26 other bonds.

*Grand bien ne vient pas en peu d'heures.**
—Walloon maxim

3. BELGIUM

Brussels is the seat of the Common Market, its administrative center, and the *de facto* capital of Europe. It is also the capital of the Belgians. Situated just beyond an east-west line which divides the Flemish-speaking population from French-speaking Walloons, the capital is bilingual with emphasis on French. Her rooftops reflect the mixed population, as does her cuisine, and the fact that *cafés* serve either wine or beer.

Belgium is a young nation, established in 1830, but her cities were among the chief medieval marts of Europe. Flanders transformed English woolens into cloth, and Antwerp, Bruges, and Ghent sold them to the rest of the Continent. Rulers came and went in quick succession: the Lotharingians succeeded Charlemagne; the Dukes of Burgundy ceded to the Spaniards; Austrian Hapsburgs retreated before the sweep of the French Revolution, but the Empire in turn fell back and gave way to the Dutch. Belgian merchants, however, plied their wares and grew wealthy. Belgium became one of the bankers of the world and Belgian investors helped build streetcar lines in cities from Istanbul to Buenos Aires, and from Poland to China. Her engineers, moreover, had a hand in drawing plans for Paris' subway, the *métro,* and her burghers lent some of the funds.

But Belgian ties to France and French culture go deeper than the métro. Though the country is a cultural amalgam of Germanic Flem-

* A fortune is not made in a few hours.

ings and Latin Walloons, her legal structure is modeled on the Napoleonic Code and, in financial matters too, Belgians owe a debt to France. *Bruxellois* owe their *Bourse* to a Napoleonic decree—an *arrêté* of the nineteenth Messidor, year IX of the Revolution, or to be exact, July 8, 1801. The Paris government designated the site: a former Augustinian convent in rue Fossé-aux-Loups, Trench-of-Wolves Street. The French, it appears, had a propensity for converting convents into market places.

The present Bourse building, a colonnaded palace dating from 1873, is on the main streetcar line between the South and North stations, two of the city's main railway terminals. It faces a square where a trio of streets meet the boulevard. Here a population of pigeons flutters around the crowd of Bruxellois heading for adjoining cafés, waiting for trolleys, or on the way to A La Bourse, a department store across the way. From the peristyle of the Exchange, the allegoric figure of Belgium looks down, flanked by the twin genies of Commerce and Industry. Inside, the Bourse displays sculptures by Rodin.

Belgium's most important mart, the *terme* or forward market, is located in the back of the building. Modeled on the French system, the Brussels terme market differs in several ways. Contrary to Paris practice, the Belgian forward market divides its account periods into units of two weeks. Stocks quoted on the terme may or may not be the most active securities: a great many Congo issues, for instance, are quoted on the forward market, but they have seen little but indifference from both traders and public alike of late. At 12:30, a bell marks the opening of this market and trading in the 72 stocks quoted in the *marché à terme* may begin. Dealing takes place in round lots which, depending on the price of the security, may be 5, 10, 25, 30, 40, 50, or 100 shares minimum.

Before the pandemonium of the opening at half-past noon, 45 Bourse employees in a back room have spent a hectic fifteen minutes collating purchase and sales orders. These are tallied to find out if buyers or sellers predominate; the clerks add figures like lightening. Recently, the Exchange consulted IBM with the thought of automating the process, only to be told that to perforate the tape or cards would alone take more than ten minutes. Mental arithmetic is quicker.

With this tally sheet in front of him giving him the list of offers and bids at various prices, the *commissaire,* a specialist appointed by the Bourse on a rotating basis from among the agents de change, is now ready to start the trading. He stands on a catwalk high above his compeers. Leaning on a rail, his back to a series of blackboards (one per security), his first job is to set the opening price. The manner in which this is done is unique to the Brussels Exchange.

The commissaire does not act for his own account; his only function is to bring orders into equilibrium. If, for instance, there are 2,000 buyers to 1,500 sellers in toto for Gevaert, Belgium's largest photo-products producer, the commissaire must find another 500 sellers among the crowd below. Thus he announces, "I buy." The brokers on the floor may then speak up, but only if they are sellers. The starting point is the previous day's price. If no one wishes to sell at that level, the commissaire ups his bid between 1 to 15 francs, depending on the stock's price.

He must then start his balancing act again. The total of buy orders "at best" or *sans limite* is still 500, but in addition he may have sellers at the higher price. Assuming another seller of 100 shares now figures on the list, the specialist is still short 400 shares. Without revealing his hand by mentioning the quantity, he repeats, "I buy," until he has satisfied his orders. If, at any particular price level, the trend according to his tally sheet reverses itself, and the price is now high enough so that more people wish to sell Gevaert, the commissaire too becomes turncoat. He will now show his hand and announce, "I am selling," an invitation to the brokers below to speak up if they have buy orders to fill. Thus a first price is set. All this takes four or five minutes at most.

Once the first price is set, the market becomes free and trading takes place *à la criée,* as in Paris. The commissaire, however, may still have unfilled orders at prices way below or way above the first price. These he lists on the Gevaert blackboard, and henceforth they act as outside limits. Trading can go on among the brokers themselves, or between brokers and the specialist who confronts them like a Roman orator. After the outside limits are noted on the blackboard in yellow chalk, the commissaire is free to take a stroll along the catwalk, take care of the quotation of other securities, or go out for coffee. Brokers then bargain among themselves within the limits and merely advise a clerk that a transaction has taken place. If there is a new price after a trade, it is noted on the board.

At ten minutes to one, another bell reverberates under the central cupola and part of the cash market is now officially open. The cash market has a total of some 500 securities and is divided into *Corbeilles* which feature the *vedettes*, the stars (the same word is used for movie stars), the 72 stocks quoted on the terme, plus 40-odd other stocks. The remaining, usually less active securities, are dealt on the *Parquet,* where trading begins a little later, at 1:10 P.M.

Corbeilles and Parquet have different systems: the Corbeilles is the more interesting. In the main part of the building, a series of desks line the walls, forming a semicircle. The effect, reminiscent of a school room, is a ridiculously small and cramped arrangement for grown men. The seats, in fact, consist of three-legged stools chained securely to each desk. Absent-minded brokers have been known to take them home. Thus crowded and cramped the "holders of notebooks," the specialists of the cash market, await customers. They are self-designated, having decided that henceforth they will centralize the market for one, or for a group of stocks, and always act for their own account.

Transactions, however, do not have to go through the specialists; brokers may simply join the crowd and yell their orders to a clerk perched on a raised platform. In practice, a good many orders go through the *teneurs de carnets*. Thus a man will sit at his pint-sized desk, packets of pink buy order slips in hand, sorting them from white sell slips as though he were playing solitaire. This is the Belgian equivalent of keeping a book. Appropriately, in French the game is called *Réussite,* or "success"; in essence, it is making a market.

On the Corbeilles, prices vary, fluctuating with transactions. Moreover, since the same stocks are also being dealt on the terme market a few hundred feet away, arbitrage is sometimes possible. Occasionally too, a specialist will sprint over to the terme market to buy so that he may fill his orders. On the Corbeilles as well as the Parquet, any number can play and an order for a single share is never ignored.

The Parquet, the last of the three staggered markets, works on a system similar to that employed in Amsterdam: there is one price for the day and all transactions take place at that level. For stocks traded on the Parquet, prices may not fluctuate more than 5 per cent from the previous day's closing. For the Corbeilles, the permitted variation is a more liberal 10 per cent.

The agents de change, the brokers, are the official intermediaries, though bank representatives are admitted to the floor as observers. The public, however, is excluded, forced to remain near the entrance on the other side of a railing, watching the action on the floor from a distance. Those who come to sit, to watch, and perhaps to trade are mostly elderly retired people, termed, *les pieds humides*, those of the damp feet. Brussels is a wet and misty city.

Although there are some 700 stocks quoted in Brussels, 25 companies account for well over half the volume. The market tends to be a relatively thin one, more sedate than Paris and with fewer day-to-day fluctuations. Estimates put private share ownership in Belgium at some 500,000, but private transactions are dwarfed by the activity of Belgian and international institutions. Both play a considerable role, though it is sometimes difficult to disentangle foreign from domestic activity. For institutional clients, one banker remarked, *"Il faut travailler le marché,"* one has to "work" the market, to prepare it so that a large buy or sell order will not throw prices out of kilter. But then this process of compensation for the narrowness of a market is true for most of Europe's Exchanges. For institutional clients, the best approach is often a gradual one; for small investors, foreign or domestic, the problem does not exist.

There are over one hundred foreign stocks and bonds traded. Brussels is a big international market and the foreign securities quoted include British and Commonwealth companies, Argentinian, Canadians, French, German, Luxembourg, Dutch, Italian, Portuguese, Swedish, and U.S. firms, not to mention bonds of international organizations.

BROKERAGE RATES

Commission rates are as follows:

Government bonds, loans of municipalities, provinces, and Congo loans range between BF3 and BF7.5 per 1,000 francs actual value. A small tax, ranging from 0.6 per mill to 1.2 per mill is also due.

Corporate bonds carry a brokerage of BF7.5 per BF1,000 actual, or 7.5 per mill.

Stocks bought on the cash market are liable for brokerage rates of 7.5 per mill maximum for securities whose market price exceeds BF500. A tax of 3 per mill is also due.

For stocks purchased on the terme or forward market, brokerage rates are 6 per mill and the tax due is 1.5 per mill.

To carry forward, that is to delay payment for stock beyond the normal two-week account period, half the brokerage is charged on the new transaction.

BELGIUM'S ECONOMY AND INDUSTRY

Unlike Holland, Belgium is one of the oldest of Europe's industrial hubs. Thanks to the collieries of Liége and Charleroi and the advice of British engineers, she built the first blast furnaces on the Continent. Her iron and steel industries started in the 1820s. Ferrous and non-ferrous metallurgy is still her forte, but time can transform an early start into a handicap. Like England's, a good segment of Belgium's industrial plant is now old-fashioned. Belgium, second in age only to Britain among industrial countries, is something of a stately dowager.

She has stayed with the staples, the traditional industries, as opposed to the more volatile "growth" groups. Basic metals, steel, mining, quarrying, and textiles still anchor her economy, with plastics, synthetics, and electronics playing a minor role. The conservatism of Belgium's holding companies has been held partly to blame, but this conservatism is rooted in economic reality. Belgium's population numbers but 9.2 million and her area is 11,775 square miles, so the home market is thus *ipso facto* small. Europe as a whole has traditionally been her market and with the liberalization of trade within the

Common Market complex, the customers for Belgian industry potentially number 175 million.

So long as Europe prospers, Belgium will prosper. For much of Europe, the tarnished side of the golden coin of prosperity is inflation; but for Belgium, inflationary pressures in neighboring countries spell opportunity. When their own internal demand outruns home production, European customers come with orders. Excess demand in the rest of Europe means full order books for Belgian producers. However, this stand-by role has its dangers. Customers are not permanent, and Belgium is thus more sensitive to trade cycles than less export-oriented nations or nations with more elastic markets at home.

In addition, Belgium's problems are those of any mature economy. The one-time forerunners, industries which formed the vanguard in the nineteenth century, are now facing difficulties. Companies producing railway rolling stock, coal, and textiles are faced with a dilemma. Though some might wish to close their plants, the assets of these plants are difficult to dispose of. There are no buyers, for the competition is in equal trouble. The alternative thus becomes disinvestment versus defensive investment, and most firms have chosen the latter. The government is already subsidizing the coal producers, but this is an exception in the Belgian scheme rather than the rule. The Belgian government is active in making available financing for industry through a number of special agencies as intermediaries but otherwise prefers to remain inconspicuous. There is no *Plan à la Française*, with its special incentives and favored industries treatment; the Belgian regional development schemes aim to entice industry to poorer sections of the country and therefore hardly apply to long-established and now ailing sectors. The burden of modernization falls solely on the industries themselves and goes a long way toward explaining Belgium's sluggish rate of over-all investment today.

Belgium boasts a frugal population and a very stable currency. Savings are high and until recently, deflation prevailed despite the fact that the rest of Europe was courting inflation. Although there is no shortage of funds, the pace of investment has generally been slow in the postwar period, or at least slow in comparison with that of neighboring countries. It is true that Belgium emerged from World War II with much of her industrial plant intact and could thus afford a slower pace of reconstruction. But the heart of the problem really lies in her concentration on traditional industries and the contretemps in store for coal, textiles, and steel.

The steel industry is heavily concentrated in the hands of Belgian holding companies and part of the problem of the industry, no doubt, devolves from the protective shelter of the holding company structure. Within the holding company itself, funds can usually be found to support an ailing plant or even a group of plants, thus delaying the day of reckoning. The holding companies have grown to be ponderous giants. Indeed, half a dozen such holdings control some 60 per cent of Belgian industry, and their ubiquity has long molded the Belgian financial scene.

Dating from a 1934 law which split off investment banking from other banking functions, a new form was created. The industrial holding company, dubbed *les holdings* for short, is a typically Belgian phenomenon and a preeminent one. Belgium has no antitrust laws, and the only legislation applicable is not national in character but international. As a member of the European Coal and Steel Community and of the Common Market, Belgium adheres to their strictures concerning combines or agreements in restraint of trade. The domestic scene, however is free and clear as far as mergers or size are concerned. Les holdings have grown and grown to Gargantuan size and some critics feel that concentration has become an obstacle to competition, with corporate "hardening of the arteries" as the result. The curious thing about the Belgian arrangement is that rather than banks controlling holding companies—the usual phenomenon in Europe—the holding companies control the banks.

The biggest holding company of all in Belgium is Société Générale de Belgique, controlling about 20 per cent of the country's industry. The Société Générale's holdings spread across nearly every sector from banking to mining, transportation to electrical and nuclear power, metallurgy, construction, glass, chemicals, paper, textiles, plus its African investments. Brufina, of which Banque de Bruxelles is a part, heads another large conglomerate. Three other large complexes are the Empain group. Compagnie d'Outremer of which Banque Lambert is a part, and the Solvay group.

The Solvay process for producing soda ash is a Belgian technique dating from the 1860s and the Solvay interests today range from chemicals to plastics with plants around the world. The Solvay group of companies has close ties with many large American and Continental chemical concerns: ICI in England, Rhône-Poulenc in France, Monsanto, and Allied Chemical, to name but a few.

Cooperation among Belgian holding companies is often close and a single company might well have its shares held by two or more of les holdings. To cite but one example, Société Générale de Belgique and Brufina share control of the largest and oldest steel company, Cockerill-Ougrée. Together, moreover, they control some two-thirds of Belgian steel output.

Belgium has always been export oriented and in fact, exports between 30 and 40 per cent of her production, some $450 per capita or the highest ratio for any EEC country. The country's exports are extremely diversified, ranging from *witloof*, the slightly bitter Belgian endives so relished by gourmets the world over, to film, machinery, electrical equipment, and steel. Perhaps most important, Belgium is the world's center for industrial diamonds. The Congo's Kasai and Katanga provinces have a hoard of industrial treasure; *diamant boart*, a diamond grit used for various grinding tools from fine dental implements to huge oil-rig bores is an essential commodity. Antwerp transforms this boart into various grades of what is basically a glittering sandpaper made of diamond dust which is bonded to specification to the metal surface of the tool. Antwerp, of course, also supplies diamonds of larger caliber for multifarious industrial purposes, as well as gem stones for the sole purpose of beauty and ornament.

Because Belgium has always considered the world her market, many of her largest companies are as well known abroad as at home. Photoproducts Gevaert, is the world's second largest producer of photosensitive materials. It recently formed a joint company with Agfa, the German Farbenfabriken Bayer subsidiary. Some 92 per cent of Gevaert's products—film for photography, medical, and office purposes—is exported to Common Market countries, the United States and the EFTA nations. Innovation, a large Brussels department store, is as well known in Paris as in the Belgian capital. The company has started a popular Parisian chain of discount stores, the INNOs, which often undersell all other food and retail chains.

Fabrique Nationale d'Armes de Guerre makes the Browning and Mauser sports rifles as well as heavier-gauge equipment such as jet engines and parts. It supplies NATO with rifles and of course armaments to a variety of armies and governments. Among the other well-known Belgian firms are La Royale Belge, a large insurance company; Ateliers de Construction Électrique de Charleroi, (ACEC), an electric and electronic equipment firm; Pétrofina, an international oil company; and Wagon Lits, long synonymous with sleeping-car comfort for European travellers. Belgian furniture manufacturers are also well known internationally and the country is pioneering in the production of prefabricated units for construction.

Generally speaking, the sectors of Belgian industry which are prospering include electrical engineering, cement, foods, and the service areas—supermarkets and banks. The glass and chemicals industries have also demonstrated good growth potential, as have the utilities which, in contrast to much of the rest of Europe, are privately held.

THE CONGO, THE TAX, AND THE BOURSE

"All good things are three," states a folk saying, but for the Brussels Bourse the proverb would have to be modified to read, "All bad things too, come in threes." Three factors have cast long shadows on the Bourse and have made it into one of Europe's more somnolent markets in recent years: the loss of the Congo; the country's dependence on coal and steel; and a recently promulgated withholding tax on dividends.

Since the turn of the century, when King Leopold II bequeathed his central African properties to his nation, Belgian talents in trade and technical fields centered on the Congo. The Congo's Katanga province is a mining engineer's dream and a geological anomaly. It is the wealthiest area in Africa, a continent otherwise poor in natural resources. Such is the mineral concentration in Katanga that the province produces some 8 per cent of the world's copper, nearly 75 per cent of its cobalt, 80 per cent of industrial diamonds, as well as significant quantities of gold, silver, manganese, tantalum, and cadmium. The Union Minière du Haut Katanga mines also yield radium and uranium, the building blocks of the atomic age. Before the extensive Canadian uranium finds of the mid-1950s, the Belgian Congo's Shinkolobwe mine in Katanga was one of the only known sources for this fissionable raw material.

For Belgium, the Congo loomed large not only because the mother country became the purveyor of the colony's mineral wealth, but because it attracted the cream of her youth, the best of her university graduates. Moreover, Belgian colonial policy concentrated on primary education but failed to provide for Congolese higher education. At independence in 1960, there were fewer than a dozen native college graduates in the whole of the Congo. The dictates of Belgian paternalism afforded a monopoly of responsible positions to whites, and often more specifically to Walloons. Flemings were often limited to minor clerical functions and sometimes these *petits blancs* competed for jobs with the Congolese *évolués,* the high-school educated Westernized middle class. So seemingly secure was Belgium's hold on the Congo and so integrated in Belgian thinking that it was considered a national refuge in time of trouble. Ironically, during the Korean War many people sent their securities and wealth to Leopoldville for safekeeping. There was even a proposal afoot to move the Brussels Bourse to Leopoldville.

The Belgians precipitously left the Congo in 1960, granting the Congolese a hurried independence; the aftermath and ensuing chaos became a world problem, with United Nations troops called in to restore peace and a semblance of civil order. However, it is the generally accepted view that the dispatch with which the Belgian government acceded to Congolese demands for independence—within six months—was a goodwill gesture. Not only did they not expect the civil war which followed statehood, but in return for their speedy gesture of goodwill, the Belgians expected to be asked to stay on in the Congo as guides and mentors. This was not to be. In addition, Moise Tshombe's attempts to create an independent state at Katanga also failed. In the words of one Brussels paper, there was to be no "*Katanga de Papa*," where Belgium could continue in a modified version of her former role.

The Belgian economy was less dependent on the Congo than was generally assumed, but the effect on Belgium's Bourses was drastic. They are only now beginning to recover from the blow. Depending on the valuation of shares, Belgium's commitments in the Congo have been gauged at between $4.5 to $7.5 billion. As of 1959, the official estimate of private Belgian holdings in Congo companies was some $2 billion. This figure includes only industrial equity and not government expenditures.

In over-all economic terms, however, the Congo provided Belgium with only about 5 per cent of her national income and an equal percentage of her imports. The aftermath of Congolese independence was that the Belgian budget was saddled with some BF6 billion ($120 million) in compensation to refugees and payments of Congolese government debts. Revenues from taxing Congolese enterprises had amounted to some BF3 billion ($60 million) which would no longer be forthcoming. The cost of servicing Congolese loans for which the Belgian government had acted as guarantor came to another BF3 billion ($60 million).

What Belgium as a whole lost was her exclusive share in the Congo's potential growth. For instance, her part in the development of the hydroelectric potential at Inga in the lower Congo which promises to make of the area a kind of African Ruhr, is now much reduced. For companies that played a leading role in Congo development before nationhood, the adjustments have been far greater, of course.

The really heavy losses were more localized. With independence the mother country lost her monopoly of shipping to the colony and of insurance on the goods shipped. For Sabena Belgian World Airlines (50 per cent government owned) this meant the loss of her most profitable air route, and for Compagnie Maritime, Belgium's main shipping line, the withering away of her main cargo route. About 20 per cent of Société Générale's holdings were tied up in the Congo, and the government too had sizeable African investments. Since 1908 when she acquired the Congo, Belgium has plowed considerable sums into the colony. At independence, however, there was a deficit of some $112 million in Belgium's account. This deficit had been growing for five years preceding the Congo's independence due to a sharp drop in world prices for copper and other basic commodities. About a third of the payments deficit was due to Belgian shipping and insurance interests.

Among the companies holding major interests in the Congo, Société Générale de Belgique figures prominently. It controlled a variety of sectors including banks, breweries, railroads, insurance, sugar, and cotton plantations. The Compagnie du Congo pour le Commerce et l'Industrie was one of its main holdings. Union Minière du Haut Katanga, on the other hand, is held partly by Société Générale, the Congolese government and British and American shareholders. Société de Bruxelles pour la Finance et l'Industrie, the holding company of which Banque de Bruxelles is a part, is also very active in the Congo as are Huilever, a subsidiary of the Anglo-Dutch firm of Unilever, Banque Empain, and the Société Commerciale et Minière du Congo.

Belgian private investors first bought heavily in the Congo and then abruptly withdrew their funds in 1958 and 1959. By the end of 1959 the flight of capital reached alarming proportions of close to $100 million, and by 1960 money was being repatriated at the rate of some $20 million per month. At this point Belgian authorities stepped in and persuaded some of the large financial institutions to stem the flow and even to make advance payments to the Congolese Treasury. Most private investors thus cut their losses but, of course, many did not get out in time. Today Congo issues can be bought at bargain-basement prices. When young professionals are asked today why they are not active purchasers of securities, the answer is invariably: "Oh, you see Papa lost so much money in the Congo. . . ."

Old habits seemingly die hard, however. The Official List of the Brussels Bourse still features headings such as *Emprunts de la Colonie,* Loans of the Colony, and *Actions a revenu variable dont le dividende fixe de 4% et l'amortissement sont garantis par la Colonie,* where the Colony guarantees the interest due. Perhaps the typesetters will eventually change the headings to conform with history.

The other factors deepening the doldrums on the Bourse are the difficulties of the steel industry, an industrial sector which accounts for 20 per cent of Belgium's exports, and the withholding tax on dividends which went into effect in 1963. Actually, Belgium's withholding tax on dividends dates back to 1961, but the recent revision has added teeth. Stockholders must now come forward and identify themselves to tax authorities if they wish to collect their full dividends. The net effect on the Bourse has been a flight of capital, as wealthy Belgians purchased foreign securities where no withholding tax applies and no names need be mentioned. Observers blame the tax as a major factor in investor disinterest in Belgian stocks, bonds, and government paper as well. For the foreign investor, 15 per cent of the dividend is withheld at source, and this may be taken as a credit against U.S. federal taxes.

CORPORATE STRUCTURE

In large outline, Belgian corporate structure follows the French model. The corporation, *société anonyme,* is the prevailing form and that closest to American business organization. When a public offering of shares is made, whether of new or well-established corporations, the Belgian Banking Commission, the *Commission Bancaire,* must be informed of the step. The Commission is a sort of SEC which, though not empowered to either approve or disapprove of such an offering, can delay it if not satisfied with the prospectus, or information given on either the company or the issue. The Commission Bancaire may suggest revisions of the prospectus and require that more detailed information be made public. Although technically government consent is not needed to raise capital, without the Commission Bancaire's approval an offering would be doomed to failure, as no financial institution would handle it and no investors would take it up.

Generally speaking, neither investment laws nor Belgian company by-laws discriminate against foreigners. No distinction is made between nationals and foreigners as a rule, and for all intents and purposes there are no restrictions concerning foreigners in Belgium, nor in repatriating principal, dividends, or interest.

Most Belgian shares are bearer rather than registered, and all shares representing an equal share of the capital must confer an equal voice in company affairs. Nonvoting, or plural voting shares are outlawed in Belgium, but shares may or may not have a par value. Belgium is the exception on the Continent in permitting no-par value stock. Consequently, quotations are in Belgian francs per share, except for bonds and debentures where the quote is expressed as a percentage. As in France, the Belgian société anonyme may have different categories of shares including preferred stock and founders' parts, *actions de jouissance*.

Belgians are more yield conscious than the French, but less so than the British. New issues are usually priced low, way below the market price of the shares. Rights issues are not as frequent as in France, but Belgian banks will usually come out with a rights issue once a year as a form of dividend payment. This is in addition to the cash dividend, as a rule.

SECURITY ANALYSIS

Belgian analysts encounter the usual difficulties current on the Continent. Pétrofina and Compagnie d'Outremer are the only companies which consolidate their accounts. Most others will merely give their holdings without the extent of their participation. This, in the words of one Belgian analyst, makes for "major uncertainty." Many companies, for instance, will simply give broad general indications of sales. Gevaert has been known to state that its sales are up 10 per cent from the year before, but since it is the largest exporter of photosensitive materials and since 92 per cent of their product is geared for export, it is possible to extrapolate a more specific figure.

Most companies will not reveal their sales figures. When asked why, the reply is invariably, "So that the competition won't know!" However, should one ask them their competitors' sales, they seem to know the figures very well. Analysis is a new business that is making slow progress. The secrecy which surrounds the holding companies is further complicated by the lack of uniformity in accounting practices and interpretation of the tax laws. For instance, depreciation means widely different things to different companies and in the last analysis seems to be negotiable with the tax authorities. Under these circumstances it is difficult for the most skilled analysts to draw any general rules.

SOURCES OF INFORMATION

Belgian brokers are the only persons allowed to trade on the Exchanges. There are so many agents de change in Brussels—735 of them representing 350 active firms—that most brokers have far too little business. Besides the Brussels market, there are Exchanges in Anvers, Ghent, and Liége with another 276 local brokers. Consequently, only a few brokers publish market letters or financial information. The banks are the usual sources of information on companies and general economic development and outlook. All the large Belgian banks publish regular market surveys and market letters, as do many small private institutions. Bank letters, however, will not actively recommend stocks; this is left to the banker–client conference.

The morning paper specializing in financial news is the *Agence Économique et Financière* and the main evening newspaper is *L'Écho de la Bourse*.

For company reports, the standard reference volume is *Le Recueil Financier, Annuaire des Valeurs Cotées aux Bourses de Belgique*. There is also a yearly edition of another volume entitled, *Mémento des Valeurs à Revenu variable cotées aux Bourses Belges* which carries the imprimatur of various banks or brokerage houses. It includes a page or so rundown on both the domestic and the foreign stocks quoted in Belgium.

Excellent material is published by the Caisse Générale d'Épargne et de Retraite, the CGER. Their yearly *Compte Rendu* includes an analysis of a large number of company reports, and their *Études Complémentaires* will tackle a whole sector, such as coal, foods, chemicals, etc. The studies put out by the economic department of the Banque de Bruxelles are also extremely comprehensive.

Considered "financial leftists," the Centre de Recherche et d'Information Socio-Politique published *Structure Économique de la Belgique, Morphologie des Groupes Financiers* which is one of the only sources of information on the activities of les holdings. The publication gives the holding companies' participations and the companies they control.

For more general economic information and statistics, good sources are: the Institut National de Statistique, the central statistical office publications; material issued by DULBEA, the Département d'Économie Appliquée de l'Université de Bruxelles. DULBEA's quarterly *Cahiers économiques de Bruxelles* is one of the best sources for overall statistics, information on the GNP, various indexes, as well as other relevant global figures.

The Fédération des Industries Belges, the Belgian Federation of Industry, is a good source for specialized information such as detailed studies of tax laws, etc.

The most widely used indexes are compiled by the Bourse with a base date of December 31, 1953. Though there are several indexes for various parts of the market, the most quoted one comprises 152 stocks representing 87 per cent of the total market. It is adjusted to reflect changes in share capitalization.

An important index—one widely referred to in any discussion of European securities—is the *Eurosyndicat Index* published by a group of European banks with headquarters in Brussels. Besides a general index, an index of each major sector is also published: Banks and Finance; Utilities and Telephone; Metal; Electrical and Electronics; Oils and Chemicals. The general index is based on the share equity of 100 Common Market concerns with a base date of December 31, 1958 or the beginning of the EEC.

4. THE NETHERLANDS

Embedded in the large stone blocks of the Amsterdam Stock Exchange facade are six signs, three on either side of the entrance: VERBODEN RIJWIELEN TE PLAATSEN, "It is forbidden to park bicycles here." Holland's twelve million people own six million bicycles. Everyone rides one, Amsterdam brokers, bankers, and office boys included. In a sense, therefore, this strange interdiction on the walls of one of the world's leading financial institutions protects its denizens from themselves. Brokers are always on the run. The sidewalk is narrow. The less nimble would stumble over their own two-wheelers in their concerted rush into the *Beurs*.

Beurs means "purse" and *Bourse* (French), *Börse* (German), *Børs* (Danish), *Borsa* (Italian), and *Bolsa* (Spanish) are later translations from the Dutch. Three symbolic purses on a sign used to swing high above a Bruges merchant's door, marking the first Exchange in Europe. His name was Van de Beurse and in the late 1450s his house became known simply as the Beurs. As other countries emulated Netherlands trading techniques, they adopted not only the form of trade but the name as well. In Amsterdam, the first formal Beurs dates back to 1611. The present building, however, is of 1913 vintage.

Appropriately, the Exchange has a sailing vessel for weathervane, a wind-blown reminder of Holland's shipping and trading tradition. Appropriately too, both *Effectenbeurs* and *Koopmansbeurs,* Stock Exchange and Merchants' Exchange, are set in the midst of today's familiar trading centers, Amsterdam's bustling department stores.

The more traditional trading companies which historically made

116

Holland's fortune are also close by. They line the concentric canals which almost encircle the old city and grace the Amstel, the river which gave Amstelredam or Amsterdam its name. River and canal were and are ideal conduits for the conduct of business. When ships arrived from foreign ports and far-flung trading posts, they moored right at the merchant's door before calling at a customer's warehouse. The trading companies fostered a unique commercial development— the first joint stock companies with actively traded shares in the Western world. The Vereenigde Oost-Indische Compagnie (the Associate East India Company) founded in 1602 is the Methuselah of stock companies. Its shares (*actiën*) were registered subscriptions of varying amounts, and almost as soon as these subscriptions were entered the commercially minded public of Amsterdam started to trade them. This development, a transition from the trade association or merchant guild to a public company of limited liability, set the stage for commercial expansion. In the words of one noted historian:

> . . . it enabled others than merchants to put their money into trade, thus increasing the available sources of capital. It united different classes of men in the ventures, and so was able to associate the technical knowledge of the merchant with political influence and judgment of the man of larger affairs. . . .*

The Amsterdam Exchange dates its origins to those dealings.

The independence of the Netherlands and the establishment of the Dutch Empire in the seventeenth century focused world attention on Amsterdam. The city became a center of entrepôt trade; it was a magnet for northern Europe as it was situated on the deltas of the Rhine, Meuse, and Scheldt rivers. During the course of the seventeenth century, the Dutch developed the best fishing fleet and merchant marine in Europe, building both quickly and cheaply. Holland became the common carrier and the "packhouse of the world." Moreover, the Dutch boasted the lowest interest rates during that period. Foreign potentates, plenipotentiaries, and princes all applied to the Dutch *stoop,* awaiting a handout from the thrifty, well-to-do Netherlanders. Few went away empty-handed; during the following three

* G. N. Clark, *The Seventeenth Century* (Oxford: Clarendon Press, 1953), p. 35.

centuries the Dutch extended credit and floated loans on a worldwide basis.

Consequently, the present day international character of the Dutch capital market has a long, venerable, and profitable history. By the end of the eighteenth century, of the 100 securities quoted in Amsterdam 44 were foreign bonds. Fifty years later, the number had risen to 71 and by 1880 the value of foreign securities was 2.2 billion guilders, compared to only Gld. 1.2 billion of Dutch domestic stock. Dutchmen were actively dealing in American securities from an early date. On August 28, 1798, a 5 per cent U.S. bond sold at Fl. 90, a respectable showing compared to a similar Russian issue then selling at Fl. 84. Yet during the Civil War some Dutch investors misplaced their money, purchasing a Confederate 4 per cent debenture. The Confederacy, moreover, redeemed only a single coupon.

By and large, American securities have served Holland well, particularly during World War II. Before the war, Netherlands interests held nearly $1.8 billion of those securities. That sizable investment was largely in "street name," so to speak, held by a series of central depositaries, or "administration offices," which in turn issued "Dutch Administration Certificates" in bearer form against the registered U.S. shares. Dutch stockholders preferred the bearer form, and an active market in American shares was maintained. With the German invasion of Holland, the United States froze those assets, blocking the enemy from redeeming them. Although the invaders acquired physical control of the shares, they found they could do nothing with them. Of course, with the underlying stock blocked, the Administration Certificates became as useless as play money.

At the end of the war, American shares held abroad once more became freely convertible. The Dutch resumed their trading in certificates—at, needless to say, much higher prices. Today certificates are still used, but large investors do not convert their shares.

Dutch bankers assert that nearly every investor holds one or more American issues. (Dutch citizens are not allowed to have security accounts outside of Holland.) However, American interest in Dutch securities is relatively new and has focused on the six "internationals": Koninklijke Nederlandsche Petroleum Maatschappij, Royal Dutch

Petroleum Company; Philips' Gloeilampenfabrieken, Philips' Incandescent Lamps Works, the General Electric of Europe; Algemene Kunstzijde Unie, or AKU, a leading producer of rayon and other synthetics; Koninklijke Nederlandsche Hoogovens en Staalfabrieken, or Royal Dutch Blast Furnaces and Steelworks, "Hoogovens" for short; Unilever, the Anglo-Dutch suds giant, producing detergents, chemicals, foods, and fats; and Koninklijke Luchtvaart Maatschappij, Royal Dutch Airlines.

The "internationals" are giant companies, even by American standards. Royal Dutch Petroleum ranks after Standard Oil of New Jersey as the second largest oil company. Rated by sales, Unilever is the seventh largest company in the world. It consists of two holding companies, the English Unilever Ltd. and the Dutch Unilever, NV. Both are listed on the Big Board. Philips' is the largest electric appliance and electronics manufacturer in Europe.

BEURS AND BROKERS

The *Effectenbeurs* is a most self-contained entity. Every service a man could want is available within the massive building, including a trilingual barbershop on the ground floor. The only thing brokers might venture outside for is *nieuwe haring,* a snack of raw young herring, held by the tail and savored on the curb. For this delicacy they must dash across the street.

Owned by the *Vereeniging voor den Effectenhandel,* the Stock Exchange Association, the building meets the needs of a modern financial center, complete with jabbering teletype machines, a control booth in the center of the floor, rentable phone booths around the sides, and a statue of Mercury, the patron saint of Stock Exchanges. Membership in the association, a private institution, is open to both banks and brokers. Currently, it costs 17,000 florins ($4,722) to join the Exchange and there are 475 members. This is a sizable body by European standards, almost the same size as the American Stock Exchange.

The scope of the market is likewise impressive for so small a country. There are over 2,300 listed securities, 800 of which are shares of foreign companies. Dutch shares are valued at over Gld. 31 billion ($8.6 billion) in 1963; in addition, there is a substantial over-the-counter market. However, in 1961, for the first time after the war purchases of foreign shares by Dutchmen exceeded the sale of domestic Dutch securities to foreigners by Gld. 120 million.

Officially, the Exchange is open only from 1:00 to 2:15 P.M. daily. In reality, it is open longer, but only transactions taking place during the time interval are published in the Official List and in the financial press. Arbitrage with other European Bourses takes place all day, while trading with New York begins at 3 o'clock and lasts till 8:30. Since the market is already closed, activity with New York only concerns the "internationals."

Any broker in Holland can also act as a specialist on the floor of the Exchange; the option is his and is of no concern to the Exchange administration. The man simply appoints himself, telling his colleagues he will henceforth deal in X securities. This procedure is symptomatic of the informality with which the Dutch approach all business dealings. Rules and regulations are minimal or nonexistent. Specialists are termed *hoekman,* but their job is not quite parallel to an American specialist or a London jobber. He is merely an intermediary, an agent, between buyer and seller attempting to balance the conflicting forces. He rarely takes a position in the security.

Specialists are to be found at the 82 *hoeken,* "corners," or spots where various categories of stocks are traded, i.e., government bonds, plantation shares, foreign securities, etc. There are two kinds of hoeken; the open corners carry on trade in active shares, while the closed corners concentrate on inactive securities. Actually, it is the amount of activity in a security which determines whether the hoeken is open or closed.

At the open hoeken four dozen active bonds and two dozen active stocks change hands, including of course the "internationals." Prices are quoted at seven distinct intervals, termed "tapes," for the duration of the trading day. Highs and lows for each period are published in the daily Official List, affording a Dutchman a fairly accurate picture of price trends.

The investor purchasing "internationals" can take advantage of a special Dutch treat—the unique device of the "average" price. If he gives an "at the market" order before the opening of trading, his purchase or sale will be executed at the day's median price. Thus there is no danger of buying too dearly or selling too cheaply by catching the market at a wrong turn. Should the client wish to give a limited order, he can still benefit from the "average price." He will get whichever is more favorable—his specified limit, or the middle price. In no event will his order be executed beyond his imposed limit. Of course, to take advantage of this device, the broker must receive the order and pass it to the specialist before the opening of the trading session.

The active international stocks rarely go begging for buyers or sellers, so the hoekman has a relatively easy time matching orders regardless of size. This is not always true for the less active domestic shares. Because of the more limited activity, the specialist fixes a single price for the day and all transactions take place at that quotation. Should there be a shortage of stock, the specialist rations his customers on a proportional basis. In order not to push up or force down prices in the less active shares it is worthwhile to give the broker or banker discretion and to include in the market order the proviso, "without forcing."

Dutch institutions insist that the middle price arrangement and proportional distribution are "most advantageous for the customer." Ostensibly, it appears that way, and all clients of the Amsterdam market are, in fact, treated equally. But it must be remembered that by and large European Exchanges have no equivalent of the Securities and Exchange Commission. The markets are no more honest or dishonest than American ones, but practices do vary and ethical interpretations differ. For instance, the Dutch "average price" is in itself strictly fair, provided that the average is freely arrived at. However, there are some Dutchmen who feel that on rare occasions the market is given a helping hand. Brokers and floor traders do a lot of mutual business and any official bid or offer, even the smallest amount at the fringes, can move the average. Reportedly this happens from time

to time, particularly when there is an imbalance in the market. It is
not apparent from the translux tape, as only prices are indicated, not
sales volume. Volume figures are published the next day.

By U.S. standards, prices of Dutch shares are high, though Dutchmen are quick to point out that this is not synonymous with "expensive." High prices naturally means fewer shares changing hands. The
Dutch seem to sell stock as they might herring or sausage and it is not
uncommon to hear brokers on the floor yelling, "I'll take two pieces,"
or "One piece for me, please."

Why the high denominations? Government tax policies and the
lack of a broad share-owning public have conspired to keep denominations of share capital in sizable lots. Par value (a government
requirement) for most stocks is Gld. 1,000 ($277) and no distinction
exists between trading one or one hundred shares. In Holland it is
customary to quote security prices in percentages of the nominal
value, except for a few "internationals" that are quoted in florins (another name for the guilder) or in dollars. For instance, a single share
of Bijenkorf, the largest department store in Holland, might cost 775
per cent, or Fl. 7,750 ($2,152). Cash and stock dividends likewise are
expressed as percentages. For the "internationals" the shares have
been split into more manageable denominations of Fl. 20 ($5.55),
Fl. 25 ($6.94), or Fl. 50 ($13.88) par value. Prices of Royal Dutch
Petroleum given in the press are usually expressed in either dollar
or florin equivalents; the same is true of Philips'. For instance, a Fl. 25
par value share may be quoted at a market price of Fl. 148 or $41.11.

All transactions on the Amsterdam Stock Exchange must be settled
within four days. There is no forward or term market in Holland and
consequently short sales are unknown. Securities cannot be bought
on margin, though some banks will lend money against deposited
securities. A put and call option market exists though it is largely
confined to the "internationals."

There is no capital gains tax in the Netherlands. The Dutch tried it
but were not pleased with the results and so repealed it. Obviously,
they are a pragmatic people. The tax produced little income for the
government and it dried up trading on the Exchange, cutting government revenue from stamp duty to boot. Though the Dutch are wedded

to bearer securities, all transactions in stocks and bonds, whether sales or purchases, are subject to stamp duty of Fl. 0.12 per Fl. 100. If the stamp duty is not paid there is no proof of possession and the government considers such sales void.

What does this mean to an American investor? Assuming that prices are more or less the same in Holland and in the United States because of arbitrage in the international shares, the only difference will be in commission rates. There would be a small saving by going directly to the Amsterdam market where commission rates are slightly lower (see the tabulation below). As noted in the chapter on England,

Commission Rates (per cent)	Value to be Charged on	Fee (per cent)
1. For the purchase and sale in the Netherlands of securities quoted in percentages		
A. Not exceeding 10	Actual	2.4
B. Above 10 but not exceeding 30	Nominal	0.3
C. Above 30 but not exceeding 105	Nominal	0.6
D. Above 105	Actual	0.6
2. For the purchase and sale in the Netherlands of securities quoted in guilders per unit	Actual	0.6

a more substantial saving arises when a stock has little or no market in the United States and its purchase is executed abroad. Otherwise the American investor faces two commission charges, plus a possible additional markup if the transaction goes through a Wall Street firm not specializing in foreign shares.

Holland makes no distinction between domestic and foreign investors. Listed foreign securities can be freely purchased by nonresidents for guilders, dollars, or any other foreign currency. Currency control regulation of trading hardly exists. Dividends and principal are freely redeemable or can be kept in a convertible guilder account. To purchase unlisted securities, however, requires a license from the Netherlands central bank. This is usually granted.

Dutch corporations have to remit a 15 per cent dividend withholding tax to the government. This sum is simply subtracted from dividends before they are paid out to the investor. Residents of the

United States can collect their dividends tax free on all the large international companies. The 15 per cent withheld by other companies can be used as a credit against U.S. taxes since the signing of a double taxation treaty in 1948.

THE BANKS

There is no equivalent of Lombard Street or Broad Street in Amsterdam. The banks are spread all over; one Wall Street representative even has his office in his suburban home. Yet, from clipper weathervane on the Stock Exchange to rooftop pulley rig which crowns all buildings affording access to upstairs warehouses, the city's trading traditions are apparent. Rotterdam's harbor is more active—in fact, it surpasses New York's in tonnage—but Amsterdam's canal caïques never stop. Commerce characterizes the capital.

"Doing business in Holland is easy—almost too easy. The same thing is true of banking," one banker remarked. The number of banks in evidence seems to bear him out. Opening a bank in the Netherlands requires only a chat with the head of the central bank, and the formalities are over. There are few restrictions on the kinds of transactions a bank may engage in. Brokerage, investment banking, financing mortgages, dealing in bills of acceptance are all fair game.

While both banks and brokers are members of the Amsterdam Stock Exchange, the banks play by far the more active role. Indeed, according to informed estimates, four-fifths of the brokerage business is done by banks, which do almost all the international business. What role then do the banks play in the market? It is generally understood that Dutch banks do not pursue an active role in determining prices as, say, the French, German, or Swiss banks do. First of all, Netherlands banks prefer to limit themselves to short- and medium-term credit. Loans to industry are their forte and, but for occasional underwritings, they rarely purchase equity for their own account.

Recent mergers among the "big four" banks may change this picture, however. The four large banks which dominated the Dutch scene and accounted for two-thirds of the nation's banking business are now two. The Amsterdamsche Bank and the Rotterdamsche Bank have combined under the new name of Amrobank. Algemene Bank Nederland will be the new name for the merged Nederlandsche Handel-Maatschappij (Netherlands Trading Society) and de Twentsche Bank. These moves were undoubtedly forced on them by growing American competition and the larger banking units found in other European countries. In terms of brokerage business, these two banks now command a large majority of market transactions. It is not yet clear how their matching of orders off the Exchange will affect business on the Beurs.

The two large banks have extensive brokerage services with research departments, though commercial banking is their more important business. They will accept any size of account and no minimum balance is required. They do not provide investment counseling but do occasionally make portfolio suggestions. However, they abjure discretionary power except in their trust accounts. Naturally, they take care of all the household chores connected with custodianship.

There are other smaller public banks in the Netherlands which also provide brokerage and general banking services. Two are of particular interest: the Nederlandse Overzee Bank and the Hollandsche Bank-Unie. The former has extensive ties with South Africa, a 25 per cent interest in Nederlands Bank of South Africa, plus offices and interests throughout Europe. Moreover, in cooperation with Hambros Bank of London it introduced the first *banque d'affaires* in Holland, Investeringsbank Amsterdam, which has connections in South America, Israel, and Turkey.

Brokerage business plays a more preferred role among private bankers and to some degree they pursue their ends more aggressively. The Stock Market is the *specialité de la maison* of the private banks. While all Dutch banks publish market literature in English, the reviews and company analyses of the private banks are longer and more detailed. Hope and Company (Benjamin Franklin borrowed money for the United States from them) and Mees and Zoonen have merged to form one bank; Pierson, Heldring and Pierson; Labouchère and Company; and Bankiershuis van Eeghen are excellent private banks acquainted with American market practices. Needless to say, the list is far from a complete index of Dutch banks. Some private banks have special accounts for portfolio management, charging a flat fee on the sum involved. Two large brokerage houses are also worth noting: Nachenius and Gleichman & van Heemstra.

CORPORATE STRUCTURE

Most Dutch companies take a limited liability form, expressed as *Naamloze Vennootschap,* usually abbreviated to NV. Bearer shares are issued against the fixed capital of the corporation, each having a specific par value. "No-par" stock is unknown in Holland, but a few companies do issue partly paid shares, e.g., 20 per cent down and future instalments whenever the company is in need of more capital. These partially paid shares are traded on the Exchange but, since owners of such shares are legally obligated to pay their full value, the stock is in registered form. This technique is preferred by insurance companies since their business requires a surplus of capital. Registered shares are also used by a few tightly held companies wary of alien domination, be it foreign or domestic.

The Dutch have devised other ways of obviating take-over dangers. Many Netherlands companies have established trusts or holding companies. The total of common stock is held outright by the trust, which then issues certificates backed by the stock. (The process is akin to a country's central bank issuing paper currency while holding the gold which backs it in its coffers.) These "Dutch certificates" are quoted on the Amsterdam Exchange as well as abroad. Owners have all the rights of ordinary stockholders—receiving full dividends, participating in rights issues—but they have no voting privileges. This obviously insures the company against any take-over bids or any dissenting voices in the management. Proponents of stockholder democracy may be shocked, but the Dutch appear happy enough with the situation. To cite but one example, Philips' Gloeilampenfabrieken, the largest non-American electronics and electrical goods producer, is owned by Philips' Incandescent Lamps Works Holding Company (Philips' NV). Twenty-eight per cent of these trust certificates are reportedly owned by Americans.

Company Analysis

Dutch companies fall into two categories: the "internationals" and the domestic variety. Information on the internationals is about as complete and comprehensive as most investors could wish. A plethora of facts are available, since they are vast companies traded in many countries. Royal Dutch, Unilever, and KLM are listed on the New York Stock Exchange and thus comply with most of the Exchange and SEC requirements concerning full disclosure. For instance, prompt quarterly or semiannual statements are made as to consolidated balance sheets (AKU does not consolidate though it publishes quarterly figures), sales, income before and after taxes, and profit margins. In brief, one gets the kind of information that might be expected from a large U.S. company.

Information on the internationals is carried in the financial sections of every self-respecting newspaper. The *Financieele Dagblad,* a daily, and *De Financieele Koerier,* a weekly, are the main business publications of Holland. However, the main stock index is prepared by the Central Bureau of Statistics, using 1953 as the base of 100. This is a relatively good index, weighted in relation to the trading volume. Fifty-three stocks are used: they are divided into the internationals and the major segments of the economy. Five internationals make up 47 per cent of the average and are often quoted separately. Observers feel that even more weight should be accorded to this group since it is usually responsible for two-thirds of the Amsterdam Exchange's volume. Banks make up 8 per cent of the index, shipping shares 8 per cent, industrials 24 per cent, and commercial issues 13 per cent.

Information on Dutch domestic companies is considerably scarcer. Quarterly reports are the exception rather than the rule. Companies pay dividends once a year and generally prefer to remain financially anonymous the rest of the time. Balance sheets are rarely consolidated. Though the Dutch may be secretive, they have a reputation for fiscal integrity. Secrecy, besides being traditional, is to some degree due to the country's tax structure. Families that own or control corporations are subject to a capital assets tax. Therefore they provide little corporate news and have little interest in seeing their securities bid up on

the Exchange, which would eventually entail higher tax bills. Furthermore, internal financing is a traditional way of raising money in the
Netherlands. This accounts for the rather few new issues to appear in
the Dutch market. Financing from retained earnings—an honored
Calvanistic penchant—also keeps dividends rather low. More public
information does, however, become available when companies are
forced either to borrow money or raise cash through the sale of new
stock.

Rights issues are fairly frequent in Holland—a practice similar to
the French one—with a large disparity between market price of the
shares and price of the rights. The detached rights can then be sold on
the Exchange, a practice indulged in by most Dutchmen. Most companies will try to maintain dividends on the new shares as well. Dutch
companies prefer this method of issuing shares as opposed to distributing high stock dividends. Holders of old shares may thus either acquire
the new shares or sell the rights without worrying about taxes. Stock
dividends from earnings are subject to tax for the difference between
the market value and the nominal value, whereas stock dividends
from the company's capital are not taxed.

The same holds true for stock dividends ("bonus shares"): dividends from paid-in surplus capital are tax free, but those from earnings are fair game for the revenue officer. Consequently, company
cornucopias often contain nontaxable stock dividends. For instance,
Philips' pursues a policy of distributing a 5 per cent stock dividend
per year. In reality, this is a form of tax-free indemnification for the
dilution of the company's capital by issuing shares that are under the
market value. The remaining international companies, on the other
hand, have adopted American procedures and issue new shares close
to the market price.

Annual reports of Dutch companies are far from uniform and information varies from company to company. Some Dutch firms still
value their fixed assets at one guilder, but this practice is slowly
fading. In 1962 many companies revalued their assets, thus giving a
more accurate estimate. Depreciation tends to be excessively generous by American standards, sometimes writing off investments in a
couple of years. This procedure, of course, diminishes the picture of

the company's earnings. However, Dutch investors are more concerned with the yield of a security than they are with the underlying earning power. As one Dutch banker noted, yield "plays a bigger role in determining prices than the profits of a company do." Consequently, professional American analysts have occasionally assumed Dutch shares to be cheap by American standards. Dutchmen do not always see it that way.

Though Holland (population 12 million; area 12,971 square miles) is an old commercial and trading center, the Industrial Revolution came late to the Netherlands. The first industrial census was held as late as 1930, or eighty-four years after Belgium's first count. Until World War II much of Dutch industry was small scale and family owned. With rather limited natural resources and a large proportion of potentially arable land under water or constantly threatened by the North Atlantic, the country had customarily based its prosperity largely on international trade and its colonial holdings in the East Indies. Shipping and plantation shareholdings were of paramount importance in the Dutch economy before the war.

Holland's recovery from the war was remarkable both for its speed and its soundness. Considering the devastation of the countryside—not to mention the almost total destruction of Rotterdam—the Dutch were again lending money abroad in 1954. After the war the economic structure of Holland changed rapidly. Japan's imperialism in the Pacific completely changed the political and economic forces in the area, even though she lost the war. The winds of change rapidly entered the void left by Japan's defeat. By 1949, the Dutch were forced to acknowledge the independence of their prime colonial holding, Indonesia. Probably over one-fifth of the national income was lost with the eviction from the East Indies. This rupture had its psychological manifestations as well. "We felt like a man who had lost one of his two legs," recalled the head of a private bank. "The very vitality of our country seemed to be sapped."

With Indonesia gone, the Dutch turned to internal development. They channeled their energies from trading, fishing, agriculture, and plantation companies to heavy industry: steel, chemicals, petroleum, paper, and textiles. The new industries grew along with the population. From 1940 to 1963 the population increased by one-third, or to the point where Holland is today one of the most densely populated countries in the world. However, its rapid industrial growth left the country with almost no unemployment problem.

Prosperity has slightly surprised the country and people are saving a good deal of what they earn. (In 1938 the national income per capita was Gld. 565 ($157), whereas in 1962 it was Gld. 3,284 ($912). National savings equal about one-fifth of the national income; the Dutch reputation for thrift is obviously well deserved. For instance, insurance is deemed important and consequently some of the largest insurance companies in Europe are situated in the Netherlands. In 1963 the Nationale Levensverzekering-Bank NV and the Nederlanden van 1845 merged to form the Nationale Nederlanden NV, the second largest life insurance company in the Common Market.

Through rather elaborate social insurance schemes, redistribution of income has increased consumer consumption. Three-fifths of all Dutch families have washing machines, though only 12 per cent have refrigerators. In such a small country cars are far from a necessity and only one out of 15 inhabitants owns one. To the visitor, Holland appears prosperous and comfortable, but not given to indulging in affluence.

While social welfare ranks high in the Netherlands, there has been no rash of nationalizing industries before or after the war. Nationalization is not even an avowed program of any of the non-Communist left parties. Indeed, some sectors of the economy are state owned and some private companies are jointly owned with the government; these are few though significant. For instance, Hoogovens, or more formally, the Royal Netherlands Blast Furnaces and Steelworks accounts for all the iron and steel production in Holland. The government owns 27 per cent of its modern plant and the city of Amsterdam owns 10 per cent.

Railroads and domestic gas and electricity are state enterprises; radio and television are run on a noncommercial basis; the state does not participate in the building industry, but housing construction is tightly regulated by the government; the shipping lines—such as Holland-America Line—are public stock companies, as is KLM, the third largest airline in the world and presently one of the least profitable. Parenthetically, KLM is listed on the New York Stock Exchange but reportedly 95 per cent of the company's stock is in government hands. (Swissair is the only European air system in which the government owns considerably less than half the equity.) Telephone and telegraph services, like the post, are government utilities.

Two vast industrial changes are destined to transform the geographical and economic face of Europe in general and Holland in particular. Due to devastating floods in 1953 which drowned 1,800 people and swamped over 430,000 acres of land, the government has undertaken a Gld. 3 billion ($833 million) Delta Plan. The object of the plan is to seal off the two southwestern provinces of Holland from the North Sea, reclaim some of the land, and rehabilitate a heretofore neglected part of the country. This twenty-five year development scheme—scheduled for completion in 1978—has been compared with the TVA in size and importance.

A recent discovery has changed the picture of Holland's limited natural resources. In 1962 huge natural gas reserves were found in the province of Groningen and off its shores in the North Sea. Under the law, in most European countries, subsoil extractive rights belong to the state and not to the landlord; Anglo-Saxon practice is just the opposite. Consequently, it is up to the Dutch government to determine how these vast gas fields will be exploited. A state-dominated consortium has been set up for this purpose. Early explorations have ascertained that these reserves are among the largest in the world. Full-scale production is expected by 1965, giving an enormous boost to the Dutch economy. While it is premature to guess which companies will benefit most directly, it is obvious that cheap power has long been one of industrial Europe's greatest needs. These gas fields should go a long way toward lowering energy prices in the whole of Western Europe.*

* H. George Franks, *Holland's Industries Stride Ahead: The New Netherlands of the 1960s* (Amsterdam: Federation of Netherlands Industries).

5. SWITZERLAND

INTERVIEWERS: Are there any typically Swiss proverbs, or perhaps humorous sayings about finance, money, banks, or securities that come to mind off hand?

SWISS BANKER: . . . No: The Swiss, my friends, don't joke about money!

In the past hundred years, Switzerland has achieved world renown for financial security, secrecy, stability, solvency, and sobriety. This reputation is something this small country (population 5.5 million; 15,996 square miles) occasionally has a hard time living with.

Starting with an alliance among three of the present twenty-two cantons, the Swiss Confederation dates from 1291. For the next three centuries, Switzerland became the home of armed mercenaries, tough legions of halberdier and pikemen. In the sixteenth century John Calvin's Reformed Church was established in Geneva. Calvinism's zealous efficiency and infatuation with good works could not assure salvation in a predestined world, but those qualities might be manifestations of that salvation. Calvin's theology supplied the growing middle-class Genevese with a *raison d'être* for their own frugality, thrift, and cunning. By bringing Christianity and commercial common sense together, he helped shape the future. For instance, interest was not condemned, as in the rest of medieval Europe, but defined and regulated.

During the sixteenth century Geneva's commercial activity expanded as its competitor, Lyon, was destroyed in the French religious wars. Situated on the confluence of the Rhône, Geneva prospered on the river traffic and an occasional corner in the wheat market. A further boost to the city's prosperity came upon Louis XIV's revocation of the Edict of Nantes in 1685. Thousands of Huguenots migrated to Geneva bringing with them capital and, perhaps more important, craft skills to a country of few natural resources. In 1815, the Congress of Vienna recognized Switzerland's perpetual neutrality, which was due, as one commentator notes, "to a benevolent Providence and an alert army."

It was not until the twentieth century that Zurich became the leading financial center of the country, though far from predominant. The tripartite nature of Swiss society (German 70 per cent, French 20 per cent, Italian 10 per cent) demanded neutrality abroad and confederation within. Neutrality is however more than a substitute for internecine strife. For the last couple of hundred years a policy of professional neutralism has stood the Swiss in good stead as arbiters in an aggressive world while they lived in peace. Geneva contains the United Nations European Headquarters, the International Committee of the Red Cross, the International Labor Organization, the World Postal Union, the Bank for International Settlements, and an endless series of other alphabet organizations that represent world bureaucracy. Mediation has achieved the status of a minor industry and the sanction of a ministerial calling.

In a pragmatic sense, Swiss frontiers are open to the hard and soft currencies of the world. Of course it is more than Swiss altruism that makes foreigners and foreign funds feel at home. First of all, the Swiss rely heavily on "invisible imports" (commerce, banking, and insurance payments from abroad), since their balance of payments since 1960 has been on the minus side. They have managed to cover their considerable trade gap with the two-edged sword of foreign capital. While the foreign influx of money has redressed the balance, to some extent it is responsible for overheating the economy with cheap money. With too much money chasing too few goods, the Swiss have had one of the more aggravated inflationary booms in Europe in the early sixties—an inflation of at least 4 per cent per year.

Recently, the "golden tide" reached such proportions that it threatened to inundate the Alps. Swiss banks are recipients of funds from the four corners of the world. The motives of the depositors are about as diverse as the countries from which moneys are sent. Money usually arrives via bank transfers or checks but has been known to appear on the scene in brown paper bags, scuffy leather luggage, and canvas money belts. Part of this Croessian deluge is "hot money," fugitive not from the law but from either the previous country's low interest rate, political instability, or impending devaluation whether real or rumoured. When bankers speak of hot money they usually refer to currency in the hands of speculators who are willing to move lire, Deutsche marks, pounds or dollars to wherever there are prospects for better interest rates or revaluation. To be sure, Switzerland is not the only country to receive hot money. Nor should one think of speculators as a class of shifty-eyed mendicants or swindlers. Involved in this game of monetary musical chairs are naturally the foreign exchange departments of all international banks, arbitrageurs, importers and exporters, commodity dealers, a host of interest hunters, international businesses, as well as some governmental agencies. All of them are interested in putting their funds to work in the most lucrative markets. Moving money is an expensive game and one has to be reasonably certain that the game is worthwhile.

Money is rarely moved into Switzerland on interest considerations alone. Switzerland's interest rates have been extraordinarily low for over a generation. In part, the reason, as noted by Dr. Franz Aschinger, financial editor of the *Neue Züricher Zeitung,* is the characteristic of "permanent liquidity" on the Swiss scene. Between 1936 and 1957 the Swiss National Bank kept the discount rate at 1½ per cent; even during the inflationary sixties it remains at 2 per cent or 2½ per cent. The liquidity ratio of the large Swiss banks often hovers around the 20 per cent mark. Consequently, the central bank lacks close contact with the commercial banks because it extends them rather little credit. The Swiss National Bank seems to exert less direct control on the economic life of the country than does any other European central bank. In fact, the National Bank is not quite a public institution; 45 per cent of its shares are in private hands. Shares are limited to Swiss citizens and they sell for approximately SF700 ($162). Instead of customary open market operations—the bank's portfolio of government securities is small—its monetary influence comes from regulating gold, the foreign exchange, and the capital markets of the country.

The picture of low interest rates has changed somewhat with the rapid growth in the last few years of the "Eurodollar" market—short-term financial transactions in dollars—but has not changed or radically altered rates on Swiss francs. Even if Swiss interest rates should be favorable, that is, higher than those of other European money centers, the cost of the swap (the contract for buying spot and selling forward currencies) may well eliminate the advantage. As one recent textbook put it: "With a given interest rate differential between two countries, interest arbitragers tend to move funds into the country where interest rates are higher, *provided* that the cost of covering the exchange risk is less than the interest rate differential."*

Obviously, Switzerland's foreign capital surplus is in the country not for any interest rate differential, but for safety and discretion. For instance, during World War II funds from all over Europe raced toward the Swiss banks. When the war was over a huge problem faced the Swiss about the assets of German nationals and the heirless assets of those persecuted by the Nazis. The American government demanded the Nazi hoards ensconced in Swiss banks. This was distasteful to the Swiss for it meant compromising their banking secrecy standards. A compromise was worked out in the Washington Agreement, by which the Swiss paid American authorities $60 million of German funds but did not reveal the names of the confiscated accounts. Heirless assets involved a smaller sum but proved to be more difficult to handle. A special parliamentary act was passed in 1962 which directed banks and other custodians to prepare lists of accounts inactive since the war. Nine hundred and sixty-one accounts were reported with assets of $2 million. The moneys will probably go to religious charities after further investigation.

Current crises reveal the same story: the Congo upheaval reportedly

---

* Max J. Wasserman, Charles W. Hultman, and Laszlo Zsoldos, *International Finance* (New York: Simmons-Boardman Publishing Corporation, 1963), p. 212.

caused the equivalent of SF1 billion ($231 million) to flood the country. Italian political instability in 1963-1964 saw perhaps even more in lire come into the country. "It would seem that every time there is a major political disturbance anywhere in the world," remarked a Swiss banker, "our banks will increase their assets by approximately $40 per Swiss citizen." Recent estimates find the inflow of capital to be running in the neighborhood of half a billion dollars yearly.

THE SWISS BANKS

Trustees of Switzerland's and the insecure world's moneys, the Swiss banks are rather singular institutions. First of all, their numbers are overwhelming. Switzerland is probably the most overbanked country in the world with 1,500 independent banks having over 4,000 separate offices or agencies. That provides one bank for every 1,360 individuals, infants included. The Swiss are fond of pointing out that there are more banking offices than dental offices, from which one can assume that your money gets better care than your teeth. Since the Swiss consume more chocolate than anyone else in the world—18 pounds per person, per year—this may be a dubious distinction.

One of the reasons for such intensive banking is the un-Continental hoarding habits of the Swiss: they don't practice it. For instance, Germans are estimated to hoard over DM6 billion ($1.5 billion) and the French have such a distrust of banks and paper money that their gold hoardings are proverbial. The Swiss on the other hand bank their savings and salaries. Consequently, money moves faster and more productively.

Three large commercial banks dominate the financial scene. They are public companies and their stock is quoted on Swiss Exchanges. Their balance sheets indicate that they are roughly the same size; moreover, their identity is often confused by native and foreigner alike since their titles in French, German, Italian, and English seem to be permutations and combinations on a single theme. Thus: the Union Bank of Switzerland is Schweizerische Bankgesellschaft, or Union de Banques Suisses, or finally Unione di Banche Svizzere. The

Swiss Bank Corporation might be Schweizerischer Bankverein, possibly Société de Banque Suisse, or Società di Banca Svizzera. And lastly, the Swiss Credit Bank goes under its German title as Schweizerische Kreditanstalt, Crédit Suisse in French, and Credito Svizzero in Italian. This of course only scratches the surface since there are another 1,497 banks, each with two, three, or four names to reckon with. Depositors have been known to develop dislexia with a vengeance.

These three banks, together with two smaller commercial banks, the Volksbank and Bank Leu & Co., account for approximately a third of total bank assets. Another third is held by the cantonal banks and the remainder is in savings banks, credit banks, and private banks. It is the three giant commercial banks and the private banks that give Switzerland its international image. Though there are less than sixty private banks—their liability is unlimited and so, it would seem, are the family fortunes behind the banks—their influence and portfolio holdings are sizable and out of all proportion to their number. Zurich is the home of the large commercial banks, even though the head office of the Swiss Bank Corporation is in Basle. The city is the capital for corporate life, twice the size of the second largest city, Basle, and is the center of the foreign exchange and gold markets. Geneva, on the other hand, is home for the private bankers. For instance, five old Genevese private banks—Darier & Cie., Ferrier, Lullin & Cie., Hentsch & Cie., Lombard, Odier & Cie., and Pictet & Cie. are situated there. They are highly regarded and much sought after for their investment advice, though legally enjoined from putting their names on the street doors lest it be interpreted as a solicitation for funds. Initials must suffice.

Any discussion of Switzerland's financial community must sooner or later bog down for lack of hard facts, statistical or otherwise. The reason for this is Switzerland's extremely effective law for banking secrecy. What would seem to be common knowledge in other countries is often shrouded in fog. Even where the subject under discussion is not a secret or detrimental to anyone's well-being, data is painfully missing. The *Economist* bitterly noted that "Switzerland remains an underdeveloped country in the field of statistics." Even the United

States Treasury had to conclude: "Deficiencies in Swiss statistics and the secretive attitude in banking and business circles concerning most transactions makes it necessary to rely on estimates. The average Swiss businessman and banker profess strong distrust of statistics-gathering by any government agency." Consequently, any generalities must be understood in this light.

Before moving on to the securities markets, it is important to discuss the Swiss banks at some length since they are the warp and woof of the markets: there are no stockbrokers per se as in the United States or *agents de change* as in France. Swiss banks, that is, the large commercial banks and the private banks, do what is called "department store" business. In other words, their services run the whole gamut of financial needs. Though both the public and private banks do mixed banking, it is obvious from their demeanor and appearance that the public is welcome in one but unwelcome in the other. The main offices of the public banks are large institutional affairs that bear a strong resemblance to American banks. An air of efficiency pervades the premises. The private banks are quite different since they are family enterprises handed down over several generations. Situated in the second story of an office building or in splendid isolation in a baronial mansion, their offices are heavily panelled in walnut or oak rather than in official marble. In them, one is more likely to be greeted by a partner in the firm than by the general manager. Whereas anyone can open an account in the public banks, private banks prefer to deal with "people of means." What this euphemism means precisely is hard to say, differing as it does from bank to bank.

Swiss bankers carry a very special cross of gold. About twice a year half of the world's sensational press points a righteous and indignant finger at Swiss financiers accusing them, among other things, of abetting the machinations of international swindlers, playing host to known criminals, helping the "other" side in proxy fights, giving aid and comfort to the Communists, playing purser to illicit drug traffic, operating a haven for tax dodgers and Americans flouting SEC regulations, and finally causing the Stock Exchanges throughout the world to fluctuate at their bidding. Just as regularly, the Swiss protest but to little avail. The charges are pretty far from the mark, but there are some grains of truth in them. Whether the Swiss should be blamed or ostracized because their facilities are used for illegal or ethically questionable practices is another matter.

Almost anyone can open a general account with a Swiss bank. However if large sums are involved banks will investigate. They will want to know the origins of the moneys involved, the nature of the business to be transacted, and possibly social and business references of those involved. If the banks are not satisfied as to the legitimacy of the account, they are not obliged to accept it. However, the Swiss have rather strong beliefs in individual freedom and privacy; they do not lightly turn away customers unless convinced of dishonesty or that the enterprise is against the national interest.

A mystique has sprung up about numbered accounts, but they are less mysterious than they seem. First of all, and contrary to popular belief, bankers will not open a numbered account unless they know the identity of the individual concerned. Second, only substantial deposits may qualify for this type of account. Third, they may already be obsolete in the era of computers and digital identity. About the only advantage to a number is the additional secrecy within the bank. These accounts are handled by a small department, and the identity of the individual is known to only a half-dozen employees. Numbers became popular during the 1930s when it became apparent that the German government had been successful in obtaining information from bank sources as to which of her nationals had assets on deposit with Swiss banks.

FOREIGN ACTIVITY

Another great source of confusion is the question of foreign activity in Switzerland, and its reciprocal, Swiss activity in foreign countries. Reportedly, 30 per cent of Switzerland's banking business is done with foreigners. The problem is compounded by the fact that estimates can be made only on open accounts; the origin and contents of closed safe-deposit boxes can, of course, not be known. As to actual foreign holdings in Switzerland of foreign stock, the Association of Swiss Bankers will do no more than quote two separate studies:

on the minimal side SF10-11 billion ($2.3-2.5 billion), while on the maximum side SF17-18 billion ($3.9-4.1 billion).

Foreign shares make up for about one-fifth of the securities deposited in Swiss banks. What percentages of these securities are American is impossible to say, but one informed observer puts the figure of $2.5 billion of American securities on deposit with Swiss banks. Approximately half of these belong to the Swiss. These are all estimates for, unlike Holland, no central depositary exists for foreign shares. If the above figures are approximately true, then Swiss holdings of American assets in open accounts are less than $1.5 billion. With the total value of the securities listed on the New York Stock Exchange past the $529 billion mark, Swiss holdings are not likely to exert an unseemly influence. The Swiss markets may not be above reproach, as we shall see, but it is unlikely that they are the cause of market cracks, particularly American ones.

Swiss secrecy dates back to 1934, at least that was the year the law was passed. Bankers almost by definition should be tight-lipped about client relationships, much in the fashion of other professional men. In the United States this is often far from the case; credit information or simply ascertaining whether there are sufficient funds to cover an issued check is a relatively simple business. The Swiss make it a criminal act to divulge financial information to a third party. The Swiss Bank Secrecy Act reads as follows:

Whoever intentionally in his capacity as an officer or employee of a bank, or as an auditor or his assistant, or as a member of the banking commission, or as an officer or employee of its bureau, violates his duty to observe silence or professional secrecy; or whoever induces or attempts to induce a person to commit such an offense, shall be fined not more than 20,000 francs ($4,630), or shall be imprisoned for not longer than six months, or both.

If the offender acts negligently, he shall be fined not more than 10,000 francs ($2,315).

Naturally, it covers foreigners dealing in Switzerland together with nationals.

Yet this does not mean that Swiss secrecy will necessarily protect domestic crooks or international swindlers. Through judicial proceedings, liens, or attachments on accounts—numbered or not—can be secured. Obviously, each case must be decided in court, but generally speaking the deciding point is whether or not the alleged deed is against Swiss, not foreign, law. A private banker in Zurich remarked that "it is no crime in Switzerland to avoid French taxes. However, if a man kills and robs someone in Germany, it is very easy to attach his illegally obtained money." In other words, it seems that criminal activity has no greater chance of going unpunished in Switzerland than elsewhere.

A GENTLEMEN'S AGREEMENT

During the early 1960s Switzerland had its fill of foreign money. While it did cover a widening trade gap, it was causing internal strains and stresses in the economy through inflationary tendencies. The Cold War, the Congo, Cuba, Algeria to name but a few, all fed the monetary flood. The National Bank called a halt by setting forth a Gentlemen's Agreement among the country's banks. Such agreements are common events in Switzerland's financial history. This particular one came into force in August 1960 in an attempt to keep foreign money out of the country's internal circulation. The agreement, which is still in force at this writing, allows foreign money to be deposited in Swiss banks, but no interest is to accrue to the account whether it was a demand or time deposit. Originally—but this has since been deleted— a charge of ¼ per cent was levied. The other point to this agreement is a prohibition on sales of Swiss securities or real estate to foreigners. Foreign shares quoted in Switzerland and foreign bonds issued in Swiss francs are not subject to the agreement. Generally speaking, while this compact exists, foreigners are denied entrance to Swiss Exchanges, unless they held Swiss securities or had Swiss francs on deposit before July 1, 1960. Swiss bankers are not overly happy with this voluntary arrangement since it is but a capital barrier to a traditionally free market. On the other hand, inflationary pressures better supported by a major world economy and a reserve currency are alleviated by this agreement.

Of course, the application of the pact is less than perfect and one banker complained that the "wording of the Gentlemen's Agreement suffers from a defect which makes itself felt from time to time: The preamble does not define the term 'gentleman'. . . ." Some private banks and custodial attorneys have winked at this accord. With a large proportion of bearer shares in the market, it is doubly difficult to enforce. Some shares are listed abroad such as Nestlé in Paris, while others are actively traded over-the-counter. One legitimate way around this prescription is to purchase stock of an open-end trust; selling these to outsiders is permitted. Such trusts are quite popular with the Swiss since the 1930s, with close to 140 in operation. Two funds wholly invested in Swiss companies are particularly well known; Actions Suisses and Swissvalor.

In March 1964 the Swiss National Bank modified the Gentlemen's Agreement by approving foreign investments in Swiss holding companies 80 per cent of whose assets are held abroad. Possibly of more significance was the new provision enabling foreigners to purchase Swiss securities from a fixed pool of Swiss shares owned by foreigners. In other words, aliens can purchase any domestic stock provided that the share comes from a non-Swiss source. Furthermore, foreigners no longer have the sanctuary of an external franc account; proceeds from the sale of Swiss securities are afforded no priority in purchasing new Swiss shares. While the new regulations make it simpler for foreign investors, foreign money is still effectively fenced out of the national economy.

SWISS SHARES AS STATUS SYMBOLS

Though the modern image of Switzerland is a country afloat on a sea of money—even the GNP per capita of $2,000 is the highest in Europe—investing is not a popular pastime or a poor man's prerogative. Involvement in the Stock Market is limited to the very few since the high prices of Swiss securities makes them prohibitive to most people. The preference for bearer securities and the lack of hard facts as to share ownership does not help clarify the situation. Parenthetically, one of the few generally accepted facts about Swiss industry is that about 30 per cent of its equity is held by foreigners, largely French, Germans, and South Americans.

Swiss industrial society has almost a plutocratic air about it. Close family associations seem to be the rule whether one is speaking of private banks, chocolate factories, drug companies, or watch manufacturers. The high prices of stock and the apparent disinterest in lowering share prices tends to reinforce this observation. Whether by accident or design the small stockholder seems unwelcome in the general meetings of Swiss companies. Without doubt, Swiss share prices are on average the highest in Western Europe or the United States. An average price of a dozen active shares on the Zurich Exchange might easily be SF3,800 ($880), while two drug firms must hold some sort of record with the price of their shares: Geigy at SF19,000 ($4,398) and Hoffmann-La Roche at SF50,000 ($11,574).

Corporate structure in Switzerland is quite similar to the French *société anonyme* or the German *Aktiengesellschaft,* though variations occur from canton to canton due to different laws. A minimal fixed capital against which shares can be issued must be SF50,000 ($11,574) and the minimum nominal value of shares is SF100 ($23). All bearer shares are fully paid up, but registered shares may be partially paid, thus obligating the owner to pay the remainder if called upon by the company. While some preferred shares exist—*Partizipationsscheine*—they are not as a rule sold to foreigners, even before the Gentlemen's Agreement came into effect. The large machine tool and heating equipment manufacturer, Gebrüder Sulzer, has such shares outstanding. Theoretically, convertible bonds do not exist within a fixed capital structure, but there are some *bons de jouissance,* participation certificates. These certificates have no voting rights, but do share in the profits. On occasion, stock options are attached to such certificates.

High share prices are due to the narrow capital base of most companies. Why, one might ask, don't the companies broaden their base and lower the price of their shares by splitting their stock? A few companies have done just this, but a legal problem exists in splitting shares since many companies have shares already of the minimum nominal value of SF100. A rights issue might be another solution but this is superfluous to many firms for they do not really need more working capital when their treasuries are usually full or bank interest rates so cheap. Moreover, another consideration is always present: more shares would dilute control.

If the Gentlemen's Agreement discriminates against foreigners for the sake of economic stability, there have been other less overt steps to prevent *Uberfremdungsgefahr,* danger from too much foreign participation. It is difficult to state what percentage of shares are in bearer form, but in recent years registered shares have become very popular. Insurance company shares are all registered and very tightly controlled. Reportedly, insurance companies will not sell shares to Swiss citizens if they live outside the country. When Nestlé began to worry about foreign participation in 1959, the company recapitalized its stock and issued registered as well as bearer shares. The registered shares usually sell at about two-thirds or three-fifths the price of the bearer. Chemical companies and heavy industry for the most part have registered shares. The three leading bank shares, however, are all bearer as are all bond issues.

Of course, there are ways of subverting both the Gentlemen's Agreement and the by-laws of the companies in question through intermediaries, but the legality of share ownership may then become problematic. Part of the great attraction of Switzerland's Exchanges are their foreign listings. The Gentlemen's Agreement says nothing about buying and selling non-Swiss securities or foreign bonds even though quoted in Swiss francs. Foreign shares are, of course, no cheaper in Switzerland, on the contrary usually somewhat more expensive owing to double brokerage, but there are ample tax reasons why people will utilize Helvetian markets.

Many American bonds and stocks are traded and listed on a dollar or Swiss franc basis. Of the 181 shares listed, 108 are domestic concerns, 27 are American, and the remaining 46 foreign but predominantly German issues. The bond market has an even more ecumenical air: of the 623 bonds, 164 are alien. The Swiss are extensive holders of international obligations since federal and cantonal loans have low yields. With a touch of pride, no doubt commensurate with their stake in international altruism, the Swiss claim to have retained more World Bank (International Bank for Reconstruction and Development) bonds than anyone else.

THE STOCK EXCHANGE

Of the three major Exchanges, Zurich, Basel, and Geneva, Zurich is the largest and most active, though reportedly foreign money plays a greater role in Geneva. All three have similar lists of stocks plus exclusive regional companies, though there is no uniform federal law regulating them. There are local Exchanges in Lausanne, Berne, Neuchâtel, St. Gall, and Coire. The Zurich Börse, officially the *Effektenbörsenverein,* was founded in 1912 and is regulated by the cantonal government. The twenty-six members are all banks since there are no brokerage houses, though some small banks are but brokerage houses in disguise. Twenty-two American brokerage firms have offices in Switzerland, but they must pass all orders for Swiss shares, provided they can be purchased, through one of the banks. Seats on the Exchange are government-approved memberships, costing SF300,000 ($69,444). Outside the Exchange exists a group of dealers, sixty-eight licensed agents, that do some over-the-counter business as well as act as *gerants de fortune,* financial advisers. Though some are extremely astute, the banks are perhaps more secure. The last major bank bankruptcy in Zurich was in 1931. The same cannot be said for the outside concession holders.

In Zurich the Stock Exchange stands between Paradeplatz, one of the city's busiest intersections, parade grounds for strolling Swiss, and a languid canal. Facing the Platz at numbers 6 and 8 respectively are two of Switzerland's banking greats, the Swiss Credit Bank and the Swiss Bank Corporation. Other banks line either side of the square and the tree-lined elegant main street, Bahnhofstrasse, station street. Facing the canal are rows of stately willows. Luxury yachts are moored democratically next to canoes, motor boats, and swans. Office workers and traders gather here during lunch, crowding a narrow catwalk named the Bären Brüggli, bears' pass, and throw bread crumbs to the birds. The reference to bears dates from pre-Exchange days.

The Exchange itself, a kind of 1930s wave-of-the-future concrete structure dominated by a round tower which houses swift elevators, is headquarters of trade for the German cantons. It reveals one of the funniest spectacles in all of Europe. Trading takes place on the top floor in two adjoining rooms divided only by draperies. The ceiling is of corrugated and leaded glass; the floor is pea green and littered with veridian slips of paper, remnants of old bids.

Work starts at ten in the morning and is usually finished by one in the afternoon, five days a week. The traders are mostly young and in shirtsleeves; some have no ties. When they are standing still, they look like normal, dignified, slightly reserved, stolid Swiss citizens. However, when they go into action, all stereotypes of Swiss dignity and reserve vanish. Gathered around the trading arena in either room, ringed by a circular wooden ship's rail about thirty feet in diameter, they shout hysterically, lean over gesticulating wildly, practically falling over the railing, swinging as on parallel bars, shouting at the top of their lungs in an attempt to outbid each other. It is hot work and the gymnastics are fantastic. In the middle of the madness sit the calm *maklers*, cantonally appointed auctioneers who conduct and supervise trading. They sit at a square desk with a pile of papers facing a small TV set. One official, unperturbed, repeatedly and patiently presses a button for quiet. The sound is that of a Biblical ram's horn and if that doesn't work, he resorts to a shrill whistle, like a circus trainer. Understandably, this is called the *criée,* crying, system.

Trading is conducted in German, though some French sneaks in. Brokers punctuate their deals with *"merci, viel dank, merci, viel mal,"* thanks four ways. The maklers read down the Official List, pausing after each security while awaiting bids and offers. On a hectic day the screaming and phrenetic gesticulating reaches an unbelievable peak. The object is to reach an opening or balanced first price. In itself the first price has no official importance. The traders have no idea as to volume and only after a price is agreed upon is the question of how many shares then broached. A Swiss "round lot" for official price purposes varies with the stock. Between SF501 and SF2,000 at least 10 shares must be traded; from SF2,005 to SF5,000, 5 shares; from SF5,005 to SF10,000, only 2 and anything over SF10,000 just

1 share need be traded. An official bond price must be at least a nominal value of SF5,000. Bonds, though, may be in SF1,000 or SF5,000 denominations. Once a security is called it can be traded for the rest of the session. In reality, after a first price is fixed any odd-lot combination is permitted.

Usual settlement practice is on the next day or at the latest within a week. However, it is possible to deal on a term basis by using the last day of the current month or of the following month as a day of settlement. Though there was once an active option market, only a small one exists today. This is a call market where the purchaser must decide by the fourth trading day from the end of either the current month or the following month whether to pick up his shares or pay the option fee. Short sales are possible, but this technique is not widely used. Precise trading volume is not revealed, though individual share transactions are noted, thus giving a rough guide to the day's activity. This in turn provides the information for stock indexes. A new daily index by the Swiss Bank Corporation has replaced the Swiss National Bank's index as the most quoted in the world's press. It is a broad-scale index of 80 different securities of 65 companies, covering 90 per cent of the market capitalization of all equities quoted. As the bank notes: "The index is the weighted arithmetical average of the price relatives. The influence of each security on the behaviour of the index is thus proportional to its importance (weighting). At the outset, the weights correspond to the initial market capitalization (prices multiplied by the numbers of securities issued). As time goes on, this weighting is adjusted after each modification in capital structure in order to reflect the changes caused thereby in the composition of securities portfolios." The base of 100 is December 31, 1958 or the same as the *Eurosyndicat* index and other European yardsticks.

Volume figures are occasionally published but they are based on an imprecise turnover tax rather than on the actual dealings. The last few years have seen a yearly average of SF22.5 billion ($5.2 billion) in Zurich alone. This represents a growth of over five times since 1950.

Swiss Exchanges are almost hypersensitive to news from the rest of the world since the country is situated in the heart of Europe. But the hypersensitiveness has other sources as well. "Our system is a little bit archaic. It functions well in good times, but in times of a crack, not at all," summarized a Zurich private banker. The high price of stock, the small capitalization of most Swiss companies, the paucity of private investors (probably less than 1 per cent of the population), all make for a thin, narrow, and sometimes nervous market. Margin practices are also partially responsible for erratic market behavior in periods of crisis. While the Association of Swiss Stock Exchanges has the power to regulate margin lending, and did in 1961 and 1962, it now leaves that prerogative to the banks. The banks can advance as much as 100 per cent of the securities' value, but this likelihood is rather slim. Fifty per cent is a customary margin figure, but the banks are under no formal obligation to lend a penny.

Swiss Exchanges came under heavy shadows after the May 1962 market crash. A graph of American and European shares would reveal that prices on the Swiss market dropped more sharply and to a lower point both in May's break and in the following October's crisis in Cuba than on any other market. For example, on Europe's "Black Tuesday," May 29, bank shares fell an average of 30 per cent. Outsiders and even some Swiss financiers were critical of the market mechanism and the role of the banks. Criticism was based on two points: prices went down sharply and on *lighter* than usual trading; and allegedly banks were liquidating margin accounts at the lowest prices while repurchasing these shares for their fiduciary account at higher prices. The cry for reform went up and the Zurich Exchange studied the situation. About the only significant step taken in consequence was to introduce a fifteen-minute mandatory recess on trading if prices moved more than 15 per cent. This is supposed to give time for cooler judgments and second thoughts.

The banks, of course, deal for their own account, their investment trusts, and discretionary accounts. They can and do marry stock, crossing orders among their branches. On Black Tuesday the banks were as panic stricken as most investors and apparently did little to stabilize the fall. In fact, a general manager from one of the Big Three banks went to the Exchange for the first time in ten years and started selling stock. Charges of self-serving and manipulation levelled at the banks have not been sustained. But then again neither was the efficacy of an auction system that has relatively few shares to sell at ridiculously high prices.

Market orders received before the opening do not necessarily get the first price since there may not be enough stock to go round. Sales or purchases are then apportioned to the interested parties. Large banks may have two identical market orders, but the final price may vary by 10, 20, or 30 francs. Not knowing the volume presents a ticklish problem: for a series of sell orders a trader will put the price down to attract buyers, but after the executions and a whetting of appetites prices are likely to close at considerably higher levels. The same is true of buy orders that push up the market only to have it fall when they are completed. This a major difficulty of the criée system when it is forced to operate with a thin inventory. An investor can temper this volatile behavior by placing limit orders. He may be left in the cold, but it affords some protection. Trading does take place after the market on the telephone, but it probably is not as extensive as in Germany.

TAXES AND HAVENS

Everyman's image of Switzerland as a tax haven is still partially true. While the last decade has seen a striving toward a unification of Western tax systems—for instance the EEC is actively pursuing a policy of Community-wide taxes—taxation will undoubtedly remain as the last symbol of national sovereignty. And as long as levy differentials and taxing concepts are dissimilar, havens will remain. One of the classic Swiss havens was Zug, a small town a few miles south of Zurich. At the end of 1963 it had approximately 300 foreign companies on its rolls, 135 of which were American firms. Three separate events have brought an end to corporate tax sanctuaries: crowded conditions in the desirable cantons, a lack of surplus labor due to tighter government control, and a change in American tax laws in 1963 by which income is taxed regardless whether it is held abroad or repatriated. Heretofore, subsidiaries of American firms could postpone taxes on foreign earnings until they were brought home.

Individual investors in Swiss securities, assuming they purchased the shares before the summer of 1960 or in a foreign market, are faced with a withholding tax of 30 per cent on dividends and coupon interest at source. Twenty-seven per cent can be used as a tax credit against federal taxes since a double taxation agreement exists with the United States. That is the extent of Swiss dividend and interest taxation of nationals or foreigners. Non-Swiss securities held in Swiss accounts are not taxed by the Swiss since they are probably taxed at their source. A tax haven, of course, exists if an American does not report profits or capital gains in a Swiss bank account. Obviously, the Swiss are not going to report these deals; it is neither their legal nor moral obligation to enforce another country's tax laws. Just as obviously, tax evasion remains tax evasion wherever its locus. Expatriates should investigate before settling down; some Swiss residents are subject to a capital gains levy while others are not. This depends solely on the canton of residence.

SECURITY ANALYSIS AND INFORMATION

A society of Swiss security analysts was started a couple of years ago, but the profession is still in its infancy. Part of the difficulty is that Swiss businessmen are more than a bit reluctant to release relevant information. Since self-financing has been customary, there was rarely a need to divulge information to Stock Exchange or bank. Swiss law requires reports from public companies, but it errs on the cautious side by prohibiting inflated figures. It says nothing about deflated figures, understatements, and undervaluations. This practice encourages large unexplained reserves that often lie like icebergs in company accounts. When Americans first "found" Swiss securities a few years back, they went to the other extreme and assumed every Swiss company was a gold mine.

Some of the better financial reporting comes from the Swiss banks since they are obliged to publish their balance sheets every quarter, though their profit and loss statements appear only once a year. Industrial companies are somewhat less informative since reporting is erratic, nonconsolidated, and sometimes misleading. Very few companies release true earnings figures or even the next best thing, sales figures. Brown, Boveri, a heavy electrical equipment manufacturer is a case in point. The company has affiliates in nine countries. Though the Swiss parent company is only a third the size of the German subsidiary, it controls the activities of the group. However, the company does not publish a consolidated balance sheet, since under Swiss law it cannot consolidate sales from the next canton let alone the next country if taxes are paid there. With holding companies almost a Swiss way of life, an analyst has his hands full.*

"How then do you know how well a company is doing?" a banker was asked.

"Oh, we read *Fortune* magazine," he replied, "they always seem to know."

Bankers skeptical of what they read in *Fortune* work by a process of extrapolation. Earnings can be estimated if one knows the profit margin of comparable American and German firms and approximate turnover of the Swiss company in question. Some Swiss analysts use a ratio of sales to capitalization; this guide can be useful if the underlying data is valid, but is not comparable to American firms which have a much wider capital base. But even in Switzerland one cannot compare CIBA with Hoffmann-La Roche, both worldwide drug concerns, since the latter never releases sales figures in the first place.

Accounting techniques often cloud the picture of a company. Plant and fixed assets, as in the Nestlé annual report, are sometimes valued at 1 Swiss franc, though some reports mention the insured value of the property. Dividends, which are paid once a year, are rarely a guide to

* One of the most famous Swiss holding companies, Interhandel, has finally come to an agreement with the United States Department of Justice concerning General Aniline and Film Corporation. This U.S. based chemical company was seized by the government in February 1942 as enemy property. Most of the company's stock was held by a Swiss holding company, I .G. Chemie. Through a complex agreement, Chemie was in turn controlled by I. G. Farben, the huge chemical cartel. For the next twenty-two years, the Swiss holding company, now known as Interhandel, claimed that that agreement had been terminated in 1940. Consequently, it was a Swiss, not German, corporation. Long litigation ensued and Interhandel might have won the case if Swiss authorities had permitted the Swiss banks to forward proof of ownership. But the government regarded this as a violation of Swiss bank secrecy and forbade it. A concord was signed between the Justice Department and Interhandel which provided for a sale of most of the company's stock, but with the majority of the proceeds of the sale reverting to the U.S. Treasury to satisfy war claims.

the health of a company since payout bears no relationship to earnings. A 2 per cent yield is considered generous. The only company to give a fuller accounting of itself is Landis and Gyr, an electronics manufacturer. Ironically, few people believe they are telling the truth. One gerant de fortune suggests quite seriously that his clients buy shares of Nestlé "on faith and because they make good chocolate."

While company statements are improving in Switzerland, the banks still appear to be repositories of investment advice. For instance, the Swiss Bank Corporation with headquarters in Basle is particularly knowledgeable as to the business affairs of Basle chemical companies. The large public banks are well informed, though far less opinionated than the private banks. By European standards, Swiss banks publish a good deal of information, much of it pertaining to Europe in general. It is rare to be charged a "management fee" in Switzerland; most banks settle for a custodian's fee for securities, the brokerage charge, and a small tax on dividends. Discretionary power is not something Swiss banks relish, but they will accept it.

COMMISSION RATES

Brokerage is almost on a par with United States commissions. For stocks above SF350, and almost everything on the Swiss Exchanges is—the commission is ⅜ of 1 per cent. To put it in the European fashion 3.75 per mill or SF3.75 per thousand Swiss francs in the transaction. Bonds are somewhat cheaper with a brokerage rate of only ¼ of 1 per cent of the market value including the interest, if the price is 100 per cent or over. If the price is less than 100 per cent including the interest, then the same rate on the nominal value of the bond. Other charges are minimal; a federal stamp of 15 centimes per thousand Swiss francs traded and 50 centimes per thousand on foreign shares listed on the Swiss Exchanges.

A small country of limited needs, Switzerland's major industries are forced to export much of their product. Germany, the United States, Italy, and France are both Switzerland's chief customers as well as her chief suppliers. In a sense, Switzerland is one of the most successful turntables in the world: by finishing or transforming raw materials for export her volume of foreign trade is over four and a half times that of the United States per capita.

Outside the banking and financial services that Switzerland offers (about 1 per cent of her labor force is in this service industry), four or five industries make up the bulk of the country's national product. The machinery and capital goods sector is dominated by Brown, Boveri, Gebrüder Sulzer, Swiss Aluminium, Landis and Gyr, though other small companies are listed. Swiss chemicals and drugs have experienced very rapid growth in the late 'fifties and early 'sixties. Geigy, CIBA, and Sandoz are to be found on the Exchanges while Hoffmann-La Roche is dealt in over the counter. Probably Switzerland's best-known products are her watches. This small country makes roughly 44 million timepieces a year or one half the world's requirements. She supplies the United States with 83 per cent of the country's needs. However, it is almost impossible to invest in this industry as it consists of 2,000 small companies, almost none of which are publicly held. Perhaps the second most popular export is Swiss chocolate. Nestlé, Alimentana and Suchard are the leaders in this field, though thirty-six other companies are also in the bonbon business. Nestlé's activities cover the whole field of food processing. Of course tourism is a major occupation, but it is largely a local business. One aspect that is far from local is the national airline, Swissair. This extremely profitable line is seven-tenths owned by small Swiss stockholders, its shares being among the cheapest in the Swiss market.

SOURCES OF INFORMATION

Newspapers:

The *Neue Züricher Zeitung* is the country's most authoritative newspaper. It publishes a monthly world review in English.
The *Journal de Genève* is widely read in the French cantons.

Reference Works:

Mannuel des Bourses Suisses, Edition Scriptar, Lausanne, is the main handbook to Swiss securities.
Guide des Valeurs Suisses de Placement is published four times a year under the imprints of various banks.

Books:

ASCHINGER, F. E. *Zurich as a Center of Finance.* Zurich: *Neue Züricher Zeitung,* 1959.

BÄR, HANS J. *The Banking System of Switzerland.* Zurich: Buchdruckerei Schulthess & Co., 1957.

BIGOSINSKI, GERRY. *Switzerland: An International Financial Center.* New York: C. J. Devine Institute of Finance, 1964.

HUNOLD, A. and BIERI, H. *Die Schweizerischen Effetenbörsen.* Zurich: Schweizerischer Kaufmännischer Verein.

IKLÉ, MAX. *"Die Schweiz als internationaler Kapitalmarkt," Struktur- wandlungen der schweizerischen Wirtschaft und Gesellschaft,* (Festschrift für Fritz Marbach). Bern: 1962.

*Geld regiert die Welt.**
—German proverb

6. GERMANY

Ohne Hast, aber ohne Rast.†
—Johann Wolfgang Von Goethe

THE MIRACLE

The German miracle, the *Wirtschaftswunder,* is now over a decade old, and Germany has entered a postmiracle phase no less prosperous than its former state of economic grace. Germany's renascence transformed her from a prostrate nation to one of the Continent's most affluent, exporting more cars than the United States, more electrical equipment than Britain, and more chemicals than France. Her gross national product is still climbing, though it has slowed down: 1959 saw a rise of 6.7 per cent; 1960 a jump of 8.8 per cent; 1961, 5.5 per cent; 1962, 4.1 per cent; and 1963, an increase of 6 per cent.

In her postwar period, Germany had a number of curious advantages. Political and economic liabilities turned into their converse. The incessant pounding by Allied bombs, for instance, wrecked her communications network and leveled many plants. The shower of incendiaries did away with factories which might have proved a liability in the postwar period. Had they survived, they would have needed major overhauling, not only to change over from war production to peacetime use, but also because they were outfitted with machinery and equipment dating from a previous era. The physical destruction

* Money rules the world.
† Without haste, but without rest.

of some and the dismantling of others proved a boon. Germany could start with a fresh slate. She built some of the newest and most efficient plants in Europe, aided by Marshall Plan funds which flowed into the country to the amount of some $3.5 billion.

The cleavage of the country into an East, Soviet zone and a West, tri-partite zone which became the Federal Republic, confronted the German government with a huge problem: what to do with the over three million refugees from East Germany and the nine to ten million "expellees," ousted from an area once German, but now Polish or Russian. The overwhelming human problem—how to house these people, feed them, and integrate them into the West German economy —proved a windfall. The refugees and expellees provided the Federal Republic with a steady stream of skilled workers and professionals and thus a plentiful and eager labor market with which to carry on the reconstruction.

Paradoxically, Germany had one more trump card. She had to bear occupation costs and later the expense of quartering NATO troops on her soil. But in contrast to her European neighbors with arsenals in readiness to fight off a possible Communist threat, Germany was spared that huge expense. As a demilitarized country, she could expend the full resources of her budget and productive capacities on the *Wiederaufbau*. Had this not been so, the "miracle" might well have taken ten years longer to accomplish.

Today, the most striking impression of Germany (population 57 million, 95,900 square miles) is of her wealth; the automobile, symbol of this abundance dominates her cities and ties up her superhighways. The phenomenon of the small car and the motor bike is evident everywhere in Europe except in Germany, where it is conspicuous by its absence. In Europe as a whole, of course, the proliferation of the automobile has led to more traffic tangles and frayed tempers than even long-motorized Americans can imagine. Continental cities with their core of ancient buildings and narrow winding streets are ill adapted to the pace of this century. Bottlenecks abound and at peak hours the population is often totally immobilized; no one can enter, or leave the business district. This explains the preponderance of vehicles with great maneuverability, small cars, motorcycles, motor tri-cycles and other three-wheeled bugs. In Germany, however, large Mercedes and American models abound. Volkswagen are seemingly intended for someone else's *volk*. They are exported in astounding quantities.

Spatially, Germany's cities are the most "American" in Europe, having given the twentieth century and its planning free rein; Germany has built anew and has built better. There is less of a housing shortage in Germany than anywhere else on the Continent. Moreover, Germans are better housed by modern standards than any other nationals, with the possible exception of Swedes and Danes. Much of the credit for this housing boom must go to the governments of the *Länder*, the states, and to the Federal Republic. In fact, close to 50 per cent of residential construction has benefitted from some form of governmental assistance.

Another aspect of the building boom has been its effect on the country's capital markets, for without a doubt construction contributed mightily to the high level of long-term interest rates in Germany. With sizeable amounts of capital needed on a long-term basis, there was naturally a great demand for mortgage loans. The banks issuing these loans refinanced them by issuing mortgage bank bonds; these bonds form about 50 per cent of the total issue of fixed-interest bearing securities.

Other financial institutions, in turn, are prime purchasers of such high-yield indebtedness paper, tying up their own capital in this fashion. Interest rates spiraled to the point where the government felt it was time to curb the construction boom it once sponsored and encouraged.

Aside from its role in stimulating and providing the spur for reconstruction, the German government prefers to leave the leading role to private business. Germany can in no sense be considered a planned economy or even one in which *dirigisme,* French-style, holds sway. Conrad Adenauer, *der Alte,* had little taste for economics, and Ludwig Erhard his one-time Minister of Economics and present successor has no use for any Plan. Author of the Wirtschaftswunder, a Bavarian and a Protestant, Erhard was a professor of economics and one of the few economists untainted by Nazi connections. At the end of the war, therefore, the American Military Government persuaded him to enter politics and since then he has been one of the guiding forces in West Germany. Philosophically and practically he insists on a free market economy. He is not the only one to do so; Germans saw government domination of industry during the Nazi decades and, as a result, most of the German public wants none of it. A large part of Ministry of Economics officials, moreover, men on Erhard's present staff, are graduates of the University of Bonn. The institution is an anti-planning stronghold, and no doubt this professorial penchant left its mark on the student body, men now in a position to effectuate policy.

Business' attitude toward planning was succinctly expressed by Kurt Hansen, chairman of Bayer, Germany's largest chemical works: "The trouble is that when you have a plan you have to fulfill the plan and that leads to terrible regulation. The French may not take such things so seriously, but if we have a law we go to hell if we don't obey it."

As for direct competition with industry, there are few government-run enterprises of any importance and the idea of nationalization more or less died in the 1930s. The government, in fact, happily divested itself of several enterprises previously under its aegis. The first to be "reprivatized" was PREUSSAG, Preussische Bergwerks -und Hütten Aktiengesellschaft, but that was done more quietly than the turning over of Volkswagen to private ownership. The government is also planning to sell stock of the coal, oil, chemicals, transport, and power complex known as VEBA, Vereinigte Elektrizitäts und Bergwerks AG. Though VEBA is as large as Volkswagen was at the time of its "reprivatization," the company is less well known and the issue is not expected to arouse as much public interest as the Volkswagen issue.

The German government is extricating itself as rapidly as possible but still commensurate with dignity from the onus of business management and ownership. In those industries where the government still holds sway, it allots itself few privileges: government-owned enterprises in Germany are usually not tax exempt. Mining and real estate are the main areas of state activity, though others developed out of war production, such as the government's dominant role in the aluminum industry. Transportation, as elsewhere in Europe, is partially state run, as are many utilities. Even the Social Democrats no longer call for state ownership and actually campaigned against it. Surprisingly, their platform in the 1961 pre-election campaign actually proposed the sale of enterprises now government run. Despite the outward trappings of a nineteenth century *laissez-faire, laissez-aller* liberalism, the Wunder was a planned and directed miracle.

On record as a supporter of the Free Market, Dr. Erhard proved himself a friend of *Finanz Dirigismus* during his years as Minister of Economics and Wirtschaftswunder author. The English, translation of this term is fiscal management, which hardly conveys the dynamism involved. German Finanz Dirigismus is the converse of French *dirigisme*. The state stays out, so far as possible, of the direct management of industries, shying away from the arduous and thankless task of acting as a pacesetter for industry. There is nothing comparable to Régie Renault in Germany and no concept of the *industrie clef,* the model for labor–management relations, wage and salary scales, and the like. Instead, Erhard took his own professorial notes literally and applied them to running the nation's economy. He also borrowed a page from motivational research and advertising, fields which interest him immensely, and has given the German economy direction by means of a system of incentives and deterrents. To encourage savings by the general public, Erhard first assigned savings a privileged tax status, and then added a system of premiums of up to 20 to 30 per cent of the principal over a five-year period, depending on age and family status. For businessmen, the choice became a simple one: in the immediate postwar years invest or be taxed; and in recent years, distribute profits or be taxed.

Retained earnings plowed back into the business are taxed at a different rate than profits distributed to shareholders. The relationship between these two levies has been wavering like a seesaw, changing every few years according to whether the government wanted to put a damper on investments or to encourage them. The laws were amended in 1951, 1953, 1954, and 1958, with minor refinements added in 1961. The present tax rate encourages corporations to distribute their earnings: distributed earnings are liable to an impost of 15 per cent, while retained earnings pay 51 per cent. According to Erhard's own estimates, self-financing by business accounted for 35 per cent of total investment in Germany 1950–1959, while for industry alone, the percentages were well over 50 per cent.

Unquestionably, tax structure and tax policies have accelerated the miracle by helping to foster a large degree of concentration in German business. Investment and depreciation privileges at one point favored large corporations as opposed to smaller businesses, a state of affairs now rectified. The *Schachtelprivileg,* a provision of the tax law, as we shall see later, is a direct impetus for the creation of subsidiaries and branches, as is the so-called "organship" clause which grants tax privileges for "mother-and-daughter" companies in formerly cartelized sectors.

Concentration, it should be emphasized, does not mean re-cartelization. Both the European Coal and Steel Community and the Common Market ban such combines in principle, with the former by far the stricter of the two. The Common Market organization affords a loophole, permitting such associations, so long as they do not interfere with trade among member states or noticeably impede competition. German anti-trust law is the most permissive of the three: it prohibits concentration in principle but permits it under certain conditions.

Dr. Erhard's views on the subject are emphatic and he has repeatedly stated at length his lack of sympathy with cartels:

. . . My opposition to cartels is not based on any charge of dishonest intentions or practices on their part, which would amount to discrimination, but simply on the view that collective price agreements as such, however defensible they may be on moral and on statistical grounds, damage the national economy . . . The eradication of protectionism, the abolition of tariff barriers, the removal of currency regulation are all aims which breathe a spirit of greater and wider freedom, which above all, provide scope at last for the untrammelled development of the individual and prevent the arbitrary use of state power. The phenomenon of cartels is not, as I see it, compatible with this trend of economic events. . . .

Prices we are told, should not be determined by the market, but only by costs, and if the cartels can to all intents and purposes guarantee price stability, they virtually become charitable institutions. Let no one imagine that I am taken in by such tactics and would not be prepared to fight once more for a free economy.*

Erhard's conflict with Adenauer over certain aspects of the Common Market was well known. His reasons for backing Germany's qualified participation in the Common Market was based on sound economic principles. Some aspects of the Common Market are problematic for Germany in the sense that it forces the Federal Republic to raise some of its tariffs. This, in Erhard's opinion, would hurt the country's industry. However, it does not mean that the Chancellor fears foreign competition—just the reverse. Foreign competition has been a big factor in creating a livelier economic atmosphere.

German industry today is large, efficient, and prosperous. The tendency to bigness evident in the country's banking structure has had some parallel in industry. Previous monopoly practices however have had to give way. The huge I.G. Farben works, for instance, were broken up after the war and today each of the three segments is still separate. The three successor companies, Bayer of Leverkusen, Farbwerke Hoechst and Badische Anilin-und-Soda Fabrik of Ludwigshafen now account for 40 per cent of West Germany's chemical production. In its heyday, the Farben combine could corral only 32 per cent of the country's chemical output. Interestingly, in the opinion of many Germans, the much criticized Allied decision to break up the cartel actually worked to the advantage of the successors, who otherwise might have had much difficulty adjusting to the Common Market and in meeting world competition. For instance, the recent and necessary switch from coal to less costly petroleum hydrocarbons as a prime source of fuel was easier for the three smaller concerns. *Ipso facto* they have greater flexibility and therefore a greater competitive advantage.

Another example of concentration is the merger in September 1964 of Phoenix-Rheinrohr and the August Thyssen-Hütte. This reorganization makes the new Thyssen company the largest steel producer in Europe with a greater capacity than the Continent's other giant, the

* *The Economics of Success* (London: Thames and Hudson, 1963), pp. 133, 136, 315.

Italian government's Finsider. Thyssen and Phoenix-Rheinrohr were formerly part of the United Steel Works, the Vereinigte Stahlwerke, AG which was broken up after World War II as part of the occupation forces' decartelization policy. The explanation for the present merger was simply that foreign competition made the step a necessity for Germany to keep pace with growth in France's Lorraine province and in Italy.

BANKERS AND BUSINESSMEN

A triumvirate of banks looms large on the German financial horizon and these giants play a leading role in the overall economic picture of the Federal Republic. The Deutsche Bank, the Dresdner Bank and the Commerzbank are not only Germany's leading commercial banks but engage in investment banking and in a very active brokerage business as well. Their role is far more pivotal to the German economy than any comparable American institution. With their nationwide network of branches reaching into every small town and major city in Germany, the "big three" not only manage a quarter of all short-term deposits of Germany's entire banking system but they are also the prima donnas of Germany's international banking business.

Germany's large industrialists and Germany's large banks have always enjoyed a close liaison, benefiting both. Traditionally, the banks participated in industry not only by providing financing but also as partners, often holding large blocks of shares for their own account. They exercised the function of the postwar French *banques d'affaires,* but with a difference. Instead of nurturing growing industries and fostering medium-sized enterprises, these German banking institutions, at the turn of the century and between the wars, aligned themselves with big industry and with Germany's industrial magnates. For small business and for the merchant class, the interwar interregnum was a troubled period as they teetered on the edge of bankruptcy. Squeezed simultaneously by the price-fixing policies of the cartels, the propensity of large industry to set up its own sales and service outlets, and by a spiralling inflation, their fortunes evaporated. The merchants as financiers bowed out. In that period the influence of business leaders in banking circles was immense; as they ranked among a bank's main clients it was possible to sway a banker's opinion by the mere size of their deposits. In times of prosperity, the industrialists led, but in leaner times the banks regained the upper hand. To a large extent, that symbiotic relationship between industry and the banks helps to put the postwar predominance of Germany's banks in perspective—in particular, the pre-eminence of the three large banks, the Dresdner, the Deutsche and the Commerzbank.

Reorganized and decentralized after the fall of Hitler, Germany's banking system has undergone yet another metamorphosis in recent years. The "big three" were each fragmented into three parts, each institution serving a particular region. That arrangement, however, was short-lived and each soon remerged. The pace of the postwar reconstruction and the amount of capital needed to rebuild German industry after the war were such that these small, financial sub-institutions were totally unable to meet industry's need for capital.

The pace of Germany's postwar miracle also helps to explain the importance of the banks today and German industry's reliance on bank capital rather than on the capital market. For industry, it was faster, easier, and often cheaper to go to the banks directly rather than through the capital market. For the banks, tax law encouraged large participation on their part via the Schachtelprivileg, or literally the "box" or "pigeonhole" privilege. Technically, it is a device to alleviate double taxation. In Germany profits are taxed twice, once under the heading of corporation tax, and in so far as these moneys accrue to an individual, he is also liable for personal income tax. However, "where a capital company participates in another capital company *to the extent of 25 per cent* it need not pay another tax on the income derived from this participation." The German banks have taken full advantage of this tax provision.

The banks' influence on industry is twofold, through the ballot and through an exchange of directors. First, the banks are the depositaries for shares held by German stockholders in every *Städtchen* and every *Land*. The shares are mostly bearer in form and, on stockholders' instructions or frequently lack thereof, the bank will cast the vote for these sizeable blocks at the annual meeting. In addition to casting ballots in behalf of their clients, the banks also cast sizeable votes for shares held for their own account. Second, the banks, and the big three in particular, have people sitting on the boards of directors of the major companies and vice versa. It has sometimes been asked whether the big three lent German industry its directorate, or whether German industrialists were on loan to the banks. At any rate the list of directors on the boards of leading German concerns reads like a *Who's Who* of finance. Some companies, in fact, have representatives of all three big banks on their boards. A 1964 study by the Federal Trade Bureau in Frankfort on concentration in German industry found that, of 318 leading German companies surveyed, bankers comprised one-third the membership of boards of directors, and almost half the companies had banker chairmen. The reverse side of the coin is that the boards of directors of the three major banks included representatives from 41 leading firms, each of which in turn had bankers on its own board. Unquestionably, the place to go for information on German industry is to the banks.

The other *dramatis personnae* on the German financial scene are the *Sparkassen,* the savings banks, and the *Girozentralen,* clearing banks. They are a relatively new influence and they can make long-term loans. Owned by municipalities, the Sparkassen's original purpose was to help small local artisans and to sell municipal obligations to the public. They are not really a big factor in stock transactions as yet, but increasingly they compete with the commercial banks in lending.

German insurance companies are not very active on the Stock Exchange either, and the plethora of public and semipublic agencies that supply long-term capital in France are absent in Germany. One notable exception is the Kreditanstalt für Wiederaufbau, the Reconstruction Loan Corporation which distributed Marshall Plan aid to German business.

The bulk of security investment is done by commercial banks, which break down into three categories: the big three; a number of other large public banks such as the Bayerische Vereinsbank and the Berliner Handelsgesellschaft; and the private banks. Of the big three the Dresdner Bank has developed its research department most aggressively in the past few years, broaching the problem of security analysis in a most vigorous fashion. The Dresdner has also pushed to the forefront of the securities business and the mutual fund industry as well. The Deutsche Bank has traditionally been a leader in the field of foreign trade and investment banking but is generally viewed as the most conservative of the trio. The Commerzbank has concentrated its efforts on expanding its commercial banking activities.

The private banks also engage in mixed banking, ranging from commercial banking to security investment. Of Germany's 204 private banks, many were created as convenient outlets for a family's industrial concern. Some of the more important ones are: Hauck & Sohn and Merk, Finck of Frankfort; C.G. Trinkaus of Dusseldorf; Brinckmann, Wirtz & Co., Hamburg; and Salomon Oppenheim and Bankhaus Herstatt of Cologne. Bankhaus Herstatt is perhaps one of the best-known banks abroad for both their comprehensive research and their index. The Herstatt Index, an internationally quoted indicator is a *sine qua non* for any analysis of German share prices. To some extent, the private banks compare most closely with the *banques d'affaires* of France, or Switzerland's private bankers. They maintain a close working relationship with all the large institutions, know what is going on, and have traditionally been geared to special situations.

When it comes to the Stock Market, do the German banks dictate prices? Some people on Wall Street believe they do. The German banks deny the proposition with emphasis. They point out that whatever influence they may have on the market is only a short-term phenomenon. In the long run, particularly for Germany's blue chips where foreign holdings are sizeable, their own buying and selling is but one factor in the market.

Unquestionably, however, German banks do exercise an important role in the market, perhaps a greater role than any other European banking system. They do hold large packets for their own account and they can trade from their position. This is not without problems, however. Part of the impetus for large buying unquestionably has come from New York in recent years. If the banks traded without a position on a large U.S. institutional order, they risked unbalancing the market or not obtaining enough shares to cover, or both. Once they had a position in a stock, however, U.S. institutions might change their minds and the banks' holdings might prove to have been acquired at too high a price. Neither system is foolproof for the bank. Moreover, in long-range terms other factors influence the market—political events, events on Wall Street, and so on. May 29, 1962, for instance, was such a day. The *Report of the Deutsche Bundesbank* for 1962, characterizes the day the German market fell out of bed as follows:

The share market in 1962 suffered a price fall of a magnitude previously unknown since the war. Whereas quotations had at first declined relatively slowly in the months from January to April, the pace of the downward movement began rapidly to quicken in May. By the 23rd of that month, that is within three weeks, prices had on the average fallen by 10% of what they had been when it began. The climax was reached at the end of the month when on 29 May, immediately after a severe collapse which had taken place a day before on the New York Stock Exchange, German shares lost about 7% of their value in the course of a single day.

The end of the Cuban crisis brought the opposite result to Germany's Exchanges. Prices recovered to the tune of a 100-point rise in the share index within a month, from an October low of 405 to 506 by the end of November.

Whatever the precise day-to-day role of the banks in the Exchanges, it is clear that their part in the postwar economy was enormous. It remains so today. First, a good deal of postwar expansion was self-financed by industry out of retained earnings and extensive bank loans. Profits were plowed back into various contingency reserves; this was the quickest way to expand. It was also the easiest and fastest way of operating. Germans had little disposable wealth for investment, and banks and institutions that are active in the market would have been the eventual purchasers of equity or debt paper in any event. Instead of going through the market, therefore, many industrialists took the frontal attack and approached the banks directly. It was also cheaper. Crucial for a company in search of capital is the cost of raising it: under German federal structure, the state or Land government levies a 2½ per cent tax on new issues of securities. For short-term capital whose maturity falls within the confines of a decade, this 2½ per cent impost on the nominal value of the issue may be prohibitive. This has led to a device known as "loans against borrower's notes," *Schuldscheindarlehen,* which might also be translated simply as indebtedness certificates. These certificates, a form of private placements, avoid the tax. A potential borrower approaches a bank which credits him with the total amount. The bank in turn will split the obligation into smaller denominations which are then offered to insurance companies, pension funds, other banks, and the like. These indebtedness certificates are not quoted on the Exchanges, do not fluctuate with the whims of the marketplace, and for these reasons offer comforting stability for the institutions holding them. In a period of political crisis or simply in a bad Stock Exchange year, the market for bonds may fluctuate markedly and prices might be caught in a downward draft. With indebtedness certificates in its portfolio, an institution can be sure that its own balance sheets always present their best profile. Schuldscheindarlehen are always listed at par value—not at market value. Interest rates on such certificates vary, of course, but tend to hover around 6¼ per cent. In essence, therefore, there are *two* bond markets in Germany: the market in *Schuldverschreibungen der Industrie,* industrial bonds, quoted on Germany's Exchanges and open to the foreign investor on a par with German nationals, and the market in *Schuldscheindarlehen,* indebtedness certificates, open only to institutions and out of bounds to individuals, German or foreign.

Unquestionably, the existence of a form of long-term borrowing which sidesteps the capital market constitutes one of its major weaknesses as an institution. For Germany's companies, however, and for her smaller companies in particular, there are many advantages in the system of private placements. For smaller firms, these indebtedness certificates save money. By not going through the market, there are no costly advertising fees to meet, no Stock Exchange introduction fees, and no underwriting risks. Moreover, these loans against borrower's notes are tax exempt.

This tax also accounts for the rather limited number of new companies coming to the market in Germany. Most new issues have been bonds, not equity. Many family companies missed their entry into the Stock Market which, by general agreement, "topped out" in

1962. "If we get steadily rising stock prices, then we will get new issues coming to the Exchange," commented one observer. Another reason for the dearth of new, small companies on Germany's Exchanges is a set of business mores which favors larger enterprises. In the United States, an enterprising inventor might simply take one or a series of patents and set up shop for himself, providing, of course, that the process did not entail huge capital and equipment outlays such as only an industrial giant could supply. In Germany, even if the technology involved is simple, the inventor is more likely to attempt to sell his idea to a large, already existing firm and hope for a lucrative niche as a result.

In the past three years, security issues provided capital for only 7 to 9 per cent of total business investment. The rest came from reserves, or from the banks. According to one estimate, bank credits supplied slightly more than half of all external financing by industry. Many German firms, therefore tend to be undercapitalized and extremely sensitive to any sudden move on the part of their financial godfathers. A sudden curtailment of credit can throw a company into a tailspin. Some companies lost ground in precisely this fashion. *"Sie haben ihre Federn gelassen,"* (They lost their feathers). A series of dramatic bankruptcies raised a flurry of questions. These failures have often been used to illustrate German industry's undercapitalization and overreliance on bank credits. Henschel, an old, established, and large engineering concern was the first to be reorganized; Borgward, a major motor concern followed in closing its doors and the Schlieker shipyards of Hamburg failed in 1962. Willi Schlieker, a postwar industrial *wunderkind* built his empire in a span of fifteen years. Often dubbed the "personification of the Wirtschaftswunder," Schlieker's downfall shocked the country. One of the country's top industrialists, he had controlled twenty-one steel mills, a shipyard, and a handful of other concerns.

The latest insolvency is that of the Hugo Stinnes group, a coal, gas, and shipping complex involving a whole packet of plants, from a Bremen engineering firm to a Ruhr producer of fork-lift trucks. The scattering of Hugo's holdings toppled another group controlled by his mother, Frau Cläre Stinnes, and by younger brother Otto. The

Stinnes case is highly complex; besides the two disparate industrial groups, the Hugo Stinnes Bank was also involved.

Can one argue from these particular cases on the general health of German industry? Most likely not, although there has been speculation that even the largest German firms may not be immune to credit pressures. After all, the fact remains that these failures were all of major, long-established firms who somehow overextended themselves. This much is clear. What else seems clear from these case histories is that the one-man or one-family entrepreneurial tradition is still strong in Germany. According to one prominent analyst, close to 75 per cent of German industry is still composed of companies, each "a family affair." One, or several major shareholders often retain control. To assure control, such men often hesitated too long before coming to the equity market, fearing a flotation of new stock would narrow their margin of command. Many such family companies missed the bull market and are waiting for a sustained market upswing. Unquestionably, therefore, there has been more leverage in the capital structure of even large German companies than might well be the case in the United States. In the United States the bond-stock ratio is 1 to 4.6; in Germany the ratio is 1 to 0.9.

Asked about these failures and what they mean, Dr. Herman Abs, Marshall Plan funds administrator, financial wizard and a *Herr Direktor* of the Deutsche Bank, said: "A few bankruptcies? What do they amount to? Ours is a free economy and in a free economy you are bound to have bankruptcies. Anyway, we [the Deutsche Bank] never lent them a mark!"

Symptomatic or not, these insolvencies were considered sufficiently significant by the heads of a number of private firms to spur some among them—Neckermann, the mail order king, Braun, the appliance firm—to go public. Asked how many new firms had come to the market since the war, one banker estimated, "Oh, not more than a dozen, perhaps." In 1963, however, Hussel, a chain of candy stores, and Neckermann went to the market in search of equity. Interestingly, they sidestepped the usual channels and instead of enlisting the underwriting services of the German banks, approached an American firm to handle the issue. Both the Hussel and the Neckermann underwritings were handled by Morgan et Cie., the French subsidiary of Morgan Guaranty. This raised a lot of eyebrows. Why should a foreign bank be called in when, as one banker pointed out, the Neckermann shares would within a rather short time find their way back into Germany?

The answer seems to be complex. First, Neckermann was wary of approaching the German banks for they already held important interests in other department stores. The Dresdner, the Deutsche and the Commerzbank usually figure prominently in any underwriting syndicate formed to float a new issue, though any number of other banks might participate as well. The big three have extensive holdings in Kaufhof and Karstadt, Germany's two largest department stores, and in die Quelle of Nuremberg, and Otto of Hamburg, who are more directly competitive with Neckermann. Afraid of pressure to alter his techniques to conform with his competitors or even of pressure to merge with the competition altogether, Neckermann steered clear of German institutions and approached a foreign bank to handle the flotation of his shares.

By attempting to spread shareholding on a more international scale, firms such as Neckermann have a better opportunity of keeping control in their own houses. Moreover, German banks underwrite share issues *à contre-coeur* and with great disinclination as a rule, preferring the simpler role of agent, who merely brings the issue to market but assumes none of the risks. Under this arrangement, should the issue fail to fire public enthusiasm, the onus is on the company not on the German banks. In the case of the Neckermann issue, the American underwriting house was not shy of shouldering the risk nor reluctant to receive the profits. The issue proved most successful indeed.

Was it a blunder on the part of the German banks to let a good issue slip through their financial fingers? *"Jawohl, es war jammerschade,"* "Yes, it was a thousand pities; he should have come to us," said one banker in retrospect.

THE EXCHANGES

One thing is certain about German Stock Exchanges: Hamburg ranks third. Frankfort, a *finanz centrum* since the seventeenth century, and

Dusseldorf, commercial capital of the Ruhr, compete for first place and the rivalry is keen. Unlike other European countries, Germany has no one major Bourse, but several almost equally important markets. History is partially to blame, for German unification is barely a hundred years old, and separatism dies hard despite a federal structure. Between the two world wars, Berlin was the business and financial center of Germany. Today, Germany is divided and Berlin split and isolated from the Western body politic. This rift, which dates from the World War II, accounts for the present decentralization of German equity markets.

In appearance, both the Frankfort and Dusseldorf Exchanges are the most modern and functional in Europe. Both are almost new, though Frankfort's *Börse* is housed in what remains of a block-long, eighteenth century building whose facade survived Allied bombs. Pairs of friendly cupids play above each window, while the roof of the three-storied building is topped by rows of dignified Greek gods and goddesses. Inside, the twentieth century dominates the scene. The antechamber, an elegant series of concrete parabolic arches, has a modern free-form chandelier in the center. On a rainy day, perhaps two hundred umbrellas are spread taunt here, arranged in neat rows to dry. Unlike most European countries, Germany does not discriminate against women on the floor of the Exchange, so there are many flowered and gaily striped parasols among the conservative male hues of dark grey and black.

The trading floor in Frankfort occupies the entire ground surface of the building, with administrative offices on first and second floor galleries. From a balcony, traders can look down on the floor, consume a leisurely coffee or yoghurt and watch the girls in bouffant coiffures quoting prices below.

If Frankfort's Börse is the epitome of quiet elegance, Dusseldorf's reflects the suppressed bustle of an airline terminal. Shaped like an elongated rectangle the trading floor rises to a three-story height, with a clerestory on the third tier. A specialists' counter and quotation board occupy one long side, while the remaining facets are occupied by bank offices. White columns support the expanse and also provide anchors for the spiral staircases connecting upstairs and downstairs offices. Secretaries scamper up and down the stairs; traders run back and forth, take telephone orders, shout across the floor, and slide to the specialists' counter to execute their orders. Teletypes clatter as arbitrage goes on between Dusseldorf and Germany's seven other Exchanges: Berlin, Bremen, Frankfort, Hamburg, Hannover, Munich, and Stuttgart. A bell broadcast simultaneously in binaural, stereophonic splendor from ceiling loudspeakers, precedes all important announcements. On the floor, there are semicircular black leather couches, butterfly chairs, and writing tables piled high with stacks of papers. Girls in flowered blouses, sheaths, and sandals, sit and collate prices and record purchases and sales.

Basic organization and trading practices are identical on all German Exchanges. Juridically, the Chamber of Commerce runs the Exchange, but actual active management is left to committees elected by members of the Exchange. There are no brokerage houses, as such, in Germany as all brokerage business traditionally has been handled by the banks. Thus all traders transacting orders for the public on the floor are bank representatives. The representatives may trade directly with each other, or bring their orders to the official specialist, the *Kursmakler,* to be executed. Kursmakler are appointed by the Land, the state of Hesse for the Frankfort Exchange, and the state of North Rhine Westphalia for Dusseldorf. Their function is to balance buy and sell orders to arrive at an official price for the securities they are charged with. Unlike the American specialists, they may not act for their own account, nor is it their duty to maintain a "fair and orderly market" by trading against the trend. For the larger German companies with an international following, the Kursmakler makes a continuous market, while for less active securities there is only one price fixed for the day.

German stocks are not bought or sold by packets of this or that number of stocks. Par value is usually DM1,000 ($250) though there are shares with DM100 par value, and DM500 par. All shares must have a nominal value. The continuous market transaction must be in round lots of DM3,000 ($750) or multiples of it. Quotations are in percentages. Thus a DM1,000 stock selling at 530 per cent would, in U.S. terms, cost DM5,300 ($1,325) a share. A round lot of DM3,000 par would cost the investor DM15,900 ($3,975). The advantage of the German system of quotation is that it is possible to see at a glance how the market evaluates any particular shares or any particular industry. Small orders below DM3,000 cannot be filled in the continuous market but are relegated to the one-price market. The prices between the round lot and odd lot quotation may vary slightly.

Bank representatives can also take their orders to floor traders or *Freie Makler,* who trade exclusively for their own account and unlike the official specialists do take positions in stocks. Should an order come in after Exchange hours, this is no obstacle in Germany. The banks are not restricted to trading through the Exchange; they may trade with these Freie Makler any time of the day or night, or among themselves. This "telephone market" is often as important as the regular 12:00 M. to 2:00 P.M. transactions. This is particularly true when American brokers come to the German market with sizable orders after the market. However, the banks are obliged to execute all orders at the day's official price set during the market session, unless they have the client's expressed instructions to deal with the Freie Makler at any other price.

Because the banks are free to trade after hours, volume figures published by the Exchanges give only a partial picture of shares traded. Thus they cannot be used to determine whether Frankfort or Dusseldorf ranks first among German equity markets. The indirect way of arriving at a comparison is through the government-levied turnover tax which must be paid on each transaction. North Rhine Westphalia pays more turnover tax than Hesse, which would give the lead to Dusseldorf. Frankfort, however, host to the head offices of two of Germany's big three, the Dresdner and the Deutsche Bank, claims it is more of an international center. Frankfort bankers fondly point out that this distinction dates back to the 1860s. After all, during the American Civil War when both the North and the South were in tight financial straights, the Confederacy approached London, and the Union came to Frankfort for funds. Moreover, today, foreign stocks listed in Germany will usually be listed in Frankfort if they are listed on only one Exchange. Swiss institutions and large U.S. buyers have traditionally come to Frankfort, while the Belgians, French, and Dutch have always been Dusseldorf oriented.

Much as the organization of the French Stock Exchanges serves as a prototype for the markets of Belgium, Italy, Spain, and Greece, the basic organizational pattern of Germany's Exchanges served as matrix for those of Austria, Switzerland, and the Scandinavian countries. However, the Exchanges of Switzerland and Scandinavia are not identical with the German pattern. Naturally, the original die has been modified a good deal in accord with national preferences and predilections, but for those interested in institutional comparisons, the German market deserves more detailed attention.

The official specialist, the *Amtliche Makler,* also called Kursmakler, is a man who is lucky enough to have to work only two hours a day, five days a week, while the market is open. He collects orders from bankers and floor traders and arrives at a series of prices for the German blue chips which are traded continuously, and for lesser stocks and odd lots which have only a single price for the day. The Makler collects the orders in verbal or written form, making a list of limit orders and market orders. Standing inside an enclave on a raised podium facing bankers and floor traders across a counter, he arrives at a price which will satisfy the largest number of transactions, matching the greatest number of buy and sell orders. The official price must be in the middle of the orders, the point at which maximum turnover can take place. What is left, the various limit orders, are collected in another notebook and reserved for the following session if they cannot be filled the same day. The Kursmakler posts the bid and asked prices: in both Dusseldorf and Frankfort the transaction is flashed onto a huge translux screen. The bid price is aptly termed *Geld,* "money," because those bidding, no doubt, used to have the cash in hand, while the asked price is *Brief* in Dusseldorf and Frankfort, or *Papier* in Munich, pertaining to the stock certificates, "letter," or "paper," which sellers must have brandished at one time. Today's traders merely shout, Volkswagen, 600 Geld, 5 Brief, meaning he is ready to buy at 600 per cent and sell at 605 per cent. The Kursmakler notes all the prices. Next to them is a notation indicating whether there is excess supply or demand at that level. The word *bezahlt* (*bz*), paid, meaning that all or most orders were executed, is used as follows:

Bezahlt und Geld (bz. G.): At this price level some orders were executed, but some demand remained.

Bezahlt und Brief (bz. B.): Some orders found their counterpart but there is still an excess of sellers.

Etwas bezahlt und Brief (etw. bz. B.): Orders were fractionally filled but much is still being offered for sale.

Etwas bezahlt und Geld (etw. bz. G.): Orders were partially filled but there was still much demand.

Bezahlt Geld rationiert (bz. G. rat.): A shortage of stock, requiring the available supply to be rationed on a proportional basis.

Bezahlt Brief rationiert (bz. B. rat.): An overabundance of stock, meaning sell orders could be executed only partially and on a proportional basis.

These notations and abbreviations are not only used by the Kursmaklers to indicate the trend of the market but are also used in the Official List and in the financial press. A market lexicon must include a few other terms.

Geld (G.): There are only buyers and no sellers at this price. The result is a stalemate and no orders are executed at all. When this symbol appears in the financial press it means that the price of the stock will rise in the next few days.

Brief (B.): Sellers had the market to themselves with no buyers on the horizon. No orders were executed, an indication that the price of the stock will drop in the next few days.

Gestrichen Geld (−G): Indicates so little demand that no price is possible.

Gestrichen Brief (−B): No price possible because of a lack of offer.

Taxe (T): Indicates no turnover. The Kursmakler arrives at an approximate price as an alternative to setting no price at all. This notation is often used with a price deviation greater than 5 per cent on stock with a narrow market. Its intent is to prevent excessive fluctuation.

Finally, if there is no offer, no demand, the stock will be marked: Kurs gestrichen (−): Quotation annulled.

There are twenty Makler on the podium, each specializing in a number of stocks. As representatives of the state whose talents should be concentrated exclusively on setting impartial prices, Kursmakler may not deal in their own names or engage in any other business ventures. The official specialist is in a sense a neutral sent into the fray. In presence and function, he guarantees the correctness of the transaction and sets a price. Admittedly, as trading is not restricted to Stock Exchange hours, this official price acts only as a reference point on which to base after hour dealings. The figure of the specialist as mediator, autioneer, and state representative makes the market a public institution, rather than a private club in which banker meets banker and arranges a deal.

As a specialist, the Kursmakler lives from brokerage. In Frankfort stocks are so distributed among them that each man will have an approximately equal income. Volkswagen, for instance has a large turnover and will provide the man who handles it with a good income. The same individual will therefore handle a number of smaller companies as well. In Dusseldorf the assignment of companies is by economic sectors and, to assure equity of income, there is a pooling arrangement among several specialists.

The Kursmakler's colleague is the Freie Makler, the floor trader. The Freie Makler gets a fee if a bank trader closes a deal through him. Though some may have several million marks and speculate for their own account, most "rather like to collect orders" and cannot afford to take too high a risk in trading from a position in this stock or that. They like to balance their books at the end of each day but may go short for a period of two days, during which time they attempt to find a counterpart. The Freie Makler, like the London jobber usually acts as a principal.

A bank representative has the option of approaching either the official specialist with his order or going to the floor trader. What will decide him to go to one or the other? First, there may be a fractional difference in price, but the main difference lies in the fact that the Freie Makler can deal immediately while the official specialist must first find a counterpart. The bank trader can also make a deal with one of his colleagues directly, without going through any other intermediary.

THE VARIOUS SUBDIVISIONS
OF THE MARKET

The Teutonic talent for sifting, cataloguing, and categorizing, proverbial in scholarly fields, is evident in more pragmatic areas as well. A steak may be ordered "English, half-English, or *durch*," "rare, medium, or cooked through," and the traveller is confronted with three types of trains: the slow train, the express, and the *eilzug,* the "hurry-up train." The hurry-up train is slower than the express.

In the Stock Market, categories can likewise confound. The investor is confronted with three markets in one, all subdivisions of the Börse: the official market, the *Amtlicher Markt*; the semiofficial market, the *Geregelter Freiverkehr,* an over-the-counter market for foreign securities, recent bond issues, and a few domestic shares as well; and the telephone market. The telephone market, an interbank, afterhour market, sees trading in any or all the stocks and bonds exchanged on the official and semiofficial markets.

The Official Market

The official market breaks down into two simultaneous subdivisions: the continuous market for the bluechips starts at 12:00 and such securities can be traded till the market closes at 2:00 P.M.; and the single-price market for stocks which have less turnover and for odd lots of the bluechips which starts at 1:00 P.M. The specialist in bluechips makes the market for both round lots and odd lots of the same stock.

The Semiofficial Market

A Geregelter Freiverkehr, "regulated free market" or semiofficial market, includes shares of smaller companies not admitted to official trading, or shares of companies who for one reason or another do not wish to make public the information required for official quotation. There is an admissions procedure for shares traded on the semiofficial market, but the information submitted by the company need not go beyond the confines of the admissions committee and is not made public. In Frankfort, the specialist in charge of this market is off in a corner; in Dusseldorf he sits on a wheeled platform. "Why is he on wheels?" "Oh, the market rolls around him and sometimes rolls *him* around."

Actually, his mobility is not symbolic but a matter of convenience. He can be pushed out of the way on heavy trading days when bank representatives race each other across the floor on the way from their bank's telephones to the Makler's counter.

The Telephone Market

A *Börsianer,* a Stock Exchange man, always carries the market with him, the official hours and prices merely setting a tone. In Germany, the *situs,* or locus, is immaterial and much of the significant trading goes on after Stock Exchange hours among the banks themselves or between the banks and their customers. The telephone market is a convenience of which foreign clients have long taken advantage. As the Stock Exchange building acts only as a convenient meeting ground for bank representatives and no total turnover figures are available, it is difficult to gauge how much trading goes on during Exchange hours, and how much on the telephone market. Estimates range from 50 per cent to far more, as when large foreign institutions were investing heavily in German equity.

THE OFFICIAL LIST

Published by the committee of specialists, the Official List, the *Amtliches Kursblatt,* offers a complete picture of the day's market activity. Of course, only the transactions which went through the market between 12:00 and 2:00 P.M. are thus recorded; the interbank telephone market is not included. The chief headings included in the list are:

Anleihen des Bundes und der Länder, federal and state government bonds;
Pfandbriefe und Schuldverschreibungen von Hypothekenbanken, öffentlichrechtlichen Kreditanstalten und Körperschaften, mortgage bonds, bonds of credit institutions and of other public corporations;
Schuldverschreibungen der Industrie, industrial bonds;
Wandelschuldverschreibungen, convertible bonds.

Under the heading *Aktien,* stocks, the list includes: industrials, bank stocks, transportation, insurance shares, the former colonial companies, and, on a green sheet, foreign stocks. No volume figures are given, only prices with an indication of whether there was an excess of demand over supply, or vice versa.

The only exception to the system of quotation as a percentage of par value is the list of German insurance shares. They are quoted like foreign stocks traded on German Exchanges, so many Deutsche marks per share.

BROKERAGE FEES AND TAXES

Commission charges on stock to private foreign investors are made up of three parts: the main charge is DM8 for every DM1,000 traded, a broker's commission paid to the bank. In addition, two other minor charges are also due. The Makler's fee is 70 pfennige per thousand Deutsche marks traded, or 7/10 per mill ($0.7^0/_{00}$ is the Continental notation); a Stock Exchange turnover tax of DM2.5 per thousand is also levied ($2.5^0/_{00}$). On government and state bonds, the charge is only 1 per mill.

Bond rates, of course, are cheaper. The basic charge is DM4 per DM1,000 of the market value, or gross amount if the bonds are selling at a premium, but of the nominal value if they sell at a discount. A

Makler's fee of 75 pfennige per thousand is levied on the market value if the bonds are at a premium, or of the par value if at a discount. The turnover tax is the same for all equities and bonds.

MARKET ORDERS

"Getting a good price," is a rather technical proposition, dependent on the trader and his timing. Getting the best possible price, selling at the top and buying at the bottom, is practically impossible at home, and the odds get worse at a distance. The foreign investor, three to six thousand miles away, is hardly in a position to catch the peaks or troughs. Most often, an investor putting his money to work in a foreign market must be content to say that Daimler-Benz, AEG (Allgemeine Elektricitäts Gesellschaft), Chemie-Verwaltung, or Farben Bayer is a good company with good prospects and whether it is purchased at 1 or 2 per cent, more or less, it is still well worth it. Nevertheless, given the limitations of distance, one can still act with dispatch. Market characteristics can work with you or against you; for this reason, technicalities are worth pursuing.

It is always best to give precise orders in any market, but when dealing in Germany perhaps even more so. There, more combinations and permutations are possible. The three most common market orders in Germany are as follows:

1. Limit orders, *Limitiert,* when the client defines the upper or lower limits at which he is willing to buy or sell.

2. Orders "at the market," are termed *Bestens,* at best, or sometimes *Billigst,* cheapest, in the case of a buy order. They are usually not advisable in Germany. If received before trading hours, such orders are automatically executed at the first price in the continuous market, or at the single *Kassakurs.* Moreover, the order will be executed in toto at one time, unless otherwise directed.

3. "For a client who knows his mind," a Dusseldorf trader commented, "the best order is a discretionary order, or better yet, a limited discretionary order. Both permit maximum leeway in timing and maximum flexibility in gauging the whims of the market."

The trader is free to exercise his judgment and can turn the market's flux and volatility to his client's advantage. The best time to execute the order is left to the bank's discretion or, if the customer so instructs, the order can be spread over several trading days if more favorable prices are thus obtainable. For instance, an order to sell DM8,000 nominal, placed *bestens interessewahrend,* best, at discretion, without specifying mark and pfennig, might be handled in this fashion: DM3,000 nominal at second quotation; DM3,000 nominal at fourth quotation and DM2,000 at the Kassakurs or single price for odd lots. In a sharply fluctuating market, the bank may execute a discretionary order fractionally or not at all.

A limited discretionary order encompasses the best of all possible worlds. It defines the limits of the customer's purse (insofar as a particular purchase is concerned) or the boundary beyond which his profit should not dip, in the case of a sale, while it takes advantage of the trader's talents. An order which is interessewahrend limitiert, a limited discretionary order, also guards against untoward fluctuations. The order might read:

"Bitte Kaufen Sie interessewahrend, aber nicht über 600%," Please purchase at discretion, but do not exceed the 600 per cent level.
Or:

"Kaufen Sie circa 600%," Buy at around the 600 per cent level. This would give the bank some leeway and it might be able to execute the order at 601.5 per cent or at 602 per cent.

Stop-loss orders are the exception rather than the rule in Germany. There are no puts or calls, the option market having been discontinued in 1931 and never resumed since. All transactions are for cash and must be settled within two days. There is no state-determined margin in Germany and the banks are free to lend money for stock purchases, or not, depending on the bank-client relationship.

GERMAN CORPORATE STRUCTURE

German law, much as Anglo-Saxon or French law, distinguishes between capital companies and private associations. The two basic forms of business organization in Germany are the corporation, *Aktien-*

gesellschaft or *AG,* and the limited liability company, the *Gesellschaft mit beschränkter Haftung* or *GmbH.*

There is one other popular form which is in essence a personal association rather than a capital company, the *Kommanditgesellschaft* or *KG,* the limited partnership. A company organized in this fashion falls somewhere between the other two previously mentioned types. Shares outstanding are usually restricted in number and not always available through the capital market. The KG, or limited partnership, may have two types of participants: the *Komplementäre,* partners liable without limitation; and the *Kommanditisten,* partners who may under certain conditions limit their liability. This type of business organizaton is extremely popular in Germany, and there are limited partnerships with a hundred or more members, which may include foreign nationals.

Asked to compare German corporate structure with its transatlantic counterpart in the United States, one banker said: "The *Aktiengesellschaften* are usually the big boys. Small stockholder participation is still in its infancy in Germany, so their attitude is 'let's not have a lot of the little boys running around and clogging up the annual meeting.' The GmbH are those who want to stay in a little club by themselves, and the Kommanditisten are somewhere in between."

The corporation, in Germany as elsewhere, is by far the most public of forms. Its basic capital must be DM100,000 ($25,000) minimum, divided into shares of equal worth, each with a minimum par value of DM100 ($25). Corporation law stipulates a supervisory council, the *Aufsichtsrat,* which in turn appoints the company's board of governors, or *Vorstand.* The supervisory council, which looks over management's shoulder, is a rather uniquely German institution consisting of between three and fifteen members, a third of whom must by law be employee representatives. In industries where trade unions are strong, they exercise the decisive influence in naming employee representatives to sit on the Aufsichtsrat.

The members of a GmbH, a limited liability company, enjoy certain advantages over their corporate brethren: they may appoint the management themselves, as the law does not require a supervisory council for this form of business organization. The limited liability company requires a base capital of only DM20,000 ($5,000). While the corporation is obliged by law to open its books to recognized independent auditors once a year (the auditors are appointed by the shareholders), the limited liability company is under no obligation to entertain outside auditors or to make elaborate public presentations concerning its activities. Because of this more private aspect of the GmbH, where both management and company affairs can be kept private, it is a preferred form in Germany. Wholly owned subsidiaries frequently assume this form.

The general rule in Germany is one share, one vote, though a few shares with plural votes do exist, remnants of the 1920s, when an influx of foreign capital gave rise to apprehension of foreign control. Aside from common shares, other categories of equity exist, as the law allows founders great liberty in setting up their companies. For instance, there may be shares which pre-empt a certain percentage of the profits before payments to ordinary shareholders are made. These are somewhat similar to the French *parts de fondateurs,* founders' parts, but are not as ubiquitous as on the French side of the Jura and the Ardennes.

There are very few restrictions on foreign participation in the German economy, the only outstanding one being that no foreigner may participate in the production of, or commerce in weapons of any kind. Foreigners can take up parts in shipping and mining and can acquire shares in public utilities with complete freedom. Moreover, there are no formal restrictions on the extent of foreign participation, non-Germans being free to acquire controlling interests in German enterprises without the necessity of obtaining permission from any government agency. The only restrictions a foreigner must comply with are foreign exchange regulations. For instance, no foreign national may buy "money paper" in Germany. Money paper, such as treasury bills, is only sold to banks to begin with, and so the restriction effects only foreign banks, not individuals.

Shares may be either bearer or registered in form. Both are freely transferable and no advantage or disadvantage attaches to either form. Bonds, too, may be either in bearer or in registered form. A glance at the Stock Exchange quotations shows a number of convertible bonds.

There are generally two types. One certificate stipulates the fact that the creditor has the right to trade in his bond for equity in the company. This is the usual form.

The second affords the creditor a special option at a discount price, should he wish to acquire stock in the future. To issue such convertible debentures, a company must first obtain the consent of several ministries of the Federal Republic. Convertibles are therefore not quite so popular a form as they are in the United States.

German companies usually pay dividends once a year. Dividends are always expressed as a per cent of par, not as so many Deutsche mark per share. German companies offer new stock fairly often and, even after such a distribution, dividends are usually maintained at the same level.

The basic company tax, the *Körperschaftssteuer*, taxes retained earnings at 51 per cent while distributed earnings, dividends, pay a levy of only 15. The law thus encourages companies to distribute their earnings to take advantage of the lower tax rate. For stockholders, dividends are taxed at a rate of 25 per cent which is withheld by the banks. This 25 per cent is what the American investor can claim against his U.S. taxes, thanks to a double taxation agreement between Germany and the United States. A new 1965 law levies a 25 per cent tax on interest paid to foreigners holding German fixed interest paper.

NEW ISSUES

Setting a price for a new issue is an exercise in compromise: the board of directors want the price in the vicinity of the stock's market price, while the public hopes for a price near par. The banker usually acts as a go-between. As dividends are often kept constant after a new issue, the company favors a high subscription price. On the other hand, if the price for the new stock is near par, the investing public need not put up too much money and the issue will be taken up with ease. New capital may not be issued below par, or below 100 per cent. Assuming that par is DM1,000, if the stock is selling at 500 per cent or 700 per cent, it becomes a rather expensive proposition to pick up the new issue. The upshot of the matter is that prices vary widely: The

Deutsche Bank in 1961 brought out new stock at 100 per cent, one new share for five old ones when its stock was selling at 878 per cent; and Farbwerke Hoechst, the large chemical concern, offered one new share for ten old ones at 300 per cent, when its stock market price was 710 per cent.

To calculate the adjusted market price of the stock after the issue and the value of the right, the procedure is the same as that used in the United States with an additional calculation. It is necessary to convert the figure expressed as a percentage of par to money terms.

Assuming that Deutsche Aktiengesellschaft stock is presently quoted at 700 per cent and that they are offering one new share at 200 per cent for every five old shares held, the market price would adjust itself to:

$$
\begin{array}{ll}
700 & \text{price of old shares} \\
\times 5 & \text{old shares held} \\
\hline
3,500 & \text{value of old shares held} \\
+200 & \text{offer price of new share} \\
\hline
3,700 &
\end{array}
$$

(5 old shares+1 new share=6), therefore: 3,700÷6=616.

The difference between the old price of 700 per cent and the new price of 616 per cent equals the value of the right; 700−616=84 per cent. When par value is DM1,000, then the value of the right is DM840.

ANALYSIS

When Americans entered the German market in 1959, they imported security analysis and American analytic techniques. Under that stimulus, the German banks first established research departments for security analysis. From an investor's point of view, company analysis in Germany ranks somewhere between that of France and the United States in difficulty; there is more information available than in France, but less than in the United States. First, there are a number of legal obligations concerning their reporting procedures which companies must meet, and the *Aktiengesetz,* the law pertaining to this area, spells out the forms required for balance sheets and income statements. Generally, they follow American formats and must by law include some thirty-three items. For the analyst, the difficulties are that hidden reserves can be extrapolated only partially from statements, and real earnings are not spelled out at all.

English understatement may be proverbial, but in the realm of company analysis, it is the German habit which is troublesome. Company law allows wide leeway in the accumulation of reserves, and hidden or "silent" reserves in particular. These are usually arrived at by an undervaluation of the company's assets, much in the manner of a Dutch firm whose million-dollar plant is down as costing one guilder. To arrive at an approximation of what a company is really worth is often a long and cumbersome task.

"Some companies," said one of Germany's leading analysts, "will give their earnings exact to the pfennig." However, this is misleading, as companies will often declare only what they intend to pay out. The Germans have developed a rather sophisticated system of calculating backwards from the amount of money companies pay in taxes over a period of several years. From tax figures, the analyst can extrapolate the company's real earnings as opposed to its declared earnings. The firm of Georg Hauck and Son and others have perfected this technique and have developed a widely accepted formula which takes all the variables involved into account. However, it must be kept in mind that as the analyst becomes wiser, company accountants become wiser too. Until a change in the tax law makes this technique obsolete, it continues to be a most valuable instrument—for those who know how to use it.

Another problem faced by the security analyst is what to do with subsidiaries. In Germany, unlike the practice in many other European countries, lists of subsidiaries and who belongs to whom is an open secret. For anyone willing to purchase a book called, *Wer Gehört Zu Wem, Mutter und Tochtergesellschaften von A-Z,* Who Belongs to Whom, Mother and Daughter Companies from A to Z, a flick of a few pages will clear up the mystery. Other books, in particular a number of recent works by Kurt Pritzkoleit will give other details such as family holdings, names of directors, banking connections, and sometimes percentage of control exercised over subsidiaries for a variety of industries.

MUTUAL FUNDS

The German mutual fund management companies with several funds under their direction are usually closely tied to one or another bank. Often they are wholly owned subsidiaries. The banks act as godfathers for the management companies, making a market for the funds, and providing research and advice for which they are paid a fee. Fund shares are deposited in the parent bank which issued the share certificates, and the bank collects a commission on trades of these shares, acting as the fund's brokers. The Dresdner Bank, for instance, has a wholly owned company, Deutscher Investment Trust, Gesellschaft fuer Wertpapieranlagen mbH, Frankfurt (Main) which is at the helm of four mutual funds whose asset values exceed $250 million, over a third of the total assets of all German funds combined. The Deutsche Bank participates in a mutual fund management company, the Deutsche Gesellschaft fuer Wertpapiersparen mbH, Frankfurt (Main); and the Commerzbank has an interest in Allgemeine Deutsche Investment GmbH, München-Dusseldorf.

All mutual funds in Germany are open end; closed-end funds are not permitted. The price of German mutual fund shares is not based on supply and demand, or the state of the market any particular day. Price is rather a function of the value of the fund's holdings. Taking the net asset value of the fund's total holdings, at the day's market price, one must add a fixed charge (varying from fund to fund) which represents the cost of issuing certificates, profit margins, and so on. The redemption price of mutual fund certificates is arrived at in a similar fashion. Investment certificates are termed *Investment Anteile,* and are not included in the daily Official List of the Stock Exchange, but are published separately.

GERMAN INDUSTRY

Germany is an economic geographer's dream, which might well explain why the field has been a German forte for so long. The country divides neatly into disparate regions, each with characteristic natural resources, and the whole is bound together by a web of waterways. A large proportion of West German industry today clusters around three areas: the Saarland, a region rich in coal with vast chemical production including ammonia, sulphuric acid, tar, benzol, and other by-products of the steel mills; the North Rhine Westphalian complex, which embraces the coal fields of the Ruhr and the shipping and shipbuilding of Bremen and Hamburg; and the Rhine-Main region, with Frankfort, and Mainz as the leading industrial cities. Frankfort, a center for the heavy chemicals, plays host to Farbwerke Hoechst, and Badische Anilin und Soda Fabrik of Ludwigshafen is nearby.

The stretch between Frankfort and Dusseldorf is Siegfried country; the Rhine flows from one region to the other. It is a green spot among the chimney pots and the slag heaps, a stretch of picturesque hills and viniculture; ruins of castles dominate the heights. Downstream past Bonn, the Rhine flows through the biggest industrial conglomorate in Germany. Heinrich Heine's "heroic Rhine" the river of the Lorelei, becomes a waterway for barge traffic.

Though coal is at its base, the Ruhr is one of the most thoroughly integrated industrial regions in Europe. Chemical, metallurgical, engineering, and textile plants are neighbors here. Besides the coke ovens and steel mills, the Cologne-Dusseldorf area is also ringed by chemical plants. Coal tar and gas, at one time mere wastes, are now the basis for the production of fertilizers, drugs, and dyestuffs. Farbenfabriken Bayer, the largest German chemical firm, 12th largest in the 1964 *Fortune* directory of 200 foreign firms, is at Leverkusen, and other pharmaceutical producers abound here. Germany's two largest department store chains, Karstadt and Kaufhof have headquarters in the area, as does RWE, Rheinisch-Westfälische Elektrizitäts-Werk, the largest producer of electrical power in Germany. As the country's largest private utility, RWE provides over 40 per cent of the nation's power needs. North-Rhine Westphalia is also the center for the production of paper, ceramics, and glass.

In the Ruhr today, many of the Rhineland-Ruhr dynasties still dominate the scene. Germany's "heavies," coal and steel, are still the demesne of a handful of families, Stinnes, Thyssen, Wolf, Krupp, and

Haniels. The *Fortune* 1964 directory of 200 largest foreign companies ranked by sales lists the steel makers as follows: Friedrich Krupp Works, 13th; Gelsenkirchener Bergwerks AG, 23rd; Mannesmann, 24th; the Gutehoffnungshütte, the Good Hope complex, 26th; Rheinische Stahlwerke, 27th; and the newly merged Phoenix-Rheinrohr and August Thyssen-Hütte, AG, not on the roster, should head the list for 1965.

The Ruhr, onetime "industrial heart of Europe," was once the seat of the combines and cartels, the munitions makers, steel trusts, chemical companies, and electrical manufacturers. By producing "guns and not butter," they attempted unsuccessfully to dominate Europe's industries and eventually Europe. In the 1920s and 1930s, the Rhineland group overbuilt and overconcentrated German heavy industry in an area in no wise equipped to support it. Once created, the huge excess capacity in steel and other production became an insoluble problem. Germany itself could not absorb the excess the Rhineland mills produced. The economic consequences of this overexpansion were, in Hitler's much quoted phrase, "export or die," and the industrialists welcomed the man who offered a solution. Obviously, Adolf Hitler's rise was helped by a concomitance of factors—a depression, widespread unemployment, political unrest, and more. Bankers and industrialists, however, must bear a large part of the blame for backing the *Führer* to compensate for their industrial myopia. They helped unleash the Juggernaut and with it World War II.

Today all this is history, a quarter of a century in the past. The families may still hold majority control in the Ruhr, but the world has changed around them. Germany has full employment, an unparalleled prosperity, and a new generation of *junge Unternehmer-persönlichkeiten,* "young management types," who have little taste for defense contracts and even less for German rearmament. The Common Market promises to achieve what the cartels attempted and failed to do and, in contrast to the pre-Hitler era, consumer production is booming in Germany as never before.

The electrical industry, chemicals, and drugs have come to the forefront along with a plethora of consumer-oriented goods and services. Despite the fact that Germany started from a postwar disadvantage, today she is second only to the United States in world volume and sales of electrical equipment. Germany has 21 per cent of world volume, whereas the United States boasts 25 per cent. The German electrical industry jostled Britain's out of its first place niche among exporters of electrical machinery. Four producers are prominent; the Siemens group; AEG, Allgemeine Elektricitäts-Gesellschaft; Robert Bosh; and Brown Boveri (a subsidiary of a Swiss company). Siemens and AEG dominate the industry with over one-third of the total. The Siemens group is the more diversified producing everything from railway equipment, computers, appliances, telecommunication and transmission apparatus of all types. The company is 9th on the *Fortune* industrial register and is one of the world's largest employers, meeting payrolls in 46 countries and presumably as many currencies. It derives a third of its sales from non-German operations. AEG, smaller than Siemens, concentrates more on consumer goods, with Telefunken, part of the AEG group, responsible for well over half of these items, including television, radio, high-fi equipment, etc.

In the chemicals, the three giant companies once part of the I.G. Farben complex lead the field. Farbenfabriken Bayer is the largest with estimated sales of over $1 billion, Farbwerke Hoechst with some $865 million in sales around the globe is next, with Badische Anilin bringing up the rear of the former Farben empire with worldwide sales of $715 million.

THE FINANCIAL SCENE

Who invests in Germany? The most active elements in the market are the banks, the large public institutions and smaller private banks, foreign buyers, and the German general public. Insurance companies usually confine themselves to the bond market. Of this cast of characters, the public is the ingenue on the Stock Exchange scene for, despite government encouragement, individual participation remains low. According to one estimate, a mere 20 per cent of the personal savings of West Germany's citizens finds its way into stocks and bonds, while 75 to 80 per cent is entrusted to savings banks, building and loan associations, and insurance.

In the pre- and post-World War I period, public participation was at its peak and provided the moorings for the market. This changed radically in the hyperinflationary times of the 1920s and 1930s. In the immediate post-World War II period, of course, there was little left to invest in, and Germans buckled down to re-creating Germany's wealth and rebuilding her industries. Moreover, savings banks and mortgage banks, the familiar lodestars, once more exerted their magnetic influence on German householders. Interest rates were modest— only 3½ to 4 per cent—but thanks to a government-sponsored system of premiums and tax exemptions, individuals saw their savings bring in bonus payments of up to 20 and 30 per cent of their total accounts. This boosted actual yields to between 8 and 12 per cent. Savings thus flowed into these institutions.

Other factors tend to discourage the small investor in Germany: the high denominations of stocks, and a certain amount of trepidation which comes with war, currency reform, and revaluation. The government has made a number of attempts to broaden share ownership, including the 1950 attempt to sell "baby bonds," debentures in DM100 denominations. This met with but small success.

A more successful attempt was the "reprivatization" of Volkswagen, in 1961, which doubled the number of small investors in Germany. "Germans are not a nation of shareholders," one banker confided, "and when they do have shares, they sit on them." Today, however, there are one million Volkswagen holders. At first, the notion of *Volksaktien,* people's shares, was thought to be ridiculous and the easy prediction was that within six months the block of stock sold to the public would end up in the hands of the banks. In fact, this has not been the case. About 75 per cent of the stock is still in the hands of small shareholders.

"How many shareholders are there in Germany?"

"Perhaps we have two million after the Volkswagen issue."

Because of the great number of bearer securities, statistics on shareholdings are vague in Germany as in much of the rest of Europe.

CONCLUSION

The German market has done very well by many investors. Despite the usual difficulties in examining European companies, there is more economic information available in Germany than in any other Continental country. This applies to statistics on the general economic scene published by government agencies and also to data made available by a whole variety of private organizations which specialize in business and economic surveys. In short, there is no lack of information. Moreover, much of it is available in English.

Besides the yearly bank reviews, the report of the Bundesbank, and the publications of the Institut für Bilanzanalysen in Wiesbaden, a service which provides a yearly rundown on companies and is extensively subscribed to by German banks, a great deal of information can be culled from the financial press. Since New York often triggers a buying or a selling wave in Germany, some professionals gauge the trend of the German market by studying the money flow into and out of the Federal Republic. Of course, they base their conclusions on a bank's daily contacts with London, Paris, and New York, and the ups and downs of arbitrage. Another approach is a statistical one. By studying the publications of the Statistisches Bundesamt, the State Statistical Service, and other economic publications, one could arrive at a significant set of figures from German statistics, whereas this would be extremely difficult to do for many other European countries.

When it comes to company analysis, the trilingual flyleaves of Hoppenstedt are excellent, as are the flyleaves of the Dresdner Bank. Neither is quite comparable to services such as Standard and Poor's or Moody's, but they offer a close parallel for the German scene. Generally speaking, the banks are the place to go for investment advice and background information. Many banks have a special department oriented to foreign clients, and they are very glad to handle accounts of whatever size. They charge no fee for advisory work but will not usually take on a discretionary account.

One of the characteristics of the Wirtschaftswunder, the economic miracle, was the accelerated rate of capital investment. Except for a three-year span between 1955 to 1958, German domestic investment as a percentage of the GNP increased steadily from about 23 per cent in 1950 to 27 per cent in 1962. Obviously, this great hunger for capital made great demands on the nation's savings and no doubt contributed significantly to the very high interest rates which characterized the German scene. Foreigners were not shy of taking advantage of these high interest rates, and foreign money flocked to Germany, sometimes to the dismay of the Bundesbank. In an effort to keep hot money out, the government, in March 1964, proposed a withholding tax on dividends paid to foreigners holding fixed-interest German securities. The immediate effect was that foreigners began selling German gilt-edged securities. The tax is still in the proposal stage but seems to have had the desired effect, and interest rates are now back at 6 per cent.

In the early 1960s, German businessmen were afraid of contracting "the English disease," stagnating production coupled with sharply rising costs. Throughout the "miracle," wage rates did not keep up with gains in productivity; now they threaten to outrace productivity. Some economists, therefore, stress that future growth will be in areas with highly automated equipment and low labor charges. Which industries will benefit from future automation is difficult to say, but some of the traditional fields of excellence will undoubtedly head the list—chemicals and steels, utilities and drugs will set the pace, with automobile and appliance manufacturers not far behind.

The drawing cards of the German market will remain as attractive as ever: a strong currency, political stability, a favorable balance of trade, ample natural resources, and a vast industrial complex.

SOURCES OF INFORMATION

Primary sources:

The weekly and quarterly reports of the Deutsches Institut für Wirtschaftsforschung, the German Institute for Economic Research.

The monthly reports and annual reviews of the Deutsche Bundesbank, the German National Bank, which are also available in English.

The monthly study, *Wirtschaft und Statistik* (The Economy and Statistics) published by the Statsbundesamt, the State publication office, and including Stock Exchange price trends, dividend yields, etc.

Börsen und Wirtschaftshandbuch (The Stock Exchange and Economic Handbook) published by the *Frankfurter Allgemeine Zeitung,* one of Germany's leading newspapers.

The *Volkswirt,* a magazine which is the *Economist* of Germany.

Newspapers:

Frankfurter Allgemeine Zeitung (a daily).
Handelsblatt (daily on Stock Exchange days).
Industrie Kurier (4 times a week).
Die Welt (a daily).
Die Zeit (a weekly).

For information on companies:

The flyleaves of the Dresdner Bank.
Hoppenstedt, Darmstadt, a business service in three languages: English, French and German.
Institut für Bilanzanalysen, the Institute for Balance Sheet Analysis.

Books:

Wer Gehört zu Wem, Mutter und Tochtergesellschaften von A-Z, (Who belongs to Whom, Mother and Daughter Companies from A to Z) published with the imprimatur of various banks, and available in English translation.

BRUNS, GEORG. *Effektenhandel an Deutschen und Ausländischen Börsen,* (Stock Trading on German and Foreign Exchanges). Frankfurt am Main: Fritz Knapp Verlag, 1961.

HINTNER, OTTO. *Wertpapierbörsen,* (Stock Exchanges). Wiesbaden, Betriebswirtschaftlicher Verlag, 1961. This is a somewhat more academic description and analysis of the subject.

For general economic background on Germany, its industries, industrial magnates, etc., Pritzkoleit's works are interesting. They include:

PRITZKOLEIT, KURT. *Männer, Mächte, Monopole,* (Men, Might, and Monopoly). Dusseldorf: Karl Rauch Verlag, 1963.

———— *Auf einer Woge von Gold, Der Triumph der Wirtschaft,* (On a Wave of Gold, The Triumph of the Economy). Wien, München, Basel: Verlag Kurt Desch, 1961.

———— *Das Kommandierte Wunder,* (The Planned Wonder). Verlag Kurt Desch, 1959.

Indexes:

The Herstatt Index developed by Bankhaus Herstatt of Cologne is an important indicator and is widely quoted outside of Germany.

The *Frankfurter Allgemeine Zeitung* publishes an index closely watched in Germany; and the Bundesamt's weekly indicator published by the State Statistical Service is another source for trend analysis.

7. AUSTRIA

One must go into the market as into a cold shower—quick in and
quick out.

—Salomon von Rothschild, founder of the
Vienna branch of the Rothschild house

Two significant turning points mark modern Austrian history. The
first was the dissolution of the Emperor Franz Joseph's Dual
Monarchy of Austria-Hungary at the end of World War I. The dissolution of the Empire has often been spoken of as a dismemberment
of the country, leaving a giant head on a dwarfed body. The head,
Vienna, had been a leading cosmopolitan center of Europe until that
war, on a par with London and Paris. With Hungary gone, Vienna in
a sense was overcapitalized—too many people administering too small
a country. Austria (32,400 square miles; 7.1 million population)
gradually became a backwater, a third-rate power living on first-rate
memories.

The next decisive factor in Austrian history was *Anschluss,* March
11, 1938, when Hitler marched into Vienna, merging the country
with the Third Reich. The Second World War was no kinder to Austria than the First had been. After the war the country was occupied
for another ten years on a four-power basis, similar to the division
of Germany. But, unlike the experience of Germany, elections were
held in 1945 and a coalition government was established. This remarkable coalition government—now two decades old—of the
People's Party (Conservatives) and the Socialists is a neat balance of
power that steers the country between Scylla and Charybdis. One

of the first tasks of the régime was to secure Austrian industry from both the east and the west. This they attempted to do by nationalizing all the heavy industries, to thwart confiscation of Austrian property which had been incorporated into the Nazi war machine. However, this step did not hinder the Russians from dismantling plants in their sector; they expropriated approximately 300 industrial plants, and removed all the equipment of the Danube Steam Navigation Company.

The State Treaty of May 1955 restored Austrian sovereignty and ended four-power control. For their cooperation, the Russians extracted $150 million of industrial matériel and nearly 10 million tons of oil. The treaty called for a neutralized Austria—a fact which has hindered Austria's desire to become a full member in the Common Market. In any event, the coalition government came out of the occupation as owner of much of the country's basic industry, a situation the Socialists favor and the Conservatives deplore. However, the situation has not greatly changed owing to the fact that the parties have been at loggerheads. Government by coalition—power is so evenly split that neither party can command a majority—is a knack of compromise carried almost to a fine art. In short, it is known as the system of *Proporz*: an egalitarian arrangement which divides all power and position between the two ruling parties. If the chairman of the board is of the People's Party, the president must be a Socialist. The Conservatives run the radio, but the Socialists control television. This system is almost as inflexible as it sounds. Consequently, a checkmate ensues when the parties agree to disagree. This frequently happens in discussion of necessary reforms of the capital market (less than 10 per cent of gross capital investment is financed through the Stock Exchange), tax reforms (Austrian companies are probably the most heavily taxed in Europe), or other assistance to the free enterprise sector of the economy.

The nationalized sector accounts for almost a quarter of the country's total industrial output, 22 per cent of its labor force and 27 per cent of its exports. Since the war, the government has invested roughly $1 billion in this sector. One survey indicated that the administration owned, directly or indirectly, 72 per cent of the stock of the nation's corporations. In 96 companies the government or local authorities have a majority interest and in 88 enterprises the government has a controlling hand through one of the state-controlled banks. For instance, the Creditanstalt-Bankverein is reported to have in its portfolio about 10 per cent of the nation's joint stock companies acquired over many years. Without very much success, the government has tried to divest itself of some industries or at least reduce its share of some enterprises. It did sell 40 per cent of the two leading nationalized banks—the Creditanstalt-Bankverein and the Österreichische Länderbank—back to the public, but it retains a controlling interest. The main government-owned activities are in iron, coal, aluminum, oil, and power. In addition the government has select firms in the steel industry (Vöest, the country's largest steel plant, Alpine Montan, Gebrüder Böhler, and Schoeller-Bleckmann); the electrical equipment and machine tool industries (Simmering-Graz-Pauker), and the chemical and oil sector (Ö.M.V. and Stickstoffwerke). Railroads, except for some minor lines, are nationalized as is the telephone system. These state-owned firms are not given any priorities over private enterprises, in part because sharp oversight by the political system makes sure that neither side achieves an advantageous position. Furthermore, there is little competition between the two sectors, since most of the nationalized companies are in heavy industry and the capital goods sector, whereas private firms are mostly in light industry and consumer goods.

A precise definition of the Austrian economy proves evasive. Undoubtedly, it is a mixed grill: part state capitalism, part socialistic, and part free enterprise. Over 300 cartels are legalized and regulated by the state's cartel commission. They regulate prices, market areas, terms of sales, and credit conditions. This is reminiscent of that other Teutonic state before World War II. Cartels regulate large areas of the economy, from the concrete of the large Perlmooser Zementwerke to the machine tool and engineering industry. This cartelization of industry appears to work for Austrian business, though its effect on consumers is open to question. Cartels may prove a problem when confronted with a more tightly integrated Europe and the rules of the EEC, if Austria should become a member. Another curious aspect of the economic structure of the country also tends to restrict competition: a quasi-feudal system of licensing by guilds regulates small businesses, and a compulsory Chamber of Commerce gathers all businesses, trades, and professions under its wing.

Austria is a member of EFTA but has been pursuing associate membership in the Common Market for reasons of trade. One-half the nation's total exports go to the EEC, largely to Germany and Italy, but only 16 per cent of her exports go to EFTA nations. The import picture is even more striking: 58 per cent of her imports come from the EEC while only 14 per cent were initiated by EFTA countries. The remainder of her import-export trade is largely with Eastern Europe. Unless she can become an associate member, Austria may be faced with a painful common tariff wall around her EEC markets. But membership in EEC would also mean that she would have to raise her tariff walls to coincide with the Community's—a step she is reluctant to take since her trade with EFTA is growing rapidly. Briefly stated, Austria would like the best of all possible worlds: to be included in the EEC in an economic sense, but remain legally separate so that she may still remain a member of EFTA and also live up to her neutrality treaty of 1955. Russia has suggested that membership within the Common Market "would be incompatible with Austrian neutrality." This is a hard nut to crack, one made tougher since the two Austrian political parties are divided on the fine points of EEC membership. It is important for Austria to trade in as many areas as possible since she has continually run a balance-of-trade deficit, one that is offset by invisible items and a large tourist industry.

As an Alpine state, Austria's economy is not dissimilar to Switzerland's though perhaps more regional. The land is endowed with a wide variety of natural resources: iron ore, lignite, salt, magnesite, graphite, copper, zinc, and others. Particularly abundant are the forests which provide Austria with a paper and pulp industry second only to Scandinavia's and Finland's in Europe. Austria's skill in precision and optical instruments is formidable. Besides products of such well-known companies as Steyr-Daimler-Puch or the rubber fabricator, Semperit Österreichisch-Amerikanische Gummiwerke, many light industries have given the country a reputation for luxury items from chocolate to crystal chandeliers or jewelry made of gold-dipped leaves of the Vienna woods. Naturally most of these companies are family owned and not listed upon the securities Exchange. One could invest in Austrian beer, Oesterreichische Brau, one of the country's larger companies, but unfortunately not in Sacher Torten.

Only a few companies are listed on the Vienna Stock Exchange, since so many of them are nationalized or completely in private hands. Of the 82 stocks listed, 7 are foreign firms, mostly German. The nominal value of all listed equity is Sch.4.3 billion ($165 million), though the market value is obviously much higher. In 1963 the value of Exchange transactions in shares was Sch.263 million ($10 million). Most of the activity in the *Börse* is in fixed-interest bearing securities since the government practices what is tantamount to fiscal discrimination against equity financing. In any given year bond issues by the government will far outweigh the number of new shares that come to the market. The yield on bonds is in the region of 6½ per cent and Austrians are more likely to own one of the 400 bonds listed on the Exchange than common stock. There was more turnover in bonds than in stocks in 1963, Sch.592 million ($23 million). There has been a fair amount of foreign interest in the Viennese bond market, particularly on the part of the Germans, Belgians, Swiss, and Dutch. The Austrian share index compiled by the Institute of Economic Research uses a base of 100 dating from immediately before Anschluss. The index is made up of 36 industrials and 6 bank and insurance companies. Its high was reached in 1962.

There are only a few restrictions upon foreign investors, among them one forbidding non-Austrians from owning ordnance companies. The government does not relish large foreign investors since memories of the 1930s are still fresh when Germany exerted pressure through her stake in Austrian companies. Direct portfolio investments can easily be made through purchases with convertible currency. Repatriation of capital and interest or dividends poses no problem, and securities can be sent out of the country. Dividends on shares are paid once a year, but interest is dispersed semiannually. There is no withholding tax on domestic bonds, but a withholding tax ("a capital yield tax") which amounts to 17.7 per cent is deducted from convertible bonds and stocks. A double taxation treaty exists between the United States and Austria so that such withholdings can be claimed on federal returns.

As a Germanic country, most of the corporate structure follows the German model. The main forms are the corporation or *Aktiengesellschaft* (*AG*) with a minimum capital of Sch.1 million ($38,461) usually divided into shares with a par value of Sch.1,000 ($38). The limited liability company, *Gesellschaft mit beschränkter Haftung* (*GmbH*), exists in Austria but is not on the Official List. The five open-end funds listed on the Exchange are managed by one holding company. They are all comprised of Austrian and foreign securities and therefore of less interest to those looking for an exclusively Austrian investment.

Most corporations issue bearer shares with attached dividend coupons which must be presented for collection. Most of a company's ordinary shares, *Stammaktien,* are in bearer form; only insurance companies have registered stock, *Namensaktien,* and some preferred shares, *Vorzugsaktien.*

Vienna, once the Paris of Central Europe, had a reputation for *gemütlichkeit,* culture and leisurely good living. Her financial mart, the *Wiener Börse,* however has enjoyed the least gemütlich of existences as *Katastrophe* of one sort or another has been its fate. Maria Theresa's first attempt to establish the Börse in 1761 was a failure and she had to start again ten years later. Subsequently, with every political upheaval such as the Napoleonic wars, World War I, the severance of Hungary from the Austrian realm, Anschluss with Germany, and World War II, the Exchange was temporarily closed.

Despite the sporatic history of the Vienna market as an institution, investors were not as hampered by the Börse's frequent closings as might appear at first glance. So called *Winkelbörsen,* unofficial markets, literally "in a nook," sprang up and a semblance of trading continued. Today, there is only one official Stock Exchange, and all trading is centralized once again.

Only slightly damaged by Allied bombings, the Exchange was destroyed by fire in 1956. Today, the Börse building has been rebuilt to the most modern specifications inside though preserving intact the outer facade, as was done in Frankfurt. The same architect who restored the Vienna Opera House also redesigned the neoclassic Börse building.

The Vienna Stock Market is an independent corporation, managed by a council which represents twenty-two financial and credit institutions. Membership consists of over 200 bankers, brokers, and traders of credit institutions. The market operates on a daily basis, working from 11:30 A.M. to 1 P.M.

The buying and selling of securities does not necessarily have to go through the floor of the Exchange. Banks and financial institutions can and do match orders without approaching the official brokers, *Sensale*. These Sensale are government appointed individuals who do not deal for their own account but act as agents between the various brokers by matching orders to arrive at the one official daily price. (Only three companies—Perlmooser Zementwerke, Semperit Österreichisch-Amerikanische Gummiwerke and Steyr-Daimler-Puch —are dealt in on a continuous basis with some price fluctuation.) Any transaction solely between two principal parties will probably be made at the official price though the Sensale was not involved. An active market also exists on the telephone in unlisted securities.

Prices are quoted in per cent of par. There are no round lots and settlement is within one or two weeks. An option market, though not prohibited, does not exist. While verbal orders are good only for the day, written orders are good until the end of the month unless otherwise stated. Actual trading is quite sedate and without the verbal madness so reminiscent of Zurich. Prices are chalked up on boards behind the Sensale and the official list is published after the day's trading.

Commission rates total 1.14 per cent on stocks and 0.7 per cent on fixed-interest-bearing securities.

SOURCES OF INFORMATION

Most information on Austrian securities is published in German, though the annual reports of the two leading banks are issued in English. The banks also publish monthly economic letters or bulletins in English, besides occasional analysis of Austrian companies. The

Creditanstalt-Bankverein and the Österreichische Länderbank are the nation's largest banks undertaking all kinds of commercial transactions besides acting as investment bankers. The daily paper with the most financial coverage is the *Presse*. A series of weeklies and monthlies which specialize in economics and finance include: *Bank und Börse, Die Wirtschaft, Internationale Wirtschaft, Der Österreichische Volkswirt,* and *Wiener Börsen-Kurier.*

Books:

HEISSENBERGER, FRANZ. *Wiederaufbau in Oesterreich,* Frankfurt am Main: Fritz Knapp Verlag, 1961.

TAUTSCHER, ANTON. *Handbuch der oesterreichischen Wirtschaftspolitik,* Wien, Basteiverlag: 1961.

WEBER, WILHELM. *Oesterreichs Wirtschafts-Struktur.* Berlin: Verlag Duncker und Humbolt, 1961.

8. SCANDINAVIA AND FINLAND

> These heroes of finance are like beads on a string—when one slips
> off, all the rest follow.
>
> —Henrik Ibsen

SWEDEN: THE SECOND EDEN?

In Paris in 1963 a Swedish economics professor soberly addressed the
Second Congress of European Sanitary Pottery Manufacturers. His
remarks debunked a myth and left the impression that Sweden, perhaps, was not Eden. Contrary to wide expectations, the good doctor
concluded that only 70 per cent of Swedish homes had flush toilets and
53 per cent, proper baths.

This singular fall from grace can not obscure the fact that Sweden
(population 7.5 million; area, 175,000 square miles) has one of the
highest standards of living in the world. Whether one speaks of the
infant mortality rate (16 per thousand) or the number of persons per
passenger car (5), Sweden's record is impressive. But at the turn of the
century the country was in a stagnant and sad condition. By World
War I a quarter of its population had emigrated to the United States.
The next half-century of peace and increasing prosperity has been
largely due to three factors. Like the Swiss, the Swedes have maintained neutrality since the Napoleonic period. Consequently, they
skipped two devastating world wars. Domestic peace was achieved
during the 1930s when the Social Democratic party came to power on
a broad promise of social welfare and labor peace. The third notable

factor in any quick survey is surely the number of Swedish technical inventions, and the skilled enterprise with which they have been exploited.

Swedish socialism—the ruling Social Democratic party has but a slim majority—is badly misunderstood because it works so well. Indeed, it is rather a socialist-professing government without socialism. Sweden ties with Switzerland for the highest gross national product per capita in all of Europe, second only to the United States. Undoubtedly, this is due to the paradoxical position of private companies retaining control over 90 per cent of the "means of production." Back in 1920 one of the planks in the Social Democratic party's platform categorically called for "annulling the capitalist right of ownership of the means of production and placing them under government control." In 1960 the tone was quite different and less bellicose: "The various forms of economic activity should be coordinated under the leadership of the state. . . . Natural resources, credit institutions, and business enterprises should be under its control to the full extent necessary to uphold the essential interests of its citizens. . . ."

Pure socialism has never had a clear-cut mandate from the electorate. On the other hand, the long line of social welfare programs that touch almost every aspect of the human condition have wide public support. A general consensus formed among these homogeneous seven and one-half million people a generation ago. Thus the tidy if somewhat pedestrian prosperity has removed the excitement and social ferment found in other European countries. No one in the established power structure wishes to rock the boat domestically or in the field of foreign policy, where they are again on a par with the Swiss in advocating neutrality.

Labor peace is one of the cardinal points of the present government; there has been no major labor strike since 1945, unemployment is less than 1 per cent and the percentage of man-days lost is reportedly one-fiftieth of that of the United States. Undoubtedly, labor harmony has been a boon to the Swedish economy and it is partially responsible for the trebling of industrial production since 1935. One must remember that Sweden, like Holland, is a newly industrialized country. Its early commercial life was founded on Baltic trade and shipping;

exporting is still an important aspect of the economy, for about a quarter of its industrial product is sent abroad. The shipyards of Gothenburg, Malmo, and Stockholm have a long tradition of superior boat construction and account for 10 per cent of world production. Though there has been a glut of shipbuilding since the Suez crisis in 1956, Sweden has retained her place as fourth largest manufacturer in the world.

Industrial expansion was based on the easy exploitation of the two principal resources of the country: timber and iron ore. These two have always been staples in Sweden and in great demand since early modern history. Even France turned to Sweden for assistance in establishing its iron industry. Colbert imported Swedish iron workers as the fame of Swedish steel spread throughout the world. By the time of the American Revolution, Sweden was the source of almost a third of European "bar iron" production.

In the context of Europe, Sweden's industrial revolution came rather late—in the second half of the nineteenth century. Refinements and technological innovations in the timber industry gradually made the paper and pulp end of that business the more profitable, and it remains so today. With the discovery of the Lappland ore fields iron ore and machine tools also became major export items. Swedish industrial development was somewhat tardy, but talented. Besides developing safety matches, dynamite, kerosene stoves, steam turbines, and refrigerators, the Swedes also led the way in perfecting ball and roller bearings, drilling equipment, electric smelters, separators, and high- and low-voltage equipment.

CURRENCY CONTROL

Naturally, specialized companies (the limited liability company is an *aktiebolaget, or AB*) arose to take advantage of these developments. By World War I the Swedes became wary that foreigners—particularly Germans—might try to take over their burgeoning industries. Consequently, the Swedish Parliament passed the first of a series of stringent decrees on foreign control and foreign capital. To begin with, immovable property (natural resources) was put beyond the reach of aliens.

Other Swedish corporations, in order not to be considered a "dangerous legal person," had to limit their number of foreign shareholders to less than 20 per cent of the voting equity or less than 40 per cent of the total share capital, regardless of the number of votes. From these complicated regulations, four types of common shares evolved. Most shares of a Swedish company—the four-fifths that must remain in domestic hands—are termed "bound" or class A shares. There also exist a few free class A shares that can be owned by foreigners. Usually each of these class A shares has one vote per share, but there are many variations from company to company in this respect. Parenthetically, it should be noted that Swedish shares are issued only in registered form, with dividend coupons attached to the actual shares (not share certificates). In actuality, once the shares are endorsed they are then traded as bearer securities. Companies will register stock, but it is not common practice. To be doubly safe and secure against foreign interests, some companies have issued B shares, both bound and free types, with but one-thousandth or one-hundredth of a vote per share. Though there are both bound and free A and B shares, generally A shares are considered as bound or tied, while B shares are usually free. It is these free B shares that are most commonly traded in foreign markets, usually at a premium over the bound shares traded on the Stockholm Exchange. The premium attests to the short supply of B shares in world markets or, on occasions, their lack of marketability.

A dozen large Swedish concerns have issued both A and B shares for separate listing. The list reads like a Blue Book of Swedish Industry: Electrolux, the maker of household appliances; Svenska Kullager-fabriken or SKF, the world's largest producer of ball and roller bearings; Svenska Tändsticks, better known as Swedish Match; L. M. Ericsson, a world-wide telephone producer and the AT&T of Sweden.

Part and parcel of this complicated control of securities are the regulations on capital movement. The underlying motivation of the Swedes appears to be an attempt to isolate Sweden's economy from the rest of the world. How much longer this xenophobia can be maintained in the face of the growing integration of the European economies remains to be seen. Certainly these barriers to capital and foreign investors would have to terminate should Sweden join the Common Market under the Rome Treaty. This may be less remote than many observers judge, for Sweden has moved toward integration rather than away from it. Only fifteen years ago in January 1950 the Prime Ministers of Norway, Denmark, and Sweden declared there was no basis for further tariff cooperation. Attempts at a Scandinavian Customs Union, they declared, would only make their economic relations too competitive. Today the success of EFTA illustrates the benefits of such a competitive customs union to member nations.

The central bank of Sweden, the Riksbank, is older than the Bank of England and probably more control oriented. The bank watches hawk-eyed over the inflow of capital. Generally speaking, aliens are prohibited from direct portfolio investment in Swedish industry. Swedish banks or brokers cannot execute initial orders for foreigners. There are, however, entirely legal ways to circumscribe these prohibitions with the blessings of the Riksbank. First, take the case of bonds. Foreigners can buy Swedish krona bonds listed on the Exchange provided they use moneys from a blocked account. In other words, an investor may use the proceeds from a sale of Swedish stock to buy bonds. The switch process works only in one direction: he cannot buy stock from the sale of bonds. There is yet another possibility for those who would purchase bonds. It is possible to purchase the switch currency needed from a pool of bond switch kronor. This pool is limited and therefore foreigners have in the past shown little interest in Swedish bonds, despite their high yields. However, these regulations are continually being liberalized and may one day be changed. All bonds are quoted exclusive of interest.

Stocks pose a different problem. B or free shares purchased in markets outside of Sweden are perfectly legitimate investments. And it it at this point that an investor in Swedish securities must begin. While foreigners cannot buy Swedish shares in Sweden, it is permissible to sell Swedish shares if they have not been owned by any person domiciled in Sweden after January 1, 1959. Therefore the procedure must be to purchase Swedish shares in other European Exchanges or in New York, send them back to Sweden, and sell them there through an authorized banker or broker. With the proceeds, the foreigner can then purchase the stock of the company he is really interested in. Initially, it is a two-step, roundabout process.

By sending the stock into Sweden to be sold, the premium is naturally lost. Having entered the market through this devious route, foreigners are still prohibited from purchasing shares in natural resources, banks, or industries of national interest such as Bofors, the renowned armaments producer. The proceeds of a sale of Swedish securities can then be applied to the purchase of other Swedish stocks within a limited two-week period. In the event that no new purchases are made, the right to reinvest is lost. In other words, every transaction for a foreigner within Sweden must be the result of a switch transaction or the purchase of bond switch or equity switch currencies. Any rights issues that arise from these holdings can be exercised directly without the previous merry-go-round. In any case, all transactions must go through an authorized agent, i.e., a Swedish bank or broker, whether the securities are kept in Sweden or abroad. All rights accruing from transactions are transferable.

Located in the medieval section of Stockholm, the Stock Exchange —*Fondbörs*—building dates from 1776 though the Exchange's inception was not until 1862. The building faces a quiet square not far from the king's palace. One flight above the trading floor are the offices of the Swedish Academy of the Nobel Prize Committee for literature. The interior of the limestone edifice is divided into small colonnaded areas; one is a lounge and library, another contains cubicles for bank offices, and finally the trading floor itself. The latter looks very much like a college lecture room with rows of school desks facing a raised podium.

If Milan is the noisiest Stock Exchange in Europe, Stockholm is the quietest. The school-room atmosphere, so prevalent in Swedish society in general, is carried over into their securities transactions. It is against the rules of the Exchange for anyone to speak except the Exchange officials who sit behind the dais. Above them is a small electric sign-board which can be controlled by both traders sitting at their desks and officials at the podium. The official performs the function of an auctioneer as he reads down the list of stocks and bonds. As a security is called, the traders work small switchboards at their desks to indicate their bid and offers. When selling and buying come into balance, then the white numerals turn red indicating the finality of the transaction and a bell is rung.

This silent electrical system was created by L. M. Ericsson forty-five years ago. If there were a great deal of activity, the system would undoubtedly flounder. As it is, stock trading is relatively light and approximately three-fifths of the transactions do not go through the Exchange. Banks and brokers can and do trade with each other, though not for their own account. The public is not active due to tax laws. The Swedish capital gains tax tends to immobilize the share market. Long-term capital gains are not taxed, but then long-term gains consist of holding profits beyond the minimal five-year period. Short-term gains are hit heavily: tax rates are based on the rather steep progressive tax on incomes, and if a profit is taken before two years then all the profit is subject to income taxes. Less of the capital gain is subject to income tax as time goes by, but in any event there is little motivation for switching.

The Stockholm Exchange is a private organization but closely regulated by the government, and even the socialists have not made suggestions to abolish it. However, at the rate brokers are vanishing this may never constitute a problem. There are only nineteen members of the Exchange—twelve banks and seven brokers—and the number has been sharply diminishing over the years. Seats, quite literally, sell for SKR10,000 ($1,934). The Exchange lists shares of 114 companies and about 500 bonds. Though there are some other Scandinavian bonds listed, no foreign companies are yet quoted on the Exchange. A few blue chip internationals are traded in the over-the-counter market. The nominal capital of the Exchange is about SKR7 billion ($1.35 billion), though the present market value is SKR23 billion ($4.45 billion). In 1963 share volume was in the neighborhood of $85 million a year, but total share transactions in Sweden amounted to about $210 million.

Trading on the Stockholm Exchange takes place between 10 A.M. and 2:30 P.M. All deals are for cash and settlement is usually made within two days. Bonds are dealt in nominal values of SKR10,000 ($1,934) though all bonds are not dealt in daily. Stocks are quoted in kronor, and round lots are usually 50 shares. However, L. M. Ericsson's round lot is 100 as are a few other companies'. The par value of most securities is SKR100 ($19).

BROKERAGE AND ANALYSIS

Brokerage rates of officially quoted common stocks are: If the share is less than SKR30, the commission is SKR0.20 per share. If the share is more than SKR30, but less than SKR60, the commission is SKR0.25 per share. If the share is more than SKR60, the charge is SKR0.35 per share.

The rate on Swedish bonds is one krona per thousand on the bond's market price. Bonds issued or guaranteed by the government are exempt from stamp duty. Otherwise, the stamp duty is SKR0.15 per SKR100 on stocks and SKR0.05 on bonds. Commission rates are likely to increase before long.

Security analysis is made somewhat easier by the publication in English of the annual reports of the larger companies. By and large, these international companies pay out less as dividends—paid once a year—than do most other Swedish corporations. Due to a double taxation agreement with the United States, the 10 per cent withholding tax can be credited to federal returns. Dividends tend to be the same year after year, regardless of profits. Even in English the reports are not always simple due to tax regulations and special fiscal tools used by the state. Swedish law requires a consolidated balance sheet but not an income statement though most large companies do publish them. Depreciation is very liberal for it is one of the ways the government stimulates private industry. As one Swedish financial service notes: "Companies are permitted to write off more than the necessary amount of depreciation on fixed assets and to write down the value of inventories, if they so wish. Many companies avail themselves of this possibility and therefore have 'secret reserves.' It should be borne in mind that no tax was paid on the amounts transferred to these 'secret reserves,' and that there is thus a contingent tax liability on the reserves."

An extensive investment reserve program permits companies to allocate a tax-free deduction of up to 40 per cent of its pre-tax income to reserves. Since this may be arbitrarily charged to the profit-and-loss account, one has to reconstitute the statement by adding these deductions back to earnings. This has led to the assumption that many Swedish companies are underpriced and that if American company statements were recast along Swedish lines their earnings would barely cover their dividends.

There are occasional rights issues, but Swedish industry leans very heavily on borrowed money, which accounts for the great number of bonds on the Exchange.

The Swedish government tightly controls the fiscal health of the nation. To counter the potential traumas of business cycles, part of a company's profit must be set aside for leaner years. Of these 40 per cent tax-free reserves, 46 per cent of the amount must be deposited with the Riksbank while the other 54 per cent can be used as working capital. This is a sophisticated technique which provides for the release of investment reserves at a time when most businessmen shy away from expansionary commitments. These "investment reserves of economic stabilization," as they are termed, can only be released by the Labor Market Board, composed of labor and management with an impartial chairman. If no occasion arises for their use within five years, they are released to the company. Investment reserves serve a dual purpose: they take excess money out of circulation during prosperous periods while they supply capital for growth in times of recession. Thus far, reserves were released in 1958-59 and in 1962, and the war against the business cycle has met with much success.

THE FUTURE

A factor of growing importance in the Swedish capital market is a newly instituted national pension fund. The fund will be accumulating moneys rapidly for use in long-term investments, an area now forbidden to the banks. A shortage of long-term funds will become a thing of the past. Rights issues, however, are likely to be more infrequent.

Sweden's economy is healthy and prosperous with fewer problems than probably any country in Europe. A comprehensive social welfare program has made for a contented people as well as a heavily taxed population. Though professing socialism, the government gives private industry a free hand. There are no threats to nationalize any industries, though the government runs the railroads, telephone, telegraph, and other utilities besides having monopolies in broadcasting, liquor, and tobacco. Much of Sweden's prosperity rests on its ability to transform and export superior finished goods. "Ours is a highly extroverted [sic] economy," remarked a Swedish banker. Forest products account for a third of her exports. Norway purchases nearly half the ships Sweden produces. Probably the largest single item the country exports is Volvo cars. Sweden's trade is largely, but not exclusively, with the European Continent: most raw materials are sent to EEC countries whereas most finished goods go to EFTA nations. The most prominent companies have set up subsidiaries abroad or have penetrated foreign markets through their superior technology. Reportedly, there are 1,100 overseas operations of Swedish firms. L. M. Ericsson manufactures telephonic equipment in Brazil and Argentina, and almost a fifth of its sales—surprisingly—are in the United States. Sweden's largest industrial complex, SKF, produces ball bearings in North America, England, France, Germany, Holland, Brazil, and Australia. Electrical transmission equipment and hydroelectric generators are the forte of ASEA, Allmänna Svenska Elektriska, the General Electric of Sweden. A third of its high-voltage machinery is shipped all over the world, from Canada to New Zealand. Other widely known Swedish products are the centrifuges of Separator,* the cars of SAAB (no free shares available) and the pneumatic tools of Atlas Copco.

Besides information gleaned from the annual reports, some material in English is published by Swedish banks. Since they are close to industrial holding companies and involved in financing foreign trade, their opinions can be helpful. They will not, however, accept discretionary accounts. The three leading banks of Sweden are the Enskilda Bank, Skandinaviska Banken and the Svenska Handelsbanken. Swedish brokers on the contrary will manage trading accounts. The most widely used stock index of thirty companies, with a base of 100 as of December 29, 1956, is published daily by the brokerage house of Jacobson & Ponsbach. Other sources of information for those who read

* Name recently changed to Alfa-Laval.

Swedish are: the financial paper, *Affärsvärlden,* and the standard reference on Swedish companies, *Svenska Aktiebolag.* An abridged English edition of the latter called *Some Prominent Swedish Companies* is also published annually.

NORWAY

Located close to the harbor and the main railway station in Oslo stands a pleasantly proportioned Georgian building, the Norwegian *Børsen* or Stock Exchange. Set in a small park and surrounded by flowers, the building dates from 1828, long before Norway became independent of Swedish authority in 1905. The interior courtyard is dominated by a statue of Mercury, though perhaps Neptune would have been more appropriate in this sea-oriented nation. Inside, the simple but functional furniture of the trading room is similar to that in the other Scandinavian Exchanges. An auctioneer seated at the podium faces the twenty-six members of the Exchange seated at black-painted school desks. Membership of the Børsen consists of ten banks and sixteen brokers.

Other weekly Exchanges exist in Bergen and Trondheim, but Oslo is the major daily Norwegian market. Trading starts at 11:30 A.M. and is usually finished by lunchtime. A list of securities is read through quickly, more to set the official price for the day than to stimulate trading. By far the largest volume of trading goes on after the market closes, when the final prices are broadcast from the Exchange. Only the more active securities are traded daily; the remainder are called Tuesdays and Fridays. The whole proceedings are supervised by the Ministry of Commerce, though the Exchange is run by a private committee.

The 186 companies listed on the Exchange have a nominal value of NKR1.3 billion ($182 million) and a market value approximately three times that figure. No foreign shares are listed nor are volume figures possible, particularly since so much of the trading is done after the market. Share ownership is also problematic even though all Norwegian shares are registered. Estimates put the number of stockholders at a quarter of a million souls. Norwegians quote shares in per cent of par: the nominal value of most shares is NKR100 ($14), though there are a few at NKR500 ($70) and NKR1,000 ($140). Transactions, which are usually for settlement the next day and thereby preclude short sales or option dealings, are in minimal round lots of NKR5,000 ($700) for shares. Transactions in bonds are for minimal nominal sums of NKR10,000 ($1,400). Dividends are paid once a year in February or March and interest is paid twice yearly, usually in January and June. Dividends paid to Americans suffer a withholding tax of 15 per cent, which can be claimed against federal taxes.

Norway (Population 3.5 million; 124,500 square miles) welcomes private investment. Indeed she appointed her most distinguished citizen, Trygve Lie (the first Secretary General of the United Nations), to encourage foreign investment. To this end, the government has liberalized trade, tax, and currency restrictions. This effort is successful in attracting direct investment but not notably efficacious with regard to portfolio investment. The Norwegians had unhappy experiences in the 1920s with foreign money and remain wary of it to this day. Foreign investors cannot own more than one-tenth of a bank's shares, more than four-tenths of a shipping or whaling company's, or more than one-fifth of a timber or forest company's shares. Besides these government restrictions, most Norwegian corporations (*aksjeselskap* or *A/S*) have a limiting clause in their articles of association which forbids alien registration of shares. Not only must the company approve of foreign investors, but the central bank (the Norges Bank) must also approve the transaction. Should dual approval be granted, an account can be opened with a bank or broker. The three main commercial banks in Oslo are the Den norske Creditbank, Christiania Bank og Kreditkasse and Bergens Privatbank.

Obtaining Norwegian kroner for investment is not a problem, since nonresidents may purchase shares with any convertible currency (defined here as any currency of an OECD country plus Canada and the United States) or against kroner from nonresident kroner accounts in banks. Nor is there any difficulty in repatriating invested funds, dividends, or interest.

Norwegian industry is undergoing a transition as it hastens to capitalize on its natural resources. Norway's economy since Viking days has always faced the sea and has thrived on fishing, whaling, and shipping. Fishing and whaling no longer play the important role they once did; nevertheless Norway's fishing fleet is still fifth in the world, and fish and its products account for about a fifth of her total exports. The whaling business has fallen off sharply owing to cheaper substitute materials and the diminished number of whales. Still there are a hundred whaling boats and nine floating factories in the fleets of the seven whaling companies listed on the Exchange. In their heyday whaling shares were highly speculative and subject to wild fluctuations depending upon the size of the catch and the price of whale oil and ambergris.

Shipping, on the other hand, continues to grow rapidly and profitably. During World War II half of Norway's merchant marine was destroyed. Rebuilding the fleet was a costly undertaking but today the country has the newest fleet afloat. About half the country's foreign exchange is earned by the shipping industry. The world's fourth largest merchant marine, 85 per cent of its business occurs between foreign ports. Parenthetically, the Norwegian America Line, Den norske Amerikalinje, is one of the few Norwegian companies whose shares are traded in New York.

Besides shipping, Norway has concentrated her energies on developing hydroelectric power. Estimates place the potential power of the country at over 120 billion kilowatts annually, far and away the largest hydroelectric resources of any country discussed here. Thus far, only a quarter of this power potential has been tapped since vast sums of capital are needed to produce power stations. The cost of electricity is one of the lowest in the world and Norway has begun exporting energy to nearby countries. Norwegians use twice as much electricity per head as Americans do. Whether all of this great potential will be utilized remains to be seen: atomic energy is still an expensive proposition, but may become cheaper before long; the huge natural gas reserves found in the North Sea may also go far in lowering energy costs throughout Europe.

The largest power company, Norsk Hydro, was started with French capital, but now the Norwegian government owns approximately half of it. The company's shares are still traded in Paris. The remainder of its shares, both common and preferred, are in private hands and it is one of the few Norwegian firms that outrightly welcome foreign investors. Most of the other power companies are owned by the state or municipalities. In any event, many industries have been establishd in or drawn to Norway because of its cheap electricity. This is particularly true of manufacturing and mining concerns which now account for roughly one-third of the net national product. Aluminum is probably the fastest growing industry, entirely run by hydroelectric power. In the last ten years smelter capacity has gone from 50,000 tons to 270,000 tons and estimates project 700,000 tons capacity by 1970. Most of Norway's aluminum is exported in crude ingot form, and little fabricated aluminum is manufactured. The opposite is true of France, Europe's largest producer, which uses more than half her tonnage for finished products. Norway's largest producer, A/S Årdal og Sunndal Verk, however, is wholly owned by the government. Other aluminum companies, Sør-Norge Aluminum, Mosjoen Aluminum, and Norsk Aluminum, to name a few, have accepted large, direct foreign investments in their shares by American, Canadian, English, French, and Swiss aluminum companies.

The electrometallurgical and electrochemical industries rely on extensive mining operations that produce iron ore, pyrites, and copper, and are the only European source of molybdenum. The chemical industry specializes in nitrogen products and other fertilizers and is the largest producer of ferrosilicon in the world. Between imports and natural resources, the production, processing, and exporting of chemicals, ferrous and nonferrous metals all play an important part of the Norwegian scene. Another sizable export commodity is paper and pulp since a quarter of the country is covered with forests. Timber products make up a fifth of Norwegian commodity exports. Two paper and pulp companies, Hunsfos Fabrikker and Vestfos Cellulosefabrik, will consider foreign investors.

Other companies that will also consider accepting foreign investors are: Frammaes mek. Verksted and Fredriksstad mek. Verksted, two shipbuilding companies; Hansa Bryggeri, a brewery; and Freia, a chocolate manufacturer. For a cross section of Norwegian industry that might not otherwise be available, foreigners can purchase shares of Orkla Grube, an important Norwegian holding company.

Though private enterprise dominates the country's economy—the usual exceptions obtain in railroads, telegraph and telephone systems —the labor government has no desire to nationalize any industries. Undoubtedly, part of Norway's substantial industrial progress since the war is due to stable and sane government. The only cloud on the economic horizon has been a tenacious deficit balance-of-payments position, as Norwegian consumers indulge themselves with foreign goods.

Some information is published in English, though not as much as in other European countries. Fortunately, the *Norges Handels og Sjøfarts Tidende,* the *Norwegian Journal of Commerce and Shipping,* publishes one page in English once a week. The standard reference work for Norwegian industry is the *Håndbok over Norske Obligasjoner og Aksjer,* published in three volumes by Carl Kierulf and Co., a local brokerage house. Other brokers publish smaller handbooks of stocks and bonds.

Commission rates are as follows: on bonds, ⅛ of 1 per cent on government bonds, municipal bonds or government guaranteed bonds, but ¼ of 1 per cent on all other bonds; on shares, the charge is ½ of 1 per cent. A small stamp tax of $\frac{1}{10}$ of 1 per cent on bond transactions is due, but approximately ½ of 1 per cent on share transactions. All government, municipal, or government guaranteed bonds are traded free of stamp duty.

Though little publicized abroad, the share index is published by the Exchange. It is a weighted index, with $1939 = 100$ as a base, and it is composed of five banks, ten industrials, ten shipping and five whaling companies.

DENMARK

The Danish Stock Exchange building, the *Fondbørs,* is perhaps architecturally the most interesting in Europe and without doubt the oldest. Built in 1624, this long, low Dutch renaissance building is situated on the harbor. Commissioned by King Christian IV, the king dedicated the building "not for the secret magics of Laverna and Mercury, but in honor of God and for a profitable use by buyers and sellers." The building's most striking feature are four dragons atop the tower with their tails twisted skyward to form the spire. The Dragon Spire was meant to defend the house from fire and enemies, a task it has thus far successfully accomplished. The inside is striking: a magnificent hall decorated with a gold ceiling, crystal chandeliers, Rembrandt-like drawings, and inlaid woods. The list of securities is not read in the main hall, but in a small adjoining room done in Danish modern. At 12:30 P.M. an auctioneer appointed by the Minister of Commerce (the Ministry runs the Exchange), reads the list to a seated group of bankers and forty brokers. The banks cannot trade on the Exchange, but do trade in the after or unofficial market in the large hall.

Sweden is the most industrialized Scandinavian nation, but Denmark is trying hard to catch up. Since World War II, the whole economic structure of this small agricultural country (population 4.6 million; 16,600 square miles) has undergone a rapid and somewhat difficult transition into an industrialized society. The troubles arise from the fact that foreign trade plays an extraordinarily important role in the gross national product since it accounts for about a third of it. Unfortunately, imports since 1960 have risen sharply and the country has suffered a deficit balance-of-payments position. The deficit has been caused by both rising wages and prices within the country and tariff barriers abroad.

The Danish government has attempted to counter this unhappy state of affairs by a series of anti-inflationary policies, the "package solution," hammered out in 1962-1963. The attempt to restore economic equilibrium has not been altogether successful, since the trouble is not wholly amenable to a national fiscal policy. The structural change in the Danish economy is caused by the rapid development of industry while the traditional farming and agricultural activities stagnate. Heretofore, the United Kingdom and Germany absorbed most of Denmark's dairy and pork products. But competition, subsidies, and lastly the protective tariff wall around the EEC has cut sharply into sales. Though a member of EFTA, Denmark has applied for membership in the EEC hoping thereby to gain admittance to its markets. Agriculture is the largest foreign-exchange earner for the country—about two-thirds of her produce is exported. Until this particular sector of the economy turns the corner, the government has taken to subsidizing farmers since their standards are considered the highest in Europe and possibly in the world. Danish butter and bacon have always graced the tables of the best hotels and restaurants.

The industrial sector started to expand in 1950, focused on the island of Zealand upon which the capital is located. Copenhagen, "Merchant's Harbor," has a quarter of the Danish population and a large part of its industry. The excellent harbor not only caters to the import-export business and shipping lines, but to shipyards as well. Across the bay from the luxurious Royal Yacht Club and the little mermaid are the important Danish shipbuilders Burmeister & Wain. The company has diversified its energies to compensate for the slump in shipbuilding after the Suez crisis. Diesel motors are not only a specialty of the firm but also of all Denmark. Electrical engineering plants and textile mills are scattered throughout the city, along with a large sugar refining plant of Danske Sukkerfabrik and beer distilleries of Carlsberg and Tuborg (Forenede Bryggerier or United Breweries). The former is a private foundation but the latter is listed on the Danish Exchange. Corporations with limited liability are called *aktieselskaber* or *A/S.*

Though a socialist state, the long commercial and trading history of the country seems to encourage private enterprise rather than state ownership. Few Danish industries are nationalized: the usual utilities and railways are, though the capital's telephone system, Kjøbenhavns Telefon, and the country's telegraphic system Store Nordiske Teleggraf Kompagni, Great Northern Cable and Telegraph, are listed. The Scandinavian Airlines System (SAS) is largely state owned, but not completely. In 1946 Sweden, Norway, and Denmark pooled their flying resources under SAS; the Swedes took up three-sevenths while the other two countries picked up two-sevenths each. Each nation's tranche is held by the country's air-transport system. These are publicly quoted companies that are partially owned by the government. Thus far this arrangement has proved a model of intergovernmental cooperation even during the critical entry of jet aircraft.

In one respect Denmark is much like Switzerland in that its products best known abroad are manufactured by small private companies of artisans. Modern Danish furniture is a case in point. This $26 million-a-year export business, a quarter of which goes to the United States, is composed of 400 small companies employing less than 6,000 craftsmen. None of these are publicly quoted companies. The same is almost true of the silver and porcelain companies, though Bing and Grøndahl and Kongelig Porcelainsfabrik are listed. Besides craftsmanship, Denmark's reputation also rests on the ability of the Danes to enjoy themselves. At Tivoli, the cultural Steeplechase of Scandinavia, the Danes have created a middle-class amusement park famous throughout the world. Its shares are quoted on the Exchange and sell for roughly DKR300 ($43).

Though Danish products—agricultural, industrial, and craft—are widely known and appreciated, few shares in Danish companies can be found in the world's markets. Perhaps the two most active shares abroad are the Danish Ford Motor Co., an affiliate of the American automobile manufacturer, and the East Asiatic Holding Co., Østasiatisk Kompagni Holding. The company is an important shipping and plantation firm which acquired many timber tracts in Southeast Asia. Much of the lumber provides the furniture industry with cheap teak. Shares of this company can be purchased in most major markets, particularly London, Paris, and Frankfort.

The foreign floating supply of this company's stock makes it a useful vehicle for entering the Danish market. Like Sweden, Denmark tries to insulate its economy from foreign take-over bids through strict control. Banks and brokers are forbidden to buy shares for foreign accounts unless as a result of a switch transaction: the sale of Danish securities in order to purchase the desired security. Consequently, Danish securities abroad usually sell for a slight premium; 5 per cent to 6 per cent is common but the premium has been as high as 10 per cent. A year's grace is granted in holding security kroner, that is, between the sale and repurchase of another Danish security by foreigners. Danish dollar bonds cannot be used for security kroner, though sometimes other Scandinavian equity may be utilized since there is a good deal of cooperation on economic and financial affairs among these countries. Even Danish kroner bonds will not avail for entry into the equity market; only other common stock will suffice. Proceeds from the sale of Danish securities, plus interest and dividends, are freely repatriated in dollars.

Volume in the bond market is much greater than it is in the equity market and much of the activity is due to dealing in mortgage bonds. Credit associations, Kreditforeninger and Hypotekforeninger, lend money against first, second, and third mortgages. Danish real estate dealings are sophisticated, well regulated, and extensive, with about half the country's land value so pledged. Since 1960 interest rates in Denmark have been the highest in Europe; most of the time the national bank's discount rate has been above 6 per cent. Consequently, companies avoid borrowing and prefer self-financing. Even the Kingdom of Denmark and the City of Copenhagen borrow abroad to get cheaper money.

Though there are 110 stocks listed, a few of them preferred issues, many are not actively traded. In part this may be due to a two-year capital gains tax added to the fact that Danes seem to prefer mortgages and debt issues with high yields above equity. Securities are issued in registered form but endorsement gives them bearer status. All shares have a par value, usually DKR100 ($14.49), and are quoted as a percentage of par. Dividends are paid once a year, in February or March, without any withholding tax deducted. As an anti-inflationary step the government promulgated a dividend stop; a ruling that prohibited companies from increasing their dividends. Round lots are DKR4,000 ($580) nominal value, though the actual price may be many times greater than this if the price is 300 or 400 per cent of par. Smaller lots of shares can be purchased in the after market. Bonds are usually dealt in round lots of DKR8,000 ($1,160). There is no option market in Denmark and settlement is usually next day. Brokerage rates are straightforward on stock, ½ of 1 per cent of the market value; on bonds DKR1.5 per thousand on nominal value.

Very few company reports are printed in English and the banks are not as market minded as they might be. Company reports are reputed to be fair, if conservative, appraisals and security analysis is still almost unheard of. For those who read Danish, the two financial papers are the daily *Børsen* and the weekly *Finanstidende*.

FINLAND

Finland may be best known for the *sauna*. To be entirely authentic, it should be enjoyed communally, complete with birch rods, a massage, and a roll in fresh snow. Both wealthy Americans and affluent Europeans are now importing and installing saunas, though foregoing the snow. It is the *dernier cri* in home appliances. Finland is famous for another luxury too: the stark luxury of good modern architecture and interior design. Many of her architects are world famous and one of the most prominent, Alvar Aalto, designed scores of buildings in the United States including many controversial vanguard structures. Though her design talents are well known, it is only recently that Europeans and Americans have awakened to Finland's growing industrial strength. Finland is a viable and modern economic state; her people are extraordinarily literate and energetic in the fashion of the other Scandinavian states. Finland is not a large country (population 4.5 million; 130,000 square miles), and by losing the war to the Russians in 1939-1940 she lost 10 per cent of her land area. The country's economic growth rate since the war has been surprising, an average of 7.1 per cent from 1945 to 1961, though somewhat slower thereafter. Considering the huge reparations of one-half billion dollars paid to the Russians, the country was left very short of investment capital. Consequently, the government had to step in to fill the gap until now it accounts for one-fifth of the nation's industrial production. Heavy participation is especially evident in energy producing and the machine tool industry. The Finnish government is not happy with this state of affairs for, like most Scandinavian countries, it prefers to leave industrialization to the capitalists. None of the major political parties have plans for further nationalization.

Finland's heavy industry rests largely on its forest preserves and its metalworking skill. Timber stands cover 70 per cent of the total land area. Paper and pulp products, locally called "green gold," are in turn responsible for a majority of the country's exports. This small country can brag of ranking third as a world exporter of paper, pulp, and forest products and her mills are comparable to those in the United States or Canada. Though most of her exports of paper and pulp go to Western Europe, the United States buys more of her newsprint than anyone else. Particularly active in this field is Finland's largest corporation, Enso-Gutzeit, a company which accounts for over 10 per cent of the country's exports. Other notable publicly listed paper and pulp companies are Nokia, Kaukas and Kajaani. Along with paper and pulp, the Finns are specialists in manufacturing newsprint machines.

Finland's new metalworking firms are rapidly increasing the nation's exports of cranes, cables, rifles, icebreakers, cable ships, and hydro-electric power plants. Europe's largest earthmovers and road graders are machines of Finnish construction. Other areas of Finnish ingenuity, such as design and architecture, are more for admiring than investing. However, as Finland's per capita income increases as it has the last few years—it is now on a par with the Netherlands—a consumer revolution is overtaking the country. Stockmann, the leading Helsinki department store and a publicly held company, attests to the spreading northern affluence and the instinctive taste displayed in her goods.

As a relatively new country, dominated for hundreds of years by the Swedes, then, by the Russians through the nineteenth century until World War I, Finland does not have an ancient financial community. Finns started trading in shares in 1862, though the first Exchange was not built until 1912 when it became known as the *Helsingin Arvopaperipörssi*. Eight per cent of the people still speak Swedish, a completely unrelated tongue. Finnish is a partner with Hungarian in the Finno-Ugrian language group: an old joke states that they were once the same language but that the Finns took all the vowels. To some degree Finnish institutions are modeled after Swedish ones and the Exchange is quite similar to the Swedish *Fondbörs*. The Stock Exchange is completely free of government control or supervision but it is administered by a committee made up of members from the Chamber of Commerce, the Bankers Association of Finland, and non-banker members of the Exchange. A baker's dozen constitutes the membership: four banks, one financial institution, and eight investment brokers. There are four "outside" brokers who can trade through the member brokers.

Trading is daily, commencing at 10:30 A.M., through use of a call-over system or the reading of the list. This does not occupy too much time since the list, in two parts, contains only 47 companies. Buying and selling are accomplished through an electric relay signboard— also the work of L. M. Ericsson—that is clearly visible to all members. When the reading is over, the prices are broadcast to the public. Most trading is done in industrial stocks, the remainder in bank stocks and bonds. Commission rates are 1½ per cent of the market value of the purchase, regardless of its size. Both bearer and registered shares are in fashion and to some degree are interchangeable when the registered shares are endorsed. Round lots differ in size, anywhere from five to several hundred shares, depending on price. Some Finnish equity tends to be low in price; the two leading banks, Nordiska Föreningsbanken and Kansallis-Osake-Pankki, have shares that sell for F.markka 2.25 ($0.71) to F.markka 3.50 ($1.10) but most company shares are much higher. Dividends are paid yearly, as a percent of the nominal value of the shares. A reciprocal tax treaty exists between the United States and Finland; an American can take a 15 per cent tax credit against the tax withheld when the dividends were paid. Finnish state bonds, usually sold in lots of FMK10,000, 50,000 or 100,000, are tied to an index that adjusts interest and amortization. Rates of interest are high, usually well in excess of 7 per cent. Undoubtedly, this is in part the price that must be paid for living next to the Soviet Union.

Finnish currency restrictions are, of course, subject to the control of the Bank of Finland. These have been liberalized of late, and it is possible to invest in Finnish securities by use of a convertible currency or convertible Finnish markkas. A commercial bank will take care of the formalities—securing the necessary permit for investing and re-patriation of the funds. Obviously, it is simpler to leave the securities in Helsinki; indeed permission for their export must be granted by the Bank of Finland. A monetary reform in 1963 simplified the currency by moving the decimal two places to the left, thus bringing the markka into line with most European moneys.

Sources of information are mostly in Finnish: a daily trade paper, *Kauppalehti,* and a financial weekly, *Talouselämä,* are the two main papers, but another weekly, *Mercator,* is published in Swedish. A few large companies publish their annual reports in English.

Besides obtaining permission to invest in Finland, there are other deterrents such as language and the proximity to Soviet Russia. After all, 23 per cent of Finland's export trade is with the Eastern bloc and thus she relies on friendly relations. In fact, it is difficult to find a Swedish national who has thought seriously of investing in Finland. On the other hand, Finland's growth rate is rapid and her industries are efficient, productive, and well entrenched. Moreover, the United States Treasury considers Finland an underdeveloped nation (though her literacy rate is far higher than America's), at least so far as the interest equalization tax is concerned.* Finland's economy, though sensitive to a difficult balance-of-payments position, seems far brighter than those of many other "underdeveloped" nations. Nevertheless, her position as a buffer, as one geographer notes, "is seldom pleasant."

* See discussion of the interest equalization tax in the last chapter. Some Special Considerations, pp. 302–306.

9. ITALY

A chi compra, bisogna aver cent'occhi;
*A chi vende, basta uno.**
                                    —Anonymous

It rains frequently in Milan, a fact which helps explain the city's most un-Latin love of work. The Milanese work longer than anyone else in Europe, earn twice as much as the average Italian, produce about a quarter of Italy's wealth, and pay 27 per cent of her taxes. The weather combined with the by-product of industriousness—smoke—has made Milanese ear, nose, and throat specialists the Continent's most prosperous practitioners.

Romans, addicted to *dolce far niente* call Milan the moral capital of Switzerland and decry Milanese materialism and efficiency. The city's tempo is akin to the restless rhythm of New York. Indeed, Milan is the cultural and financial hub of Italy; it is Turin's rival as an industrial complex. Milan contains Italy's most famous opera house, *La Scala,* the country's most important Stock Exchange, *la Borsa Valori di Milano,* and her most eminent industrialists and publishers. Pirelli, the huge rubber firm has headquarters in Milan as do Montecatini, the mining and chemical complex, la Rinascente, Italy's largest department store, and Snia Viscosa, the du Pont of Italy. Mondadori, Einaudi, Rizzoli and Feltrinelli, the country's foremost publishers make their homes here, as do many of the largest banks.

---

* He who buys needs a hundred eyes,
  While he who sells needs but one.

Before the jet made geography irrelevant, Milan's location fostered her pre-eminence. The plain of Lombardy was a junction heavily traveled by traders from France, Switzerland and Austria. Goods coming to Venetian docks from the East had to cross Mediolanum, the swampy centrum which became Milan, to make their way north. Today Milan is still a Continental caravanserai; the city has such a full calendar of international trade fairs and conferences that a tourist without hotel reservations runs the risk of spending the night in a nook of Milan's forbidding Sforza castle.

To be a Milanese stock broker is not without perils. The occupation may be hazardous in Bologna, Florence, Genoa, Naples, Palermo, Rome, Turin, Trieste, and Venice as well, but Milanese brokers seem to be the most vulnerable. Here, the public has been known to respond to a downward spiral and falling prices with ripe tomatoes, transformed on impact into *salsa di pomodoro* when hurled at one of the 132 state-appointed brokers, the *Agenti di Cambio* of the Borsa.

The origin of the missiles is the public gallery in the mezzanine. Situated above the trading floor, the investor has point-blank range; only the inept or the careless can miss the yelling swarm of brokers crowding around the four *grida,* or *corbeilles,* stations of trading for diverse groups of securities.

Italy's investors are heavily concentrated in Piedmont and Lombardy. Milan, focus of the industrial North, is the small investor's stamping ground. A generous lending policy on the part of the banks and the sharp rise in prices from 1958 through 1961 undoubtedly enlarged the Milanese appetite. Italy's incredible postwar growth brought many speculators into the market; for a while it seemed a surer way to riches than the national lottery. With stock prices at an all-time speculative high in 1961, economic reality returned as a series of political crises undermined investor confidence. Communist victories at the polls (though only one in four Italians vote for the Red line), shuffleboard governments, and the gradual drift toward the Left by successive régimes, plus the nationalization of the electrical industry in 1962 all helped to push share prices down. By 1964 the share index stood at half what it had been in 1961.

A recently instituted tax on dividends, moreover, compels investors to reveal their identity to tax officials in order to collect or forgo a portion of their due. This has led to an unprecedented flight of capital and many wealthy Italians have simply withdrawn from the market. Some, however, have come back "through the back door," by means of anonymous Swiss accounts as "foreign" purchasers of Italian shares. In short, there were few buyers and a great deal of uncertainty. Drastic slides eliminate the profits of months in a matter of hours and lent credence to the frequent moan heard in Italian financial circles: "Foreigners think our market is like a roulette!"

In 1964 the Italian market hit a three-year low. Despite the frenetic antics of her markets, the economy of Italy (population 50 million; 116,370 square miles) is prospering and expanding at a rapid rate.

Hidden in the maze of streets behind La Scala, the Borsa dominates the Piazza Affari, or business square. Banks line the piazza and confront the Exchange, a renaissance building à la Mussolini. Grey, massive, and grand, it is also pompous; columns run its height, topped by heroic statues. The roof is a triangle with two extensions, reminiscent of pieces from a huge erector set.

During Exchange hours the square is strangely still. It breathes the eery quiet of a surrealist painting and could be a de Chirico in three dimensions. The only sound is the hawking of vendors selling fruits and vegetables in adjacent streets. Inside, the noise is deafening as traders shout to each other on the run. The dim lighting suggests the twilight atmosphere of a nightclub. A single light four stories overhead looks down like a huge cyclopean eye, bathing the mob of gesticulating brokers in tones of deep rose, pink, yellow, and green. There are other lights over the four grida, circles some fourteen feet in diameter around which trading takes place, and these can be aimed like spotlights at a night baseball game.

Milan's Borsa is the dimmest and noisiest in Europe, but it is also the most jovial. It has the happy conviviality of a huge men's club. Brokers greet each other and shake hands dozens of times a morning: *"Ah, commendatore. . . . Dottore. . . . Direttore. . . . Presidente. . . , va bene, perfetto, grazie d'accordo—arrivederci."* Sociability is the pleasantest part of the day's work.

Trading takes place at the balustrade surrounding the grida. Brokers scramble and scuffle and nearly come to blows in an effort to make their bids and offers heard above the din. A Stock Exchange official sits in the middle, recording prices and eating aspirin. Assignment to this ear-splitting post is handled on a rotation basis. The pandemonium begins at 10:00 A.M. every weekday and reaches its height at 11:30 A.M., when the *chiamata del listino* takes place, the reading of the list of securities to determine a closing price. This is the day's most active market.

For the rest, the Milan Borsa has the other accouterments of an Exchange—a huge quotation board, telephone booths on the sides, a clock, loudspeakers, and an open visitors' gallery which some brokers, no doubt, wish were glass enclosed like that of the London Stock Exchange.

The Milan Exchange, the most active in Italy with about 70 per cent of the country's total volume, is not the oldest. Venice has that seniority, with an Exchange dating from 1600. The Trieste Exchange was established by the Austrian Regent in 1755, while Milan had to wait till 1808 for Eugene Napoleon's decree to set up her Exchange. It is one of the curiosities of history that Napoleon Bonaparte and his relatives established the Bourses of Belgium and Italy, France's own Exchange having already been legitimized by royal decree a few centuries earlier. All Napoleon could do for France was to order a new building for the Paris Bourse.

On the French model, the only legitimate intermediaries are the Agenti di Cambio and their representatives. Considered public officials under Italian law, the fraternity of the Agenti is strictly limited in number. The banks are admitted to the Exchange only as observers and, though they may marry orders and deal for their own account, they may not deal directly. They must go through the intermediary of the Agenti. Italy's Stock Exchanges are under the control of the Ministry of Treasury which delegates an inspector to watch over the Exchanges. He is "the antenna of the government." "What, Presidente, is his concrete function?" "Oh, he looks on; he collects rumors; he sniffs the trend of the market. He reports what is being said on the floor, the trend of government bonds, opinions on politics, but has no direct influence on the Borsa. The Italian government never intervenes directly in the affairs of the market."

The government can also rely on the opinion of the Stock Exchange Deputation, an almost exact parallel to the French *Comité des Bourses*. In Italy, this regulatory body has a representative of the *Banca d'Italia,* a representative of the Exchange Clearing House, and representatives of the Chamber of Commerce. In practice, however, the active administration of the Exchange is left to operating committees of brokers.

The Agenti must devote themselves single-mindedly to the business of the Stock Exchange and may not engage directly in any other business activity. They may not deal for their own account.

Italy's Agenti di Cambio are perhaps the most nimble-fingered in Europe. To communicate with their clerks above the din brokers use hand signs: a quick shake-off motion of the hand means, "what a lot of sellers;" a typing motion refers to Olivetti; a C made with thumb and forefinger is for "Catini" short for Montecatini; two fingers over the eye stand for E or Edison; for Generali they draw a general's cap in the air. Obviously sign language can be used only where no mistake is possible; in a country with a half-dozen typewriter companies, a typing motion could refer to any one of them. In Italy it refers only to Olivetti.

The opening price is an average to take care of the maximum of bids and offers. Trading takes place between 10:00 A.M. and 1:00 P.M. With the reading of the list of securities the blue chips open punctually at 10:00 A.M., and the closing reading for these same stocks begins at 11:30. The time in between is "free trading time" when brokers may deal with each other. Prices are in lire per share. Italian stocks are traded by so many lire per share, *la quotazione per titolo,* while bonds are quoted in percentage of par, *la quotazione per centuale.*

Securities with smaller turnover have only one price—a closing price, determination of which begins at 11.00 A.M. The banks may deal after market hours, but these transactions are not official transactions nor are they recorded by the Exchange. Like many other things in Italy, brokerage rates are negotiable. Brokers are not compelled to charge official rates and competition has forced prices down. Expenses incurred in each transaction are:

1. Commission rates (maximum): 0.7 per cent on the value of shares; 0.4 per cent on the value of bonds; 0.15 per cent on the value of government bonds.

2. Contract Stamp amounting to 0.05 per cent on bonds and 0.9 per cent on shares.

3. *Ufficio Italiano dei Cambi* fee, a small commission on currency conversion.

Transactions are settled once a month, *fine corrente,* though should a customer desire to pay cash on the spot he gets a discount equal to the money rate up to the end of the month. Should he wish to carry forward, i.e., not pay for his stock at the end of the month but get another thirty-day period of grace, *fine prossimo,* he must pay the interest on the money for that period. He does not have to pay another brokerage rate (as he does in France). In Italy, such a carrying forward is considered merely a further extension of credit rather than a simultaneous sale and repurchase.

An over-the-counter market is held once a week in one of the back rooms of the Exchange. The stocks of smaller companies are traded over the counter, as are all bank stocks. There is also an option market; both puts and calls can be purchased for one to three months.

Clearing operations are handled through the *stanza di compensazione,* an agency which is part of the Bank of Italy.

MARKET ORDERS

The usual market orders prevail in Italy with some additional variations. The most frequently used orders are:

1. Orders *al meglio,* at best, are executed in the same Stock Exchange session and do not specify price.

2. *Ordine curando* are discretionary orders leaving execution to the trader's discretion on both timing and price.

3. Limit orders fall into several subcategories: First there is a limit order with a *"circa"* clause, meaning that the broker should do the best he can with a little leeway granted, should this prove necessary. The

thematic variations are limit orders with a *"piccolo circa"* clause appended or, alternately, one with *"largo circa."* These are equivalent respectively to half and double *"circa,"* should one wish to qualify the degree of leeway desired.

It is common practice for Italian brokers to include the brokerage in the net price to the Italian client. Therefore in specifying a price, the foreign client should always mention that brokerage must be included.

In Italy, market orders are considered valid for one Stock Exchange session unless otherwise specified. The client should he wish, can give an order *a revoca,* good until cancelled, which is valid till the end of the Stock Exchange settlement calendar, or orders specifying *volando,* "rushing" or literally "flying," which are good for fifteen minutes only, and are used in arbitrage transactions.

The stockholder may, of course, mention whether he wishes his order executed at the opening or closing price. The latter is usually the most active time of the day's market. Stop-loss orders are rare.

Round lots vary from company to company and depend on the price of the stock with the exception of the following securities for which minimum amounts are fixed at 500 shares: FF Meridionali "Bastogi"; Snia Viscosa; Anic; Rumianca; Montecatini; Fiat; Olcese. For Assicurazioni Generali, the minimum is five shares. As a rule, round lots conform to the following table:

Stock Exchange Price (lire)	Round Lot (shares)
to 50	10,000
51– 100	5,000
101– 500	1,000
501– 2,000	500
2,001– 10,000	100
10,001– 30,000	50
30,001–100,000	25

THE OFFICIAL LIST

The *Listino Ufficiale,* the daily Official List gives minimum and maximum price spreads for particular securities in addition to the closing prices and the number of shares or bonds that changed hands.

If no transaction has taken place, that security is listed with a note *n* or *N, prezzi nominali,* indicating nominal price. If no counterpart can be found, there is an additional note, *denaro* (*bz.G.* in Germany), if there is an excess demand, and *lettera* (comparable to the German *Brief* or *bz.B.*), if there is too much supply.

The Listino also gives basic facts for each stock or bond, such as the nominal capital outstanding, the par value, interest or dividend payments, and so on. The List starts off with government paper and government guaranteed bonds. Next are debentures issued by special agencies such as the Consorzio di Credito per le Opere Pubbliche, the Fund for Public Works, the Istituto Mobiliare Italiano (IMI), the largest special credit agency, the Istituto per la Ricostruzione Industriale (IRI), the Institute for Industrial Reconstruction, and the Ente Nazionale Idrocarburi, the government's natural gas and oil monopoly. They are followed by securities issued by Italian provinces and municipalities.

Industrials are listed in alphabetical categories, starting with *Alimentari,* food, and ending with *Tessili* and *Trasporti,* textiles and transportation. Stocks are likewise listed under such category headings.

The last page of the Listino gives information on puts and calls, foreign exchange rates, the calendar of settlement days, and the Borsa's monthly volume of transactions. The back page is reserved for special company announcements, capital increases, and the like.

The number of securities presently quoted in Milan totals 394, which breaks down as follows:

Government loans	19
Government guaranteed loans	20
Land Credit Institution loans or loans of similar institutions	99
Municipal and provincial loans	5
Bonds and debentures of private companies	110
Share issues	141
Total	394

No foreign shares are traded in Milan, but there are two foreign bond issues included in the Official List.

THE GOVERNMENT SECTOR

In Italy there are very few industries in which the government does not have a hand. "In fact, if the milk business were ever nationalized," quipped one broker, "the Italian cow would become a government holding company."

Patrons of thermal baths may well thank the government, for these establishments are state monopolies, as are the railways, the post office, the highways, and the forests. The two giants on the Italian industrial scene, however, are two huge government holding companies which together direct well over 50 per cent of the Italian economy. Usually referred to in initials they are IRI, the Istituto per la Ricostruzione Industriale, the Institute for Industrial Reconstruction, and ENI, Ente Nazionale Idrocarburi, the natural gas and oil monopoly.

IRI, first created in 1933 to bouy up a floundering banking system and further industrial reconstruction is now Italy's largest industrial conglomerate. Bank failures were common in the 1930s and Italy's three large commercial banks, the Banca Commerciale, the Credito Italiano, the Banca di Roma were in trouble, along with many smaller institutions. To restore waning confidence and guard the interest of bank depositors, IRI took over these banks' assets including their industrial holdings, which had become increasingly illiquid. With a wide cross section of Italian industry thus in its hands, including a controlling interest in the three banks themselves, IRI was transformed from an emergency receiver for bankrupt banks and companies into titular manager of the government's new extensive holdings.

Today IRI is a complex of 125 joint stock companies encompassing about 30 per cent of the country's industrial capital. There are five main subsidiaries in the IRI orbit, and these in turn control the companies in a particular sector of industry. Most of Italian shipping, for instance, is the domain of Finmare. The shipyards and shipbuilding are the province of Fincantieri, whose yards boast well over 80 per cent of Italy's shipbuilding capacity. Rolling two-thirds of the country's steel production, Finsider's subsidiaries produce everything from pig iron to tubing, structural steel, and cement. Assorted engineering companies, aircraft, railway rolling stock, machine tools, appliances, electronic equipment, and optical instruments are all part of the versatile Fin-mecanica complex which includes Alfa Romeo, well known to racing and sportscar enthusiasts.

Finelettrica was formerly responsible for one-quarter of the country's electric power resources, but these activities have now been taken over by the newly nationalized electric company Enel. When the electric industry was nationalized in 1962, in order to tempt the Socialist Cerebus to cooperate with the coalition government, over 200 companies were added to the government register.

The "Fin's"—Finmare, Fincantieri, Finsider, Finmecanica, and STET (urban and interurban telephone service)—are only partially government owned. The usual procedure is for the government to retain majority ownership but to leave the rest to private investors. It is thus possible to buy stock in many of the nationally owned indus-tries, a rather safe investment to be sure, for the government has never permitted any of the IRI group to default or go into bankruptcy.

Besides the partially controlled IRI empire, the government sector also includes companies under complete IRI control. They include: radio and television; Alitalia's air fleet; the autostrade network; the largest commercial banks; a miscellany of paper, glass, and plastics companies, and a business school to train both foremen and adminis-trators at the top levels of IRI management.

IRI's empire was created by chance rather than design. A public entity, it has been called "a hospital for sick enterprises" and it did, in fact, at various times channel public funds into ailing companies. Though one or another sector might need bolstering in the public interest at some time, IRI runs its companies as private concerns and keeps a sharp eye out for their profit potential. It is safe to say that Italy's future industrial development and the growth of the *Mezzo-giorno,* the impoverished South, in particular, rest to a large extent on the shoulders of the state and of IRI.

The Institute for Industrial Reconstruction, IRI, is a curious com-promise between capitalism and corporatism or socialism. Ernesto Manuelli, president of Finsider, the second largest steel complex in Europe, has pursued an aggressive policy which has quadrupled pro-duction from its prewar peak. "As far as we are concerned," he emphasizes, "the Italian government is only our biggest shareholder." The government, as most shareholders do, leaves management to the managers. Finsider and other IRI subsidiaries are largely autonomous.

Wherever possible companies in the IRI group have gone to the equity and capital markets for funds rather than rely on government subsidies or a shifting of funds within the IRI structure itself. This has been successful in many cases as a glance at the Official List will show, indicating the plethora of bonds outstanding. In the early postwar years, to encourage creditors to come forward, the government guaranteed both the interest and the principal, which made it easier to place this paper with institutions which by law must buy government guaranteed paper. Since there was seemingly no dearth of funds, the government has abandoned that practice in recent years and has forgone the guarantees.

Paradoxically, despite its size and the chunk of the economy under its control, IRI is a far cry from corporate socialism. In orientation, IRI's role seems far more akin to the traditional Italian paternalism of key industrialists such as Fiat and Olivetti. The dynamic vanguard of the state is Ente Nationale Idrocarburi, ENI, the petroleum and natural gas empire. The huge oil and gas complex is entirely state owned and its dynamism derives from two factors: the personality of its former chief, Enrico Mattei, killed in 1962 in a plane accident; and the fact that but for gas and hydroelectric power the country's natural resources are limited. This limitation means that existing resources must be marshalled to the utmost to provide fuel for the manufacture of Italy's most important industrial exports—machines, autos, locomotives, sewing machines, and precision instruments.

Mattei, whose philosophy might be likened to that of the left-wing Socialist, Nenni, was unquestionably one of the most important men in Italy. He was convinced of the overwhelming importance, if not dominance, of American oil interests on government. Equally convinced that the big international oil companies were intent on keeping Italy from sources of supply and out of the international market, Mattei retaliated by an aggressive policy of wooing the Afro-Asians and opening the door to Soviet petroleum. At the time of his death he was planning to link his ENI pipelines with Russian lines beginning in the Urals and flowing westward to the Danube. Two years after his death, ENI is still pushing ahead and expanding. It too has joined the hunt for natural gas in the North Sea north of Holland, an area which promises infinite riches from an unfathomed amount of natural gas.

As an instrument of public policy, IRI's achievements have met with conflicting appraisals. Public ownership is not necessarily public bliss. Inevitably, state ownership revolves about problem areas or problem industries, which private capital has thankfully abandoned, or whose burdens private capital is unwilling to shoulder. In Italy, the North has the industry, the wealth, the high standard of living, and the employment. "Genoa, Turin and Milan have the Midas touch. The rest of Italy looks on." The South has the problems. Below the Eternal City, the Italian boot is squeezed not only by geography but by abject poverty. The Mezzogiorno, Sicily and Sardinia, are part of the other Italy, a preindustrial region where 40 per cent of the country's population ekes out less than 20 per cent of her gross national product. Historically, the region encompasses the old kingdom of the Two Sicilies, a Bourbon fief with Naples as its capital. Although Italy's political unification, the *Risorgimento,* is over a hundred years old, its economic unification is still to be achieved. The South is as yet an area of unemployment, underemployment, and illiteracy. Indeed in many respects it is more medieval than modern with its preponderance of small, craft industries and its marginal farming.

In order to entice industry to the South, a basic communications network was necessary: roads, electrification, water supply, the *sine qua non* which make industry possible. To create this infrastructure, the government set up a special agency, the Cassa per il Mezzogiorno, the Fund for the South, which provides the administrative link through which to channel development. The Cassa has launched a rather successful campaign advertizing Italy's best resource—a presently unskilled but trainable labor force. Other enticements to firms setting up shop in the South include: a decade of exemption from income tax; a discount on the national turnover tax and other local levies; a 25 to 50 per cent reduction on freight rates; and exemption from customs duties on machinery and materials imports. Loans are generous and the government will advance up to 70 per cent of the cost of land and equipment for new industrial plants at extremely low interest rates.

The most important steps, however, have been taken through IRI which has set up plants in a wide variety of sectors including electronics, radar, steel, cement, and paper. By law, $\frac{3}{5}$ of IRI's new investments must be in the South and $\frac{2}{5}$ of its total expenditures. ENI has set up a petrochemical complex at Gela in Sicily and a number of plants elsewhere. A huge steel plant is rising at Taranto to supplement others at Piombino and Naples. These projects do not solve unemployment but constitute a first step.

A related problem has been Italy's engineering sector. Many of these plants are in the Mezzogiorno and layoffs due to lack of orders would simply accentuate the difficulties of an already ailing area. IRI thus supported the sector, funneling funds from other healthier holdings. IRI may attempt to run its individual enterprises by normal business criteria, but its over-all public policy must be geared by social and political considerations.

Many foreign firms are taking advantage of opportunities in the Mezzogiorno, including Litton Industries, Abbott Laboratories, Goodyear, and other American concerns. IRI and ENI companies enjoy many privileges which give them an advantage in competing with private industry. Thus, one way to get on to the favored side of the track is to participate in a joint venture with a state-run company. Both Raytheon and U. S. Steel are successfully trying this approach.

"IRIzation" is not strictly a one-way process. IRI has on occasion disposed of shares in profitable concerns. Such shedding of shares is necessary for any holding company, for in order to finance the expansion of some companies, others must provide the proceeds.

What are the respective roles of government and the public in providing new moneys for IRI? One inherent problem, of course, is where and how these sums should be raised. By rights issues and new stock to be taken up by the public? By state increase of its own part of the equity? Or a combination of the two?

The government as the largest shareholder is faced with a series of further alternatives. Should most of the moneys go to troubled sectors or firms for which public policy dictates support? Or should they go to healthy, productive enterprises to provide the building blocks of national expansion? In actual practice the state must do both. It must from time to time contribute new share capital to the healthiest of firms for otherwise the IRI holding companies or the producing firms themselves would be forced continually to turn to the bond market. This would throw off the balance between equity and debt, creating greater leverage and also increasing fixed interest charges beyond prudence. Moreover, unless the state takes up new equity capital, its own holdings would be more and more diluted each time an offering of new shares is made to the public. The government's majority control could thus be gradually whittled away. Obviously a delicate balance must be maintained. For the private stockholder investing in IRI firms, however, one thing is certain: the government's presence and participation act as a kind of guarantee.

BANKS AND SECURITY ANALYSIS

The banks in Italy as in most Continental countries are the primary source of information on securities. They also publish general studies on the Italian economy. "They issue surveys when they have time," whereas company analyses appear regularly. "The long studies are for internal circulation only," one banker stressed, "but everyone in Milan gets them. I think they are circulating even in Moscow." "If we know you," he continued, "you have no problem getting material. We will mail it anywhere in the world." In Italy, another analyst quipped, "For private circulation only, merely means that the material is distributed free; it cannot be sold."

The banks document their studies to the fullest extent possible and, by general consensus, their analyses constitute "what it is possible to know in Italy." The Agenti di Cambio do not generally publish market letters, though there are a few exceptions. Compared with bank material, these letters usually stress the more speculative side and often contain a collection of rumors.

Analysis is an unusually difficult problem in Italy and, perhaps for this reason, no society of analysts or any other professional organization exists. This is not to say that there are no informed observers of the financial scene. There are—but many of them are connected with banks or other large financial institutions. Even for the institutional observer, difficulties constantly arise.

First, Italian national statistics are skimpy, and often the only figures available come from the industry federation or trade association and tend to be biased. Statistical categories established twenty or thirty years ago are outmoded today but are nonetheless still in use. The figures frequently do not reflect actual growth. For instance—to cite but one example—they still collect statistics on the department stores which ruled the retail horizon twenty years ago, ignoring more recent arrivals. Distortion is inevitable: five or ten years ago there were but 50 department stores worthy of the name in Italy; today there are some 200, of which Upim and Standard are the biggest chains.

There are few compulsions written into Italian law about revealing information. Each company must meet the formal requirement of publishing a balance sheet once a year within four months of the end of the fiscal year. "But sometimes," one Italian complained, "you find three lines for assets and four lines for liabilities and that's that. Most incomplete!" There is no legal requirement to itemize or give details. In fact, some Italian enterprises have been known to keep three books: one for themselves, one for the banks, and one for the fiscal authorities. Naturally, this does not hold for Italy's blue chips.

There is nothing in the law books about revealing subsidiaries or extent of participation either. However, in Italy, unlike France, subsidiaries formed jointly with competitors to develop new products are not popular. The parent company owns at least 51 per cent and usually 100 per cent. "Perhaps it is the Italian temperament," one industrialist commented, "but unless a subsidiary is wholly owned, there is trouble." Since the law is silent, some companies reveal their subsidiaries, some do not.

Italians have a national allergy to paying taxes. The government's way of getting around this is a fragmented series of levies on every possible type of income and wealth. Italy's tax system is probably the most complex in Europe, and the complexity on the central government level is multiplied on the communal and municipal levels. Companies, for instance, pay a basic tax on net corporate income which comes under the heading of *imposta de ricchezza mobile* (tax on moveable wealth). The central government's due is 18 per cent on the first L4 million and 20 per cent on the remainder. In addition, the commune collects from 1.75 per cent to 3.5 per cent, and there are contributions to the Chamber of Commerce and two surtaxes for relief programs. In addition there is a "collector's fee" which is usually 5 to 6.5 per cent of the total tax basket.

A corporation tax, *imposta sulle società,* is also due; it is a levy on capital and reserves. This amounts to 0.75 per cent of a company's capital and reserves and, if income exceeds 6 per cent of capital and reserves, an excess income tax of another 15 per cent is due. Taxes are also due on real estate, land, and buildings not used in the normal course of business, and a variety of miscellaneous levies including the turnover tax, the *IGE,* which comes to 4 per cent of the invoice per transaction.

With this welter of negotiable taxes, no technique has been developed to extrapolate a company's true worth or actual profits by calculating backward from taxes. Unlike Germany, where the technique was perfected, in Italy a company's taxes are not a fixed factor. "In Italy, everything is a little hazy," stated one Italian. "It is a continuous fight between the government and the individual. No one believes anyone else. You say X; the government says 4X. You hope to get away with 2X! For companies it is the same."

EXCHANGE CONTROL

At present there are no obstacles to a foreigner's buying or selling Italian securities. If he goes through an authorized bank, his *lire conto estero,* or foreign account, makes it possible to collect dividend or interest, repatriate the principal without hindrance or restriction as to time or amount. Investments of foreign capital are protected by law number 43, of February 7, 1956. The lira is now freely convertible into any other currency. According to an agreement with the International Monetary Fund, the lira is pegged at between 620.50 to 629.50 to the dollar and may fluctuate freely within these limits. It should be noted, however, that the present climate of convertibility is a recent phenomenon. Italy, like most of Europe at one time or another, had exchange controls. These regulations are not based on law but on a general administrative decree of the Ministry of Finance. Should the Ministry for any reason alter the present working procedures, it could be done without notice, and foreign funds might again be blocked. The trend, however, would seem to be in the other direction and in favor of the continuing liberalization of exchange. The Italian government is, in fact, trying to encourage foreign investment, both direct and indirect.

Usually shares, endorsed, dated, and notorized, will be held for safekeeping by an Italian bank. However, should a stockholder wish his shares exported to the United States, there is merely the formality of affixing a stamp, *circolante all'estero,* attesting that the shares are circulating abroad. The shareholder's signature may be authenticated by an Italian consul, commercial attaché, or bank.

ITALIAN CORPORATE STRUCTURE

Italian corporate structure does not differ markedly from that current in the rest of Europe. The most prevalent form is the corporation, *Società per Azioni* or *S.p. A*. The limited liability company, *Società a Responsabilità Limitata,* or *S.a.R.L.,* also limits the partners' responsibilities to the extent of the company's assets, but with one basic difference: under Italian law the S.a.R.L. cannot issue shares or raise money by issuing bonds. These are the prerogatives of the corporation and of the limited partnership with shares.

The *Società in Accomandita per Azioni,* the limited partnership with shares outstanding, is also an extremely popular form. Even as large a company as Pirelli, the rubber firm, has a holding company organized as an accomandita per azioni. With this organization, a company may issue stocks and bonds, though the latter may not exceed the company's paid-in capital as stated in the most recent balance sheet. The same restriction, however, applies equally to the corporation, though in both instances it may be waived for reasons affecting the national economy or if the loan is secured by collateral. Generally speaking, the ratio of debt to equity in Italy is one bond for 2.8 stocks outstanding, as compared with the United States' ratio of 1: 4.6.

To form a corporation or a limited partnership with shares, the founders need a minimum of L1 million ($1,600). To found a limited liability company, on the other hand, one need not be a lire millionaire since L50,000 ($80) will suffice. Conversely, if one has in mind the creation of a large corporation with capital exceeding L500 million ($800,000), money alone will not suffice. The Ministry of Industry and Commerce and the Interministerial Committee for Credit and Saving must be consulted. The same procedure must be followed when a capital increase of over L500 million is contemplated.

The rule of thumb for shares is a par value of L1,000 ($1.60) or multiples thereof, though there is wide variation on this, and shares exist with par value of L200 and L6,000. All common shares have equal value and confer equal rights on their holders. As current practice dictates elsewhere in Europe, other classes of shares may be created with special privileges regarding profit, and those classes may share in the capital in the event of liquidation. Preferred shares also exist; Snia Viscosa, Fiat, Olivetti and la Rinascente have issued preferred stock, *azioni privilegiate*. There may also be shares of redeemed stock, *azioni di godimento,* similar to the French *actions de jouissance,* which usually carry no voting rights but have a call on parts of the profit before it is distributed to holders of other equity. For shares issued after 1942, the rule is one share, one vote, but for equity issued earlier, the rule need not apply. According to Italian law, the founders of a company may allegate special privileges to themselves, such as a cut of the net profit up to and including 10 per cent, but only for five years.

For the small foreign shareholder, there is no problem in investing in Italian companies. No company by-laws exclude foreigners, but some insurance firms have a rule stipulating that any new investor must be approved by the board of directors. Elsewhere in Europe, such a clause is often used to exclude foreigners, but not in Italy, unless a takeover is feared or exceptional circumstances prevail.

Holding companies are a popular form in Italy and, because of their participation in numerous companies, offer diversification to the investor purchasing their shares. Among the largest are La Centrale, Bastogi, Pirelli e C. (the holding company of the large rubber firm), and Società Edison, formerly an electric holding company. They run the companies in their portfolios and usually limit themselves to a group of related sectors. Società Edison's holdings, however, are more diverse than most. This recent development is traceable to the nationalization of Italy's electric industry, and Edison's holdings now range from petrochemicals to women's wear, and food processing.

There are no mutual funds as such in Italy for the simple reason that present tax structures make them impractical. The government, however, is considering changes in these regulations. Closed-end funds do exist but have so far failed to fire public enthusiasm. Invest, an investment trust, and Sifir, a finance company, are part of the La Centrale complex and are listed separately in the Listino Ufficiale under Finanziari, finance companies. Under this heading too, can be found the list of government holding companies.

Today, all Italian shares must be registered. (The only exceptions are some shares issued in Sicily, Sardinia, and Trentino-Alto-Adige.) Registration of shares, dating from a decree of December 1957, created one of the greatest upheavals on the Italian financial scene. In fact, so much ingenuity was deployed in avoiding this ruling that the government passed a second and a third law to accomplish what the first failed to do: determine the identity of shareholders. In order to claim his whole dividend, a shareholder had to come forward and identify himself to the tax people. What was the result? A massive flight of capital from Italy.

Another step in the guerrilla warfare between the Italian fiscal authorities and the Italian stockholder was a 15 per cent tax on dividends, including a requirement that the bank file the stockholder's name when he claims the remainder of the dividend. With the passage of this law, many Italians took the easiest if costlier way out, and many large stockholders have simply forgone their dividends. This has been true despite the fact that the government, to encourage cooperation, took the extraordinary step of promising a sort of amnesty for past dividends due. "They promised to honor 'past virginity' but there is no trust at all between the contributors and the tax collector." Normally the stockholder would have had to pay the delinquent dividend tax on a retroactive basis. Many large shareholders simply sold their holdings and repurchased them in Switzerland as "foreign" investments. The small shareholder is no more trusting than his wealthier colleague. If his income is low, he should in theory get a refund. Italians, however, simply don't believe it.

Italian business did not take long in finding a way around the newly instituted 15 per cent dividend levy. A variety of steps were taken by many large companies, including Pirelli, Fiat, the largest of all Italian companies, and Montecatini. One possibility works as follows: The company declares no dividend at all, but decides instead that what would have been the year's profit will be funneled into a special reserve. Once safely tucked away in this pocket, the moneys will be distributed to stockholders as stock dividends. All distributed profits are fair game for the revenue man, irrespective of their form, whether from reserves or from earnings. However, stock dividends are not taxable if they come from moneys paid in above par during rights issues. The point is a rather technical one: when a company puts out a new issue, its new shares may be priced at par or above. This differential, or premium above par, goes into reserves also but is immune from taxation. The board of directors of Fiat thus claimed that its distribution from reserves came from these differentials and were, in fact, a sort of refund to shareholders, rather than a dividend in disguise. Whether this technique will pass muster remains to be determined and will no doubt be tested in the courts.

In March 1964, however. the government once more changed its mind on the withholding tax, cutting it from 15 per cent to 5 per cent in an effort to bolster a sagging market. Italian investors now have a choice of revealing their names and having 5 per cent withheld, or remaining silent, having 30 per cent withheld, and no questions asked. Most, so bankers' estimates run, will choose the higher levy and remain anonymous. "You can't apply Swedish techniques in Italy. We just aren't that disciplined."

The foreign investor with no reason to remain incognito will have 5 per cent deducted at source and may claim this against his United States tax declaration. Parenthetically, there are no capital gains taxes in Italy, either long term, or short term.

NEW ISSUES

New stock may take a variety of forms. A company may issue free shares, a form of dividend distribution. If more capital is needed, new shares may be issued at a fraction of the par value, the remainder to be paid later; they may be issued at par or above par. In Italy, the new stock is usually priced at par or very near it. When there is a big discrepancy between par value and the share's market price, a premium, termed *sovraprezzi,* is added. This premium is earmarked for a separate reserve held by the company. Fiat, for instance, in a recent rights issue offered new stock priced at L500 with a L500 bonus. The stock was then selling at L3,000 and the offer was one new share for every two then held.

Because of the policy of pricing at or near par, a company must issue large amounts of stock, sometimes up to 25 per cent of its capital in one offering. For sizable new issues, exceeding L500 million, permission must be obtained from the monetary authorities who also have a say in approving the terms of the flotation.

Private companies going public usually start on the over-the-counter market, graduating eventually to the unofficial market. When there are enough shares outstanding and enough interest to warrant it, their stock moves up to the Official List. This progression is only seldom achieved with benefit of an investment bank. "Banks don't do the investment banking. Nobody does. This is one of the troubles with this market."

BONDS

Bonds, unlike shares, may be either bearer or in special cases registered, and a whole range of debt paper is current in Italy including various kinds of convertibles. Fixed-interest-bearing securities and government paper must be purchased for cash for delivery the following day, though one day of grace is allowed. They are quoted in percentages of par and are traded in nominal amounts. Par value is usually L1,000 ($1.60). Government bonds, for instance, are traded in lots of L100,000 *"tel quel,"* that is, including interest accrued from the last semiannual coupon. Industrials, in contrast, and Italian Treasury debentures are sold "plus interest," that is, the interest is not included in the price and must be calculated separately. When the interest has thus to be added on, the bond is said to be quoted "dry," *la quotazione al secco*—without sauce! Interest from bonds is paid in full semiannually, and no taxes are withheld.

The Italian bond market has a number of bonds with special lottery features and other attractions. A Credito Industriale Sardo issue carried a bonus prize of a L250,000 credit for travel on Alitalia flights. A Finsider bond was convertible to stock in two of its subsidiaries. IRI Finelettrica and IRI STET (telephone) also feature convertible issues. Taking the government's lead, Edison has recently issued a similar convertible bond.

Bonds yield 5 to 7 per cent nominal, on average, and the terms of their issue are kept closely to the criteria of the Inter-Ministerial Credit Committee, the liason body between financial institutions and the financial community, on the one hand, and the Bank of Italy and the Treasury on the other.

For Italy's leading industrial firms, the bond market is a good source of funds, but smaller firms find flotation expensive. Moreover it is a capital market to a large extent dominated by IRI, ENI, IMI and other issues of state agencies. Only firms whose names are household by-words in Italy can hope to compete successfully. Smaller companies have recourse to a series of special credit agencies, since the commercial banks restrict their lending to short-term loans. For medium- and long-term funds, the best sources of money are IMI, Mediobanca, Efibanca and Centrobanca, which are jointly responsible for about 50 per cent of all long- and medium-term industrial credit.

Mediobanca, Efibanca and Centrobanca also fill a role similar to that of the merchant banks of England or the French *banques d'affaires*. These institutions may have large holdings in companies for their own account, bring them to the market, a function outside the province of normal commercial banks in Italy. Mediobanca is also instrumental in bringing new issues of both government and the private sector to the market. Four big international issues placed on the market in Italy in 1961 and 1962 were handled by a consortium of banks, plus Mediobanca.

IMI, the government-sponsored Istituto Mobiliare Italiano is the largest of the special credit institutes. Long-term credit is its speciality, and it will float public loans on the capital market two or three times a year. IMI also works on the interinstitutional level, sidestepping the capital market.

PROSPERITY AND INFLATION

Both prosperity and inflation can be contagious. Italy first caught one and is now catching the other. Her industrial production is still increasing at a faster pace than that of the rest of Europe; rates of 10 per cent a year were not unusual in the postwar period and were leveling off at a still impressive 8.2 per cent for 1963. But the tarnished side of the golden coin is inflation. Italy's problem is too much money chasing too few goods. Wages are outpacing productivity and domestic production cannot keep pace with demand. Consumption in recent years has been growing almost twice as fast as Italy's GNP.

Italy's spending spree is pushing prices upward. Only dictionaries and ballpoint pens have held the line. Everything else is more costly and, in fact, more costly than the cost-of-living indexes reflect. Based on a basket of goods and services fixed just after the war, the index is misleading on the conservative side. Moreover, it does not reflect actual costs in urban areas. Here price pressures are aggravated because increasingly, Italy's population is leaving the Mezzogiorno, Basilicate and Calabria and migrating to the industrial North, to Lombardia, Piemonte and Valle d'Aosta.

Italians have begun buying goods on credit with Latin exuberance. The boom is built on "butterflies" as Italy's promissory notes, the *cambialis,* are fondly called. In a way, they mean instant money. A purchaser of a car or household appliance, for instance, will sign a voucher for each month's instalment. The dealer in turn uses these as cash or bank checks, passing them on to pay his own debts. Eventually the butterflies flutter home to a bank to be discounted.

In the South, the temptations of easy credit have often been too great, and the number of people who overextended themselves became alarming.

Such monetary lepidoptera, of course, create great inflationary pressures and the government adopted a series of measures in an effort to clamp down. Moreover, with credit easy and business good at home, Italian businessmen neglected the export market, adding to the country's trade deficit. This overconcentration on the home market plus increasing imports of food have fattened Italy's balance-of-payments deficit and intensified her difficulties.

The decade 1953–1963 saw a doubling of Italy's output of goods and services. But industry, and northern industry in particular, prospered while agriculture in the South first advanced and then merely managed to tread water. The weather was partly to blame, but the explanation must also take into account the exodus of labor from the farms to more lucrative jobs in industry. The net result was a dramatic increase in food prices, leading to increased imports of food, which in turn have helped create a foreign exchange problem.

Italians are not only leaving the frequently marginal and sporatic employment of the agricultural sector but are often leaving Italy as well to find employment in the Ruhr, in Hamburg's shipyards, Swiss hotels, Norwegian pulp mills, and Swedish steel mills. The Common Market has paved the way for the Europeanization of the Continent's work force, and for Italians this has spelled opportunity. In the last decade, nearly 1.5 million have found jobs outside Italy, reducing her unemployment and underemployment problems and aiding her payments position by remitting foreign currencies.

Italy has, in short, undergone a full industrial revolution in the postwar years, as well as a consumer boom. With the terrific expansion of her economy and the advent of mass instalment buying came a shortage of money. In 1963 and 1964 the government's attempt at austerity measures coupled with the withholding tax on dividends led to a flight of capital. Sometimes it comes back to Italy in the form of foreign loans, sometimes not. The effect on the capital market has been a kind of crash diet, if not a starvation diet. Money used to come back to Italy to find its way into Italian bonds but for sometime, this has no longer been the case. The political situation and the market's weakness have frightened many away. "Italians trust the government's ability to pay, but they don't trust the government!"

The government, aware of the crisis in confidence has tiptoed very carefully where money matters are concerned. There is great reluctance in Italy to tamper even with the denomination of the lire for fear of shaking confidence. The French, for instance, converted old francs into new francs by merely moving the decimal point two places to the left. The Italians still hold on to the 625 lire-to-the-dollar rate and no move to make it 6.25 lire to the dollar is in sight. A good portion of Italians, in the Mezzogiorno in particular, are monetarily unsophisticated. To them, moving the decimal two places would make their money worthless. The authorities thus proceed with extreme caution. The most they have done is to change the size of the outsized L10,000 notes called "bedsheets" or "tablecloths." "Ah, but the 'bedsheets' were a good thing for the country," one banker noted. "You see, these large banknotes were so impressive that people kept them in the drawer, withdrawing them from circulation. Thus banks didn't have to pay interest. It helped curb inflation."

WHO INVESTS IN ITALY

For Italian industry, the consumer boom and the Common Market have meant expansion, opportunity, and competition; but the three factors taken together spell problems. Simply stated, the main problem is money for further growth. In recent years lower profit margins are making self-financing less practical than it formerly was, and more firms will be looking to the Stock Exchange and capital market for funds. Italy's Borse, however, have had a three-year low and the general public is seemingly more interested in antiques than in equity. As it is, stocks are not widely held in Italy. The Italian Exchanges are very much the professional's domain, with the country's big industrialists playing a role in supporting the shares of their companies. Of the institutions in Italy, only the banks are really active on the Exchanges. The insurance companies may not invest in stock. Pension funds are nonexistent, as money simply remains in the keeping of the parent company, forming an addition to its working capital.

Statistics on shareholdership are hard to come by in Italy, but estimates hover at around one million as the total of shareholders. Montecatini, one of the largest companies in the country, has some 200,000 shareholders. "We can only gauge these things indirectly," stated one banker. "For instance, at the annual meeting of Rumianca recently, there were 94 shareholders, holding close to 7 million shares. That should give you an idea."

Only with difficulty can Italy's savers be persuaded to put their money into stocks. A recent effort in this direction was a sort of Monthly Investment Plan initiated by *Quattrosoldi,* a Milan magazine backed by one of the city's banks.

A number of thunderclaps have shaken the Borse in the past three years and the storm seems only now to be abating. Heading the list of difficulties is political insecurity. Italy has seen a series of Cabinet reshuffles and this game of musical chairs at the ministerial level culminated in the "opening to the Left." The market has not yet recovered from the impact of the nationalization of Italy's electrical industry. The government will reimburse stockholders of the now nationalized electrical sector to the tune of some $3 to $4 billion. The exact figure is yet to be determined, but the sums will be paid in annual instalments over the next decade. However, a number of companies with Rumianca, the chemical firm, in the lead have taken the problem in hand themselves.

Rumianca's offer was simplicity itself: the company was offering a new issue of stock and, in payment for the shares, Rumianca offered to take either cash or to accept stock of the now nationalized power companies. It was able to sell its new issue to the public with the greatest of ease. As a creditor to the government the company was then in a good position to bargain for state loans and other financial favors, such as advantageous interest rates.

The third bolt was the shaky financial position of Olivetti, Italy's leading manufacturer of business machines. "Olivetti simply never emerged from the Underwood," one financier commented, referring to the Italian company's acquisition of the ailing American typewriter firm a few years ago. To put Underwood on its feet drained Olivetti and, moreover, the South American market, one of Olivetti's prime overseas outlets, weakened drastically because of revolutions and inflation in Brazil and elsewhere. A group of Italian financial interests, led by Fiat came to the ailing firm's assistance by extending credit and purchasing half of Olivetti family holdings. New management was installed and Olivetti was forced to divest itself of its costly computer operations. General Electric again stepped in, as it had in France with Machines Bull, to convert the data-processing division into a separate company. Olivetti has always been in the vanguard of design and advertizing and set the tone in Italy for enlightened and progressive paternalism in worker-management relations. Like Willi Schlieker in Germany, Olivetti symbolizes Italy's postwar renascence, though of course the firm antedates the war.

ITALIAN INDUSTRY

"Milan is a city of shopkeepers who became industrialists," one Milanese admitted. "Torino, there's the city of true industrialists!" Fiat, Italy's proud automobile producer is located in Turin and has molded that city in its energetic image. Olivetti is at nearby Ivrea, and the Turin area is dotted with plants producing parts needed by the two giants. RIV, the biggest Italian manufacturer of ball bearings, is within a stone's throw, as are the auto body builders, Pininfarina, and Bertone, though Innocenti is in Milan.

Unquestionably, Fiat leads the field in automobile production. The Agnelli family's products are rolling on all of Europe's major highways and the company is expanding faster than any other Continental producer. In the decade since 1953, Italy increased her production of automobiles sixfold, and Fiat was responsible for the bulk of that surge. Besides the familiar small cars, Fiat also makes commercial vehicles, diesel engines, gas turbines, railway rolling stock, and aircraft. It has its own iron and steel plants and, together with Montecatini, runs a nuclear reactor. It is the largest corporation in Italy.

The chemicals are dominated by Montecatini, the largest and most diversified chemical complex, whose products range from marble to fungicides, plastics to paints, and pharmaceuticals to glass. Società Edison also has wide holdings in chemicals and ranks second, with ANIC a fast growing third. ANIC is 51 per cent owned by ENI, the government's natural gas and oil monopoly.

The appliance field, which has been causing such a backlash of competitive concern in the rest of Europe, is led by family-owned companies. The refrigerator war which alarmed French, Dutch, and German producers who felt their markets threatened, was led principally by Ignis, Zanussi and Zoppas. All three are privately held as is the undisputed leader in the washing-machine field, a firm with the unlikely name of Candy.

Electric equipment is produced by nearly all large companies, including Fiat, Pirelli, the large rubber firm, Olivetti, Ercole Marelli of Milan, and CGE, a subsidiary of America's General Electric Corporation. Also active in the sector are San Giorgo and Breda, both partially owned by IRI.

Among the drug producers beginning to make their mark on the international scene are Carlo Erba and Ledoga-Lepetit, while textiles are led by Snia Viscosa and Châtillon.

Much of Italian industry is relatively small, and a fair proportion of it is as yet in family hands. Italy's clothing and shoe industry, for instance, sectors which have long made fashion headlines abroad, are in this category. Many of the luxury products too are the product of small shops, which is possibly why they have been able to lead the field in design.

Italian industry is an excellent competitor within the Common Market and in some areas has been able to undersell her neighbors. Competitors complain, attributing it to the Italian government's extensive incentive program. Perhaps so. Without question, however, Italy has the furthest to go of the EEC countries in raising per capita income. The government is under pressure from the vociferous and well-organized Left to do just that. While no further nationalizations are planned—and in fact it appears that the government has taken too much on itself already—the move toward industrialization has caused severe inflationary conditions. How the Italians will handle this political and economic problem remains to be seen. In any event, *la Borsa* is bound to reflect the conflicts, failures, and successes of the battle.

The battle can be measured by the widely used stock index of the newspaper *24 Ore*. The index is composed of fifty-five companies, thirteen of which are small textile firms and nine are utilities. Consequently, the latter give the index a heavy weight in the nationalized sector. The base year of 100 is 1938. A more modern index is published by the other business and financial newspaper, *Il Sole*.

SOURCES OF INFORMATION

Books:

ANGIOLINI, MARIO. *Giurisprudenza di Borsa, 1925-1951*. Milano: Instituto Tipografico Editoriale, 1951. A book on Stock Exchange law and regulation.

GARRONE, NICOLA. *Le Borse Valori, Economia, Ordinamento, Technica*. Milano: Casa Editrice Dottore Francesco Valardi, 1956.

GINELLA, EGISTO. *Moderno Trattato di Borsa (Borsa Valori)*. Milano: La Stampa Commerciale, 1928. This is the classic reference work.

MARTINI, NICOLA. *La Borsa, Origine, Ordinamento, Funzione*. Milano: Edizioni SASIP, 1942.

Newspapers:

Il Globo is Rome's financial daily.

24 Ore, is the financial paper of Milan and the most complete financial paper in Italy.

Il Sole is another Milanese financial paper.

Company information:

Guida dell'Azionista, Ragguagli su tutte le Azioni quotate in Borsa e sulle Società Emittenti. Edizione SASIP. Published every year with the imprimatur of various banks, this booklet gives a page précis on each company whose stock is quoted on the Exchanges.

General information and English sources:

LUTZ, VERA. *Italy: a Study in Economic Development*. London, New York, Toronto: Oxford University Press, 1962.

The Milan Stock Exchange, Explanatory Brochure for International Clients. (Published 1963, G. B. A. Foglia, Member, Milan Stock Exchange.)

Useful Information for Investing in Italy, Credito Italiano. (Issued yearly.)

Vade-Mecum for Foreign Investors in Italy, Banca Commerciale Italiana, Ufficio Studi. (This extremely useful general guide is published annually.)

10. SPAIN

Spain is rejoining Europe after a generation of isolation. Though Spaniards have long used the Pyrenees as a fortress and xenophobia is hardly a new trait, historically speaking, Spain's aloofness from the rest of the Continent dates from the Civil War. Any description of her economy must start with this great watershed of Spanish history, the Civil War which lasted from 1936 to 1939. The country was literally torn asunder by insurgent Nationalists and the Republicans or Loyalists; about a million people were killed and thousands went into exile as the Republican government was overthrown with the assistance of Germany and Italy. The Axis powers used Spain as a proving ground for their World War II weapons, destroying her cities and scorching the countryside. Spanish industry, what little there was, was totally disrupted. Though the issues were different, the Spanish Civil War was comparable to the American war between the states in that the economy went into a state of shock and the fratricidal conflict endured for more than a generation.

No sooner did the Civil War end with the victory of General Franco than the Second World War began. Spain was not only left to

*If fools did not go to market,
bad wares would not be sold.

her own devices but was also ostracized and isolated after the war, owing to her pro-Axis neutrality during that war. While other nations, even the defeated Germans and Italians, harvested their share of Marshall Aid, the Spaniards were left out in the cold. In 1953 at the height of the cold war a pact was negotiated between the United States and Spain for military bases on the Iberian peninsula. This was a significant turning point in the Spanish economy, for during the next decade the United States channeled a half-billion dollars in military aid and $1.2 billion in economic aid to that nation. Though Spaniards often complain that they received no Marshall Plan funds even though they were one of the most staunchly anticommunist countries in Western Europe, they cannot legitimately complain that recent American aid was insignificant. On the other hand, it must be remembered that much of Spain's success was initiated by local efforts. Private enterprise has played a large role even though the government has received much of the publicity.

Spain (population 31 million; 195,000 sq. miles) started her own operation bootstraps shortly after the Civil War in 1941 through a development corporation closely linked with the government. Though it insists it ". . . is neither a government agency nor is it a private enterprise, it functions as a private corporation fully answerable to the government. . . ." The Spanish development corporation, *Instituto Nacional de Industria* (INI), was modeled after the Italian experiment, Istituto per la Ricostruzione Industriale (IRI). Indeed, the corporatism of Fascist Italy greatly appealed to the Spanish régime and it compounded this philosophy with its own indigenous brew of Falangism. By organizing the national economy into twenty-two vertical groups of syndicates that include employees plus representatives of management and government, the administration can keep close control of the economy. Both strikes and lockouts are illegal, though the former have been appearing with greater frequency of late. Free enterprise is a basic tenet of the Spanish government, and recently it has made moves to withdraw support from INI and possibly sell off some of its wholly owned industries.

Three-quarters of INI's capital is in basic industries—shipbuilding, hydroelectric power, iron and steel production, chemicals, mining, and food processing. The remainder is largely in military ordnance and transportation equipment and facilities. Sixty-five enterprises are gathered under the INI umbrella, seventeen of which are wholly owned. INI has a majority interest in thirty-one companies and a minority interest in seventeen. Many of these companies are listed on the Exchanges and are actively traded. INI's total investments are thought to be in the neighborhood of $1.2 billion. Much of the financing of INI companies comes from the nation's savings banks since they are obliged to purchase a large percentage of government or government guaranteed obligations. Enterprises under INI control are run on a profit basis; however, the profits from one company may be used to make up the deficits of another. Termed enterprises of national interest, they enjoy a guaranteed financial structure. Private companies have a difficult time competing in sectors occupied by INI companies. The latter also seem to enjoy certain privileges in the realm of taxes and tariffs. For instance, take the case of SEAT (Sociedad Española de Automóviles de Turismo, S.A.), the largest automobile manufacturer in Spain. The company was established by a joint venture of FIAT (the Italian auto manufacturer), INI, and a group of Spanish banks. One estimate puts INI's share at 51 per cent (a figure easily checked in INI's annual report), the banks' at 32 per cent, the general public's at 12 per cent and FIAT's at 5 per cent. The company enjoys high tariff barriers against foreign competition and favorable tax credits on the investments of its earnings. Though INI's future appears to be in doubt, this holding company is so large that it will not lose its significance or influence very quickly.

THE DEVELOPMENT PLAN

The boom in the 1950s came to a halt in 1959 when the balance-of-payments position ran into sharp difficulties with the almost complete exhaustion of monetary reserves. An across-the-board pay rise of 30 billion pesetas ($500 million) for all Spanish workers in November 1956 along with a steep rise in prices created strong inflationary forces, further raising prices of her meagre and noncompetitive exports. Huge imports in the late 1950s were not balanced by any sizable increase in exports. The isolated and highly protected economic structure began to crack under modern stresses. Through the urging of the Organization of European Economic Cooperation, a stabilization plan was undertaken in July 1959. The currency was devalued by over 40 per cent, wages were frozen, taxes increased, credit tightened, and to some degree import restrictions were lifted. The Stock Market which had fallen from its high in 1956-1957 reversed itself in 1960 after a short recession, as the economy took on an air of expansion. The stabilization reform proved to be quite successful with a strong advance in exports abetted by large emigrant remittances from some 400,000 Spanish laborers spread throughout Europe. Inflation ceased. A not-so-surprising jump in tourism—a major Spanish industry— also followed due to the new favorable exchange rate. On top of that, Spain was "discovered" as a developing nation and foreign capital began to pour in.

Another aspect of the reform was also successful. Spain had hoped to insulate herself against foreign economic forces through discretionary regulations intended to limit imports and exports. That policy succeeded only too well during the inflationary period in creating demand while limiting access to foreign products through strict quotas. Without creating the wherewithal to satisfy that demand the régime had a tiger by the tail. Antiquated industries were perpetuated; they catered to internal needs through inefficient production and without the stimulus of foreign competitors. The lifting of import restrictions then set the stage for revamping many industrial plants.

A recent study by the World Bank—the most comprehensive on the Spanish economy to date—notes that only 25 per cent of the capital goods industries are fully competitive, but other estimates put the figure at half that. Probably a quarter of Spain's industrial plant is beyond salvation and must be replaced, while the remaining 50 per cent will undoubtedly be modernized over the next few years under the new development plan projected to run from 1964 to 1967.

As in so many other countries in Western Europe the plan is run by the new breed of technocrats—comparatively young specialists who have drunk deeply at the springs of modern economic planning.

Though economic controls are not new to Spain, economic planning is. The plan is an indicative one in that it is similar to the French scheme of outlining feasible goals for the various sectors of the economy. The goals are set by committees of labor, management, and government; these are voluntary objectives for private business concerns but are binding on the state and public enterprises. Master blueprints indicate the scope of the undertaking; they occupy thirty-one volumes. A few figures will point out its scale: total investments under the plan will come to Pse.335 billion ($5.5 billion); the GNP during these four years will increase by 26.2 per cent, and income per capita will rise from $365 to $475. Señor Laureano Lopez Rodo, Commissioner of the Development Plan, hopes the economy will maintain an investment rate of 9 per cent per year.

The Spanish development plan is extraordinarily ambitious, but it must be, in view of the tasks ahead. Spain is a country made up of many distinct and diversified regions. Geography and tradition have conspired to keep Spain a land of many parts. There are still huge estates in the south and only small marginal farms in the northwest. Nor has nature treated Spanish agriculture to any largesse. There is constant drought throughout the country which leaves three-fifths of the land arid. Soil erosion and deforestation have been a fixed feature in the Spanish economy for centuries. All these factors have led to rather erratic harvests, often necessitating imports of the produce Spain is best equipped to grow. The leading Spanish crops are wheat, potatoes, olives, grapes, citrus fruits, cotton, and others. While there has been a great increase in mechanization on the farms and widespread use of new fertilizers from the chemical industry, two out of five Spanish workers still till the land though agriculture accounts for only one-quarter of the national income. The development plan is taking steps to strengthen the agricultural sector by increasing irrigation, reforestation, and significant land reform to better distribute cultivable soil. Agriculture is an important element of the economy since it presently accounts for half the country's exports.

Regionalism also plays a significant role in the industrial sector. Most of the capital goods producers are in the north—Bilbao, Santander, Saragossa, and Barcelona are the main centers. The large mineral resources of the country are also in the north. Other areas of Spain have their industries, but it becomes more difficult to generalize about them since they tend to be local or decentralized and composed of numerous small production units. There are about 400,000 enterprises with ten or less employees, but only 150 with more than one thousand. In any event, part of the development plan is devoted to the less developed areas where industry is scarce and unemployment high. Through the use of incentives, businesses are being encouraged to expand by credit preferences, reduced taxes, by allowing imported equipment to enter duty-free and often by subsidies of as much as 20 per cent of a plant's cost. The government has had a flood of Spanish and foreign industrialists applying during the plan's initial stages. The areas designated are Burgos, Huelva, Corunna, Seville, Valladolid, Vigo, and Saragossa. It is hoped that these new industries will raise Spanish exports—one of the weakest aspects of the Spanish economy —besides making her less dependent on foreign suppliers.

As Spain grows closer to Europe, restrictions that hampered the flow of capital into Spain have for the most part been lifted. Indeed, in Spain as throughout Europe, the tendency is to abolish or liberalize all restrictions concerning direct or portfolio investments. Naturally, such investments have to be made with convertible or transferable pesetas, that is pesetas acquired from the sale of a hard currency (Belgian, French, or Swiss francs, American or Canadian dollars, German marks, pounds sterling, Dutch florins, Italian lire, Austrian schillings, Danish or Norwegian kroner, Finnish markkas, and Portuguese escudos) on the Spanish market. Such investments can be repatriated along with capital gains and rights issues. Nonconvertible pesetas do not enjoy the rights to transfer abroad capital and profits originating from such investments. Foreigners may purchase Spanish government bonds, corporate bonds, and common stock in most enterprises. There are, however, some restrictions on foreigners; they cannot acquire an interest in any companies involved in national defense, the national information services, and in public utilities, except where the government has made allowances. Limitations also exist in shipping, mining, and motion picture production, where only a 25 per cent participation is permitted.

In the last few years, as Spain has repealed restrictions on foreign ownership and has unshackled the economy from a series of controls, foreign investors have come flocking. In 1959 foreigners invested only $5 million in Spain. This figure rapidly increased in the next few years and it is currently estimated that their commitments in the country are well past the $400 million mark. The development plan has started a fresh flow of funds; the authorities estimate that $1.3 billion of net capital investment will be realized from foreign loans, commercial credits, direct investment, and the Stock Exchange.

THE BANKS

Most of the equity investment has been purchased directly from the banks rather than from the Exchange. Spanish banks, unlike their Continental counterparts, were in the habit of investing their reserves in long-term loans and industrial shares. They sat on "a mountain of shares," a banker remarked. The Spanish banks in a sense are holding companies usually representing family interests close to the banks. It is probably not unfair to say that most of the wealth of the country is tightly held by surprisingly few people. Reputedly, 50 per cent of the capital of all corporations of Spain and control of 696 major companies is in the hands of six major banks. Since most of Spanish industry is small and often inherited within intimate family circles, this is not surprising. The banks are emerging from under this mountain of shares because of foreign purchases and a new bank reform law of April 1962, destined to change the structure of Spain's banking industry.

Spain has five banks which control roughly 65 per cent of the banking industry's total deposits. In order of size they are: Banco Español de Crédito; Banco Hispano Americano; Banco Central; Banco de Vizcaya, and Banco de Bilbao. Until recently these banks were active in all aspects of commercial banking, in addition to acting as investment bankers. While most of the profits came from the usual commercial lending practices, a significant portion came from their association with industrial firms, either in the capacity of part owners, financial counselors, or proxy holders. The reform, modeled on the postwar French reforms, has concentrated more regulatory power in the newly nationalized Bank of Spain. The government will now be able to control credit through uniform liquidity ratios; before the reform no specific reserves were required and cash reserves varied greatly. The other element of the reform was the creation of the development bank—*banco industrial y de negocios*—brother of the French *banque d'affaires*. Each major bank will set up a new development bank to sponsor new industries and eventually bring them to the Stock Market. Of the dozen new development banks, some are supported by private capitalists. The new development banks will specialize in medium- and long-term loans to industry but, they will not be able to place more than 10 per cent of their resources in any one company or have a majority of a company's equity. On the other hand, the commercial banks will have to lighten their portfolios to meet a new requirement that the value of their portfolios and plant should not exceed their own common stock plus their reserves. The banks have until 1967 to comply with this regulation but the object of the reform is already clear; to lessen the grip of the commercial banks on the country's industries.

THE STOCK EXCHANGE

Philip IV established a *casa de contratación,* a house of trade, at the height of Spanish power in 1652. Today's counterpart, the *Bolsa de Comercio,* the Stock Exchange, is a majestic building with a neoclassic facade that dates from 1893. Situated on one of Madrid's main boulevards, the Paseo del Prado, its colonnaded entrance faces the green geometry of a formal garden and park, the Campo de la Lealtad, the Field of Loyalty. Inside, the whole central wing of the building is occupied by the imposing Salon de Contrataciones, a lavishly ornate hall of regal proportions. Two tiers of arches encircle the floor, crowned by a third which forms a clerestory. Multicolored and gilded columns of marble lead the eye up to a ceiling of translucent Moorish tiles which forms a majestic oval skylight running the length of the building. Between the columns are frescos, crests, and gilded shields, proud symbols of the provinces of Spain and former overseas colonies of Cuba and the Philippines. The latter, of course are no longer subject to Spain's hegemony, but to remove them would destroy the artistic unity, so they remain, testimonials to a bygone era.

Spain's reputation as the most Catholic country in Christendom finds expression in the Exchange's architecture. The floor is arranged in the form of a truncated cross, the usual plan for a cathedral. In the central area an ornate railing encircles the trading arena. In the nave of this parquet floor a square column topped by a clock and a bell dominates the scene. During trading hours, usually from 11 A.M. to 12 noon, brokers and clerks empowered to deal gather along the railing, while bank representatives excitedly gather on the other side. Trading takes place in ten-minute periods for the various groups; bonds, bank shares, utilities, building companies, mining, metallurgy, and the rest. All trades are made at the one prevailing price for the day. Securities are quoted in percentages of par and the nominal values are usually Pse.500 ($8.33) or Pse.1,000 ($16.66) for shares, and between Pse.1,000 ($16.66) and Pse.100,000 ($1,666) for bonds. Activity is not very great since there are as yet but few stockholders; nevertheless, the arena hums with *"digame, digame"* (tell me, yes I am listening) and *"doy"* (I sell) and *"tomo,"* (I buy) and (I take). Brokers move around the floor clockwise as trading is signaled by the tinkle of the bell.

The shares of most Spanish corporations, *sociedad anónima (s.a.)*, are in bearer form with attached dividend coupons payable once or twice a year. Interest on bonds is usually paid once a year. Bearer shares are not as freely negotiable as one might assume, since all securities transactions must pass through a broker. Some companies have registered shares but there is no apparent advantage in them. All market transactions are on a cash basis, though settlement rarely meets with the two-day requirement. Brokers complain that shares from or to another part of Spain seem to travel by burro. Most Spanish orders are *por lo mejor,* at best, though more specific orders are used. Orders are good for a month. Short selling is almost unknown and margin accounts are equally rare.

Rights issues are frequent with some companies since many Spanish companies are undercapitalized. The banks, for instance, go through the process almost annually, usually issuing rights at the stock's nominal value or higher, but always well below the market price. Spanish investors look forward to the rights since they substantially add to the dividend, which for banks is fixed by law. That their equity is being diluted does not seem to cause grave concern.

Brokerage rates in Spain are low: government bonds cost Pse.1.25 per thousand pesetas of the transaction's market value; on other public debt the rate is Pse.1.75 per thousand pesetas; on stock the rate is Pse.2.50 per thousand pesetas traded. There is also a stamp tax of one peseta per thousand.

Perhaps even more prestigious than banking in Spain's financial hierarchy is membership in the *Illustre Colegio de Agentes de Cambio y Bolsa,* the Illustrious College of Brokers. Being a stockbroker is a great honor and most lucrative. The Colegio is the professional organization for all 130 Spanish brokers. However, membership on the three Exchanges—Madrid, Barcelona, and Bilbao—is quite distinct. For instance, the 40 *Agentes de Cambio* of Barcelona may not trade in Bilbao, or vice versa. The 50 Madrid brokers are restricted to Madrid, though it is unlikely they would want to trade elsewhere. Madrid may not be the leading manufacturing city of Spain, but it is the financial capital of the country. Consequently, the Bolsa handles many foreign transactions besides the orders generated by Spain's largest city. Of all Spanish security transactions, Madrid probably accounts for half whereas Barcelona may have 30 per cent and Bilbao the remainder. The large banks appear to prefer the Madrid Bolsa and therefore account for most of its orders while Barcelona seems to be more of a broker's market. Some Barcelona brokers have aggressively pursued clients with market letters and research reports, but Madrid brokers usually have no research facilities. Nor do Madrid brokers bother with custodianship. Custodial fees were fixed thirty years ago by law and the low rates have made the banks the natural depository. As agents, Madrid brokers execute orders but do little else.

Approximately 90 per cent of the volume on the Madrid market is made up of shares of fifty companies, which can also be traded on other Exchanges. There are some 870 securities listed in Madrid with a market value of roughly $8 billion. Of late, volume has naturally increased with an average of Pse.16 million ($266,666) worth of securities traded daily. An Exchange publication estimates that New York in one five-million share day does more business than Madrid does in three years. However, this estimate is not quite accurate since many transactions are routed through the banks. As previously noted, many foreign institutions have bought shares directly from bank portfolios. Though foreign investments may not pass through the Exchange in the American meaning of the term, they must pass through a broker. Since all transactions must be notarized, usually by a broker, they may be said to have gone through the market though the transactions have not gone through the floor of the Exchange. Bolsa volume figures are at best fragmentary since many brokers do not report all transactions.

Membership in the Illustre Colegio is for life and new members are admitted in part by appointment and in part by competitive examinations. Now it is less of a closed club; since 1941 half the vacancies are filled by appointments from the ranks of the brokers' senior clerks. All members of the Colegio must be trained in either law or economics. Members must put up a surety bond of Pse.250,000 ($4,166) which must be deposited with the Bank of Spain. The Exchanges are run by the *Junta Sindical* of the Colegio, the ruling council of the professional organization under the direction of the Ministry of Interior. Besides taking care of all the administrative details, the Junta Sindical can stop trading if prices fluctuate either up or down more than 5 per cent in a single day. They may also step in and buy and sell from their own position, in a sense acting as specialists. The money for their portfolios is their own; the Junta Sindical manages its members' investments, since according to its rules, the brokers may not deal for themselves.

As a group Spanish brokers are, comparatively speaking, probably the wealthiest in Europe. Average earnings are reported to be about Pse.6 million ($100,000). Commissions from the sale of government bonds and the stocks of nationally owned companies go to the Junta Sindical. The commissions eventually revert back to member brokers with the interesting result that each Agent de Cambio in effect has a guaranteed annual wage. He gets his percentage and has a sure income even if he should never set foot in the Exchange. He also collects interest from his Pse.250,000 surety bond.

Perhaps the most profitable part of his function occurs when he is acting as a notary. All financial dealings such as mortgage, real estate, or business loans must be notarized to be considered legal contracts. Consequently, there are three parties to any transaction: the borrower, the bank, and a member of the Illustre Colegio. Without the latter's signature, or rather his *rúbrica* (his personal symbolic squiggle which is his trademark), the deal would not be valid in Spain. A broker is the preferred signatory: a notary's fee is somewhat higher.

With interest on his own capital, a cut of the Junta's portfolio, brokerage fees, and a percentage of bank transactions, brokers in Spain are undoubtedly the wealthiest professionals in the market. They do not need to run after business—it comes to them. This contributes to great dignity in office and a total lack of aggressiveness, often characteristic of other practitioners of the art. One broker expressed his attitude succinctly: *"Siempre hay que dejar que el otro gane algo"* (let the other guy make something too).

Apparently all was not always dignity and restraint, for a Bolsa ruling bars lethal weapons within its portals; all guns and swords must be checked at the door. All is not high seriousness and decorum either, and Spain's Exchange has its share of jokers and *bon mots.* Some government debentures, the Amortizables, are called *amor libre,* free love, because they are *libre de impuestos,* tax free. A metal company, Manufacturas Metálicas Madrileñas, is Mau Mau for short.

Security analysis is still a very new business in Spain. The banks publish full balance sheets but their profit and loss statements may not tell the whole story since loss reserves are usually far in excess of actual losses. Other discrepancies in bank statements range from not consolidating investment profits to arbitrarily understating loans and deposits. One Paris investment banker close to the Spanish scene estimates that "real book value per share in all five cases [the five leading banks] is substantially above market price."

Bankers and brokers familiar with other European countries find the reports of Spanish companies relatively good; though not prompt, they are thought to be accurate to a degree. A characteristic trait of Mediterranean countries is their inability to achieve efficient or equitable taxation. Businessmen are often taxed on their sales rather than on their profits with a final determination open to negotiation. This has led some companies to understate their production. At times—or so persistent rumour has it—the government has asked companies to show less profit to avoid aggravating wage claims. In any event, it is generally believed that Spanish companies sell at modest price-earnings ratios.

Too much, perhaps, has been made of Spain's backwardness. It is not to be compared with the Congo or some benighted area in Southeast Asia. It is a cultivated, civilized nation with a rich history even though marred by long periods of adversity. As a stepchild of Western Europe, Spain has slowly moved from the shadows of moral and geographic isolation. Spain is reentering the community of nations by joining the Organization for Economic Cooperation and Development, OECD, and General Agreement on Tariffs and Trade, GATT. She applied for associate membership in the EEC in 1962, a necessary step if she is to integrate her economy with the rest of Europe. Since Spain sells most of her agricultural produce to Europe, or—to put it another way—Europe takes 70 per cent of her farm exports, a denial of access to these markets could have a severely detrimental affect upon her already weak trade position. Once under the cloak of the Common Market, Spanish industry would be forced to modernize more quickly by the pressure of cheap foreign goods. Estimates suggest that seven thousand small and medium companies will not be able to withstand the absence of tariff walls.

Obviously, there will be growing pains in any association with the Common Market but, if the past few years are any indication, Spain's renascent economy should be able to weather the storm. Heavy investments in basic industries such as iron and steel and chemicals have given the country some new plants; the plants of Altos Hornos and Empresa Nacional Siderúgica (ENSIDESA), two of Spain's larger companies. Both are publicly traded on the Bolsa though the latter is largely owned by INI. With too much steel on the market, both firms have encountered a profit squeeze. The same is true of the chemical industry, the fourth largest sector of the economy after iron and steel, construction, and food production. In addition, it is plagued by many small production units. The most famous chemical company in Spain is Explosivos producing civil and military explosives and a leading producer of fertilizers. The future should see a great demand for construction, hitherto one of Spain's most neglected areas. Hydroelectric stations have grown rapidly, but railroads, roads, and housing projects are expected to be the next goals of intense development.

As the standard of living is raised, consumer goods will be sought after. A few years ago shares in Spain's largest department store, Galerias Preciados, were sold to the public and to American interests. The company has done remarkably well, indicating there is a broad market for mass-produced goods. The same is true of beer consumption (El Aguila) and car production (SEAT or Motor Ibérica). The latter has received an impetus from the first oil reserves newly discovered in Spain by Compañia Arrendataria del Monopolio de Petroleos (CAMPSA). The company is a government monopoly—similar to National Telephone of Spain and the tobacco monopolies—but private investors can buy its shares on the Exchange.

Spain is still beset by grave difficulties, but optimists believe she is on the verge of a German-style miracle. This second largest European country is strikingly poor in some respects, has an industrial plant which is uncompetitive, inefficient, and outmoded, a vulnerable agricultural system, a weak balance-of-trade position, and an uncertain future in an integrated Europe. On the other hand Spain's pride are an industrious and self-respecting people. She has low labor costs, a diversified economy, ample natural resources and hydroelectric power. Spain's balance-of-payments is in a strong position due to large "invisible" items, such as tourism.

The decisive factor in Spain's future may well be political rather than economic. Who will replace the *Caudillo,* General Franco, and what form of government will be ushered in? All are not content with the present régime, but the anomaly remains that most Spaniards would not be without it. There seems little chance of a civil war or revolt to bring about a change of administrations. Nor are all content with present economic progress and foreign influences. One Spanish editor summed it up: "It looks as if the new Spanish generation, plus foreign know-how and capital, may literally carry this horse—whether the horse likes it or not—to the finish, over a race track strewn with those who were not able to adapt themselves to the new going."

SOURCES OF INFORMATION

Accurate information on the Spanish economy is hard to come by and even when obtained tends to be tardy and statistically questionable. Secrecy—for no apparent reason—dominates the bureaucratic mind. One American-oriented financial service found it a Herculean task simply to estimate how many elevators were working in Madrid. Luckily, an excellent summary of the Spanish press is published weekly by the Spanish Economic News Service, available in either English, French, or German. The service also publishes a daily newspaper in Spanish. Most of the major banks publish flyleafs on major companies —usually the companies closest to the banks. Perhaps the best known are: the Banco Central; Banco de Bilbao and its subsidiary company, Compañia Española de Informacion Financiera (CEIFISA); Banco Urquijo; and Banco de Vizcaya. The Illustre Colegio of Barcelona publishes the *Boletin Financiero del Servicio de Estudios e Información.* Also useful is the Ministry of Commerce's publication, *Información Comercial Española,* a monthly. The most comprehensive study was undertaken by the World Bank: *The Economic Development of Spain,* published by the Johns Hopkins University Press, Baltimore, 1963.

*Com a mulher e o dinheiro, não zombes, companheiro.**
—Portugese proverb

11. PORTUGAL

Mais valem amigos na praça, que dinheiros na arca.†
—Portugese proverb

Ever since her great era of exploration, the era of Henry the Navigator and Vasco de Gama, Portugal has seen the tides of history swirl around her but pass her by. She was first among modern colonial powers and she extended her dominion to India and the Malay Archipelago. Her navigators circumnavigated Africa and explored the coasts of the dark continent, making it possible to outsmart the Turk who sat astride the trade route to India, leveling steep tariffs. This new all-water route to the spice lands broke Turkish domination of the eastern Mediterranean and proved extremely profitable to Portugese traders dealing in the blue chip of the day—pepper. Europeans craved condiments, and a voyage to Calcutta for pepper paid for itself sixty times over.

Another lucrative though less noble trade was the Portuguese initiation of the African slave trade in 1434, long before the rounding of the Cape of Good Hope in 1488. Though the slaves often died because of Lisbon's inclement weather, they afforded the Portugese with the first profits from the voyages of exploration.

The spice trade, in fact, was not as profitable as the textbooks suggest and it taught the Portugese a bitter business lesson. Colored cloth and baubles were not for the wary traders of the East; Indian

* No jests with my wife or my money, comrade.
† Friends in the market are worth more than money in the chest.

traders demanded and got specie for their spices, and the newly minted gold from African mines went to India, not to Portugal. Consequently, to finance the voyages for pepper, Portugese kings borrowed heavily from Antwerp bankers, paying between 40 and 48 per cent interest on loans. The attempt to dominate the spice market proved too much for the Portugese and before long, one historian notes, they were "operating a bankrupt grocery business." What they got out of the voyages and what has stayed with them to this year, at least, is a colonial empire. In fact, Portugal is, despite serious trouble in her African possessions, the largest colonial power in all of Europe outside Russia.

The early Portugese empire was remarkable in that such a small country managed to wield power in such an enormous sphere. This fact remains astonishing now for, in present-day realities, Portugal is something of a third-rate power. Nevertheless, this small country (population 9.2 million; 35,000 square miles) still controls and governs a vast empire: Angola and Mozambique, to name her two largest "overseas departments" have a combined population of 11 million and a land area that is over 22 times the size of the mother country.

The wave of nationalism sweeping Asia and Africa has shaken this colonial empire too, but until now has left it relatively intact. The Portugese have lost Goa to India and with it their last enclave in that subcontinent. In Africa, the revolt that rocked Angola in February 1961 has dragged on inconclusively, but Portugal, unlike other colonial powers—such as Belgium—is determined to hold fast and has been spending large sums on her military pacification efforts. Mozambique on the other hand has shown few signs of rebellion until recently.

Portugal will indubitably continue to fight to remain in these territories which play a significant role in her economic life, providing the wherewithal to balance a trade-deficit position. Mozambique, for instance, provides many of the raw materials for Portugese industry and does so at fixed price levels, well below world prices. Cotton and sugar are sold exclusively to Portugal: an estimated $50 million more would have to be spent annually if the Portugese cotton industry had to rely on other sources. To a lesser degree, the same is true for other commodities such as cashew nuts, sisal, timber, and tobacco. Unable to get normal prices for her crops, Mozambique has suffered a chronic balance-of-trade deficit, creating a strain on the escudo area. This vicious cycle supports Portugal's antiquated industries and provides the metropolitan country with her high standard of living.

What holds true for Mozambique is also applicable to Angola, where coffee, oil (the refineries are largely owned by Pétrofina, the Belgian company), diamonds, and other mineral resources are exported to Portugal at cut-rate prices. Portugal is perpetually short of investment capital to explore Angola's mineral reserves, even though Alfried Krupp has called them "the last great undeveloped African mineral asset." On the other side of the coin, the territories rely heavily on Portugese imports, completing the mercantilistic picture.

What effect the loss of these overseas departments might have on the Portugese economy is difficult to envisage, but it would surely be significant. One economist estimates that one-third of Portugal's national income is derived from these territories. Should they be lost before Portugal has had a chance to modernize her industry, the blow could be severe. As a member of the EFTA, Portugal enjoys special tariff treatment in order that she may build up her domestic industry. Instead of dismantling her tariff wall in eight years, this provision allows a twenty-year period, until 1980, to eliminate the protective elements in her tariffs.

This means that Portugese products in 1967, the year that all internal tariffs between EFTA members are removed, will enter the other six nations duty free. This advantage has not escaped the notice of many foreign businessmen who are rapidly constructing plants in Portugal to get in under the wire. Besides the favorable tariff position, other factors are equally important to new industry: low wage rates, relatively low taxes, low-interest loans by the government for businesses that conform to the development plan.

Though only little more than half the country has been brought under cultivation, metropolitan Portugal has good crops of olives, grapes, wheat, citrus fruits, figs, corn, and oats. Large timber stands supply resin and turpentine for export, and the cork oak trees provide one-half of the world's demand for cork. Forestation projects promise a great increase of paper and pulp supplies within the next few years. The great vintage port wines come from the northern part of the country while the nation's other great export—canned sardines and tuna—comes largely from the southern province of Algrave. Fish canning and other food processing are the area's major occupations.

Viniculture was stimulated by a British appetite for these sweet wines going back to the eighteenth century and the treaty of 1703 which gave Portugese wines precedence over the French. The port wine trade centers about Oporto, the nation's second largest city, and is largely controlled and financed by British wine merchants. This Portugese-British economic liaison is ancient, dating from King Dom Dinis in 1294, and was sealed by the signing of a commercial treaty between the two countries. Britain has always considered Portugal her oldest ally.

Industrialization has come belatedly to Portugal, a fact reflected in her GNP per capita of $270 and in fixed capital investment per capita, a mere $50. Both figures are the lowest in Western Europe. Granting the limited natural resources of the country, part of the blame for industrial tardiness nevertheless, must be placed on the doorstep of Dr. António de Oliveiras Salazar. This professor of economics has enjoyed near-dictatorial powers as head of state since 1928. Though he came to power as Minister of Finance, at one time or another in his long career he has run every important department in the Portugese government. This dictatorship of the professor and secret police has been rather a mild one, at least domestically, though institutionally similar to other corporate states the twentieth century has known.

The republic has a constitution which calls for a presidential election every seven years by direct vote and for a prime minister, in turn appointed by the chief of state. There is a legislative branch of the government, the National Assembly, but the real power resides in the Corporate Chamber. This body consists of 135 members representing various professions and vocations. Employers belong to guilds and workers to syndicates, which together make up trade associations which guide and regulate economic activities. All legislation must be subject to the opinions of the Corporate Chamber. Consequently, interested parties are immediately heard from and tend to be subject to their own control. While free enterprise is given a good deal of lip service—indeed, the Portugese government owns very little industry —corporatism has left the way open to monopolies and exclusive permits. Owing to high tariffs, protected industries have flourished, but this in over-all terms has stymied Portugal's growth by keeping competition out. To counter this tendency, *dirigisme,* or state planning has taken a hand, and the two six-year plans have since 1953 been aimed at broadening the country's industrial base. The plans have fallen short of their goals owing to the Angolan rebellion, though Portugal's GNP is now rising by approximately 5 per cent per year.

The Angolan rebellion began in March 1961. Almost immediately the Portugese *Bolsa* reacted sharply, as investors in African companies dumped their shares on to the market. Actually, in the postwar era the Portugese Stock Exchanges reached their high in November 1954 and fell to their low in November 1962. Ever since the Angolan rebellion, the volume on the Bolsa has fallen as investors liquidated their holdings and purchased real estate instead. A fairly sharp recovery took place in 1963 and 1964.

Should the Portugese government stabilize the situation in Angola and continue to keep Mozambique isolated from rebellious elements, then one might expect a revival in the Portugese market. On the other hand, should Angola and Mozambique win their wars of independence, one might expect a prolonged period of depressed prices and inactivity on the Bolsa similar to the one encountered on the Brussels *Bourse* after the independence of the Belgian Congo.

Presently there are two Exchanges in Portugal, one in Oporto and one in Lisbon. Lisbon, of course, is the main financial center of the country and the home base of Portugal's important banks. Though an association of merchants dates back to 1293, modern regulations governing the operation and functioning of the securities markets date from 1901. The Exchange is organized under the Ministry of Finance and brokers must be licensed by the state. All transactions must go through one of these state-appointed brokers, *corretores.* Volume on the Exchange is small, and it is estimated that one year's transactions total not much more than a million shares.

The main corporate form is the *Sociedade Anónima de Responsa-*

bilidade Limitada or *S.A.R.L.* The last industrial census in 1955 reported 654 corporations in existence. Of that figure 136 companies are listed on the Lisbon Exchange; two are foreign corporations and some had their capital raised in pounds sterling. Many companies have both bearer and registered securities. Dividend payments are once or twice a year upon presentation of the coupon attached to the shares. Interest on bonds is paid semiannually or quarterly. Prices of Portugese securities are quoted in escudos; the nominal value of bonds are usually Esc.1,000 ($34.96) or Esc.2,000 ($69.92) whereas equity usually has a par value of Esc.100, 250, 500 or Esc.1,000. There is some advantage in registered shares from the point of view of the taxpayer, since taxes are withheld at source and come to 16.5 per cent for registered shares, but may be as much as 33.5 per cent on bearer securities. Whatever the amount withheld, these taxes can be claimed against U.S. federal returns. Foreigners may freely buy Portugese securities without any formal restrictions. Dividends, interest, and capital are all freely transferrable abroad. However, any direct import of funds into, or export of funds from the overseas territories requires special permission from a government official in charge of exchange control, the *Inspecção Geral de Crédito e Seguros,* the Inspector General of Credit and Insurance. But these restrictions do not apply to the large number of *ultramarinas,* the overseas securities traded on the Bolsa.

Actual dealings on the Exchange are for cash and settlement is the next day. There is no delayed term market at present, though there was one some years ago, nor is there an option market. Portugal is the only country in Western Europe where it is cheaper to buy than to sell. Commission rates for purchases are Esc.1.5 per thousand on the transaction's market value, but Esc.2.5 per thousand on the sale. All transactions are subject to a stamp tax of Esc.1.5 per thousand In brief, the rates are probably the cheapest in Europe.

Most large banks will execute orders for clients within price limits or on an at-best basis. This is understood to be no more than 5 per cent from the previous day's price. Portugese banks, by and large, will not however accept discretionary accounts.

Information on the Portugese economy is difficult to come by since not much is published and very little is in English. Two companies do publish their annual reports in English, the Anglo-Portugese Telephone Company, Ltd. and the Lisbon Electric-Tramways Limited; both are largely financed by English money and can be purchased as easily in London as in Lisbon. The former company is scheduled to be nationalized in January 1968. Very few shares of large Portugese companies are as yet held abroad.

The Stock Exchange, of course, publishes a Daily List, and the two leading financial publications are *O Jornal do Comércio,* a daily, and *Economia e Finanças,* a monthly. Both are in Portugese. A useful publication giving page-long background and facts and figures on Portugese companies is *Aplicação de Capitais.* It is a yearly and appears under the imprimatur of Pancada, Moraes & C. A. Banqueiros, a Lisbon bank. Other large Portugese banks are the Banco Espírito Santo e Comercial de Lisboa; Fonsecas, Santos & Vianna; Banco Lisboa & Açores; Pinto & Sotto Mayor; Portúguês do Atlântico; and Totta-Aliança.

A thorough report on Portugal was published by the European Free Trade Association in 1964: *Structure and Growth of the Portugese Economy* by V. Xavier Pintado.

12. GREECE

Fortune is ever the ally of the prudent.
—Greek proverb

Paradoxes abound in Greek life. It is the oldest European civilization yet one of Europe's newest nation states. It developed political democracy but remains a monarchy. It is extraordinarily rich in the spirit but poor in natural resources. It was on the winning side in World War II but was one of the most thoroughly devastated countries in Europe. It has more people than it can adequately support (8.4 million; 51,200 square miles) but looks toward union (*enosis*) with Cyprus. It is an agricultural economy but due to circumstances and the lure of industrial progress the nation is trying to transform itself.

The transformation has been aided by a good deal of outside help. After the war and the communist guerrilla action that followed, the United States poured substantial amounts of military and economic aid into the country. Marshall Plan assistance to Greece topped $3.5 billion. Unhappily, an inflation in the early 1950s reduced the efficacy of that help and discouraged accumulation of savings by the people. The Greeks met the problem of inflation head on— not by running the printing presses, a classic solution—by cutting the banknotes in half to make them go twice as far. Through little fault of their own, the Greek reputation as a borrower of capital has not been auspicious. Many prewar government loans, both in dollars and sterling, fell into arrears. In 1962 and 1964 these loans were rescheduled. However belatedly, the payment of old debts is an attempt to improve the investment climate.

When the Greek civil war ended, economists strongly suggested

277

that a restoration of Greek credit should be the first order of business. They reasoned that the transformation and modernization of Greek society would lean largely on foreign finance. That could be obtained only if the government settled all prewar debts and guaranteed foreign investments through legal safeguards.

Foreign capital received such guarantees through a special legislative decree in 1953 which cannot be amended by normal legislative processes. Since this law was enacted, direct investment started to migrate toward Greece. As one of the few underdeveloped nations in Western Europe, the Greeks are making a massive attempt to transform their agricultural economy into an industrial one. The main difficulty here is that agriculture, dairy farming, forestry, and fishing are the main sources of income and employment, responsible for nearly a third of the gross domestic product and four-fifths of Greek exports. Though manufactured products account for 20 per cent of the GDP, only 3 per cent are for export. The government is trying strenuously to strengthen its export position since much of the country's economic future is tied to foreign trade. One leading Greek economist has written: "Looking ahead, the major underlying weakness of the Greek economy derives from the sluggishness of its exports." But at this stage of development, more and more imports are needed for the basic fabricating plants. Consequently, Greece has a growing balance-of-trade deficit, though luckily the balance-of-payments position is nearly covered by substantial invisible earnings.

These invisible items consist of shipping charges (the Greeks have the third largest merchant fleet in the world), insurance fees, tourism, and emigrant remittances. Such earnings will play an important role in the economy for the next twenty years; this is the time calculated by the EEC as required for the nation to become a full member of the Community and to attain the equivalent per capita income. To achieve that end Greece must increase her industrial output at a rate of 10 per cent while the remainder of the Community increases its output at only 4 per cent. Tourism in 1963 brought 750,000 visitors to Hellas and netted the economy about $100 million, but difficulties over Cyprus cut into the tourist trade in 1964. Emigrant remittances also contribute substantially to the economy because Greek citizens are attracted by the general shortage of labor throughout Europe. Over a quarter of a million Greeks are scattered throughout the Continent. While it is difficult to assess moneys sent home accurately, estimates put the figure at another $100 million.

The main export commodity of Greece, tobacco, has fallen on hard times. This oriental leaf has accounted for one-third of total exports, but in the last few years adverse scientific and medical reports on tobacco and health have lessened demand. Moreover, Greek tobacco is of a very fine quality, not a necessary ingredient for the now more widely used filter cigarettes. Not only have the prices of tobacco weakened, but increasing the use of fertilizers has also raised yields and produced surpluses. The only saving grace in this picture is the fact that Greek tobacco contains less nicotine and arsenic than other leaves do.

While Greece produces other crops—wheat, cotton, citrus fruit, vegetables, olive oil, melons, potatoes—there are barely enough basic staples to go around. Surprisingly, even olive oil must be imported to cover the popular demand. Rural areas are poverty stricken and personal incomes are estimated at one-fifth those in Athens. Indeed, the per capita income of the country is less than $400. In order to counter this poverty, the government is trying to alter some of the basic fundamentals of agriculture through extensive investments in irrigation, soil conservation, and fertilization. Fertilization appears to hold great promise, for Greece has one of the lowest fertilizer consumption rates in Europe. Chemical Products and Fertilizers, one of the largest Greek companies, has dominated the field for a long time but is now meeting competition from foreign interests in association with the Commercial Bank of Greece. The government is also sponsoring a large nitrate fertilizer plant in Ptolemais.

As an associate member of the Common Market, Greece receives preferrential treatment for her manufactures within the EEC vis-à-vis nonmember states. This umbrella will continue to protect her incipient industries until they can stand on their own. The government and private development banks are trying to broaden the base of Greek industry by inviting foreign interests to undertake tasks that are beyond Greek means. Acquiring proper technology is as important as corralling capital. Capital formation is difficult since most companies are quite small—only 80 are large enough to be listed on the Exchange.

Other problems basic to industry are the shortage of energy and the meagre mineral resources of the nation. Hydroelectric power is increasing, but lignite is still a widely used source of energy. Recently, Standard Oil of New Jersey started a series of projects near Salonika, termed the Pappas-Esso complex, to include an oil refinery, a petrochemical works, and an ammonia plant. The other huge undertaking of late, is the Aluminum Company of Greece, in which the French company Péchiney is the largest stockholder. Starting new enterprises is of course expensive; the Esso project will cost $200 million and the aluminum factory $120 million. However, labor is inexpensive and the country affords a base for penetrating the Middle East.

Tucked away in the southeast corner of Europe on the litoral of the Mediterranean, Greece stradles Europe and Asia. Its deep water port of Piraeus (Athens) plus the other ports of Salonika, Volos, and Patras are adequately serviced by the large Greek merchant marine. These facts have not escaped the notice of other Europeans. The Germans have invested in textile and cutlery plants, the French in aluminum, the Swiss in machine tools, the Italians in ceramics. Even the Americans have recently entered the scene with three dozen separate enterprises or joint participations with domestic firms. Just as Greece was discovered a few years ago by tourists, so now foreign business interests are plowing fertile grounds. This is especially true of the heavy industry sector. Metallurgy, machine tools, chemicals, and transportation equipment are the major industries expected to grow at the rapid rate of 12 per cent per year until 1971.

Located largely in Athens, Greek industry has always been of modest proportions. Business institutions are similar to French models and the banks are not dissimilar to French *banques d'affaires*. They tend to be specialized, participating directly in industrial concerns and providing short-term credits. Corporations must have a minimum capital of DR5 million ($166,666) and the shares must have a par value of not less than DR100 ($3.33), but in reality nominal value is anything but uniform. This, however, is not significant since prices are quoted in drachmas. Most shares are in bearer form, though registered shares of insurance companies, banks, and utilities are traded. A few companies have preferred shares and some have founders' shares, but these are rather rare. Securities usually have attached dividend or interest coupons, payable on an annual basis. While there is no withholding tax on bond interest, there is a withholding tax on stock dividends if the amount is over 1,000 drachma. The rate then is approximately 25 per cent—except for shipping companies and bonds and preferred stocks of developmental investments whose interest and dividends are tax free—though this can be claimed against federal income tax since a double taxation agreement exists.

While direct foreign investment is welcome, private portfolio transactions must be approved by the Ministry of Finance if one is to safeguard the eventual repatriation of the investment. Otherwise, investment becomes largely an *ad hoc* situation, to some degree determined by the state of the foreign exchange market and the supply of dollars. As one bank notes, ". . . it should be added, however, at this point that in general funds imported from abroad for the purchase of existing securities (as contrasted with new issues) do not enjoy repatriation rights." One is on the uncertain shores of the Levant.

There are few nationalized industries in Greece, but the government does maintain a monopoly on the telephone and telegraph systems and on some railways, but not the Hellenic Electric Railways which has the greatest number of shares outstanding and one of the highest market values of Greek companies. The government also owns some electric companies and the usual monopolies on matches, salt, kerosene, and alcohol.

The Athens Stock Exchange, *Chrimatistirion,* started its official operations in 1876. Before that traders and seamen swapped gold and stocks in coffee shops, and selling of gold and silver still continues within the Exchange—the only Exchange in Western Europe where this is practiced. Though the government passes on the rules and regulations of the Exchange, its immediate operations are in the hands of a committee of brokers. The Exchange membership consists of 35 brokers but no bankers. Membership is only DR2,000 ($67), but members must post security of DR1.2 million ($40,000) as part of a compensation fund to protect both the public and professionals. Memberships are not transferrable.

Trading takes place between 10:30 A.M. and noon six days a week. A list of the 50 bonds and 80 shares is read through on an auction basis and the results are published in the daily Official List. Transactions are either for cash or for settlement at the end of an account period of two weeks or for continuation for several accounts. Dealings for the account must be settled every fortnight on the basis of a price fixed by the Exchange, in the fashion of the Paris *Bourse*. There is no option market. Commission rates are ½ of 1 per cent of the market value for bearer securities and $8/10$ of 1 per cent for registered securities. There are no other charges.

Stock ownership in Greece is still very small and many companies are traded infrequently. In 1963, 200,338 shares were traded, down from 260,641 in 1962. To put it another way, the value of the year's transactions in 1963 was DR148 million ($5 million) whereas in 1962 it was DR269 million ($9 million). Bank shares are the most actively traded group. Half a dozen commercial banks do most of the country's banking: The National Bank of Greece; The Commercial Bank of Greece; The Ionian and Popular Bank of Greece; The Bank of Piraeus; The Commercial Credit Bank and The Army Share Fund Bank. Banks, of course, will negotiate trades and attend to a securities account. In addition—Swiss banks take note—they will open accounts designated by code numbers, though they will not open anonymous accounts.

SOURCES OF INFORMATION

Some English information is published by the banks and some material such as the Official List is published in Greek and English. However, financial information generally is hard to come by, and one Greek economist recently wrote: "The lack of adequate and consistent accounting information about assets and profits is a great barrier. It is difficult to evaluate the merits of the individual companies. There are substantial differences between companies and even between one year and the other. Profits often mean very much what the management of the company wants them to mean and hence it is difficult to calculate earnings in accordance with applied criteria of economic performance."

For those who can read Greek, the main daily financial newspapers are the *Express* and *Naftemporiki*. The latter also publishes a daily condensed English edition. *Economikos Tahidromos* in Greek is the weekly magazine, though Hellenews mimeographs an English publication, the *Weekly Athens Newsletter*.

Perhaps the most thorough studies of the Greek economy are those published by the Center of Economic Research in Athens. Besides being published in English, they are up to date and authoritative. Two of their publications provide general surveys:

PAPENDREOV, ANDREAS G. *A Strategy for Greek Economic Development.* Athens: Center of Economic Research, 1962.

KOUTSOUMARIS, GEORGE. *The Morphology of Greek Industry.* Athens: Center of Economic Research, 1963.

SOME SPECIAL CONSIDERATIONS

AMERICAN DEPOSITARY RECEIPTS

Americans investing abroad are faced with a variety of pleasures and problems. One advantage is the chance to invest in renascent European economies that may double their gross national products and standards of living within the next decade. Investments in these economies will mean high yield and capital appreciation. On the other hand, European share ownership presents problems that an investor should be aware of. Whether an investor likes to see his domestic securities under lock and key or is satisfied to keep them in Street name is simply a matter of taste, provided they are not in a margin account. The situation is somewhat different with foreign paper, and delivery of securities is a complicated procedure due to government and exchange regulations, tax laws, and variant corporate practices. However, many steps have been taken to smooth the way for Americans—as well as Europeans investing in American companies—but the procedure is still complex.

Perhaps the first thing an investor must remember is that outside of the United States and Canada, share ownership is a less personalized business. People's Capitalism or Shareholder Democracy are Anglo-Saxon concepts. Typically, in the medium-sized and smaller European corporations managerial reins are firmly grasped by the majority stockholder and his family. This has been so for generations. Consequently, European companies often tend to regard the outside investor with some suspicion and wish to evade him.

There are no personal *billets-doux* from the management indicating they are doing a fabulous job for the shareholder or how wise and intelligent he is for investing in this particular company. In the old days the prevailing corporate dictum was "the less said the better." There has been a marked change for the better, particularly among the blue chips, but some annual reports are still so evasive that it's difficult to identify the company's product, and even what industry it belongs to.

The majority of stockholders see little reason to confide in their minority confrères. Moreover, they rarely confide in the government. Insider holdings, to the great dissatisfaction of revenue agents, are seldom disclosed. The small investor feels that the extent of his involvement is no one's concern but his own. Thus, Continentals have insisted upon and obtained freely negotiable securities that leave no trace: *bearer shares*. Registered shares are the typical variety in the United States and Great Britain, but bearer shares are most common throughout the greater part of Western Europe.

Bearer shares of foreign securities are rather inconvenient for Americans. During the early part of the twentieth century, physical possession of a security meant a long insured sea journey to the new owner. Such a trip was costly and time consuming. When the new owner finally saw his purchase, he wondered if it was his first foreign security, if someone had not made a mistake: his acquisition resembled a bond more than an equity. Attached to it were dividend coupons—like interest coupons—that had to be clipped and sent to the corporation's home office or perhaps, if he was lucky, to a New York agency. If the coupon had to trek home, his dividends would be paid in foreign currency which had then to be converted. The process was, of course, lengthy, full of possible errors and at the mercy of fluctuating money rates. Moreover, he remained in the dark as to subscription rights and general corporate news. Indeed, he had a hard time finding out the market price at any given time. When he went to sell his foreign shares they had to be sent from whence they came: chances of finding active markets in the United States were not great. If he died before the shares were sold, his attorneys had to venture into foreign courts to probate the will. Since the difficulties entailed in purchasing foreign securities were so great, not many people felt it to be worth the candle. They were undoubtedly right!

During the 1920s a group of brokers, investors, and arbitrageurs came up with the serious idea of a negotiable receipt for a foreign stock. There have been attempts at this since the turn of the century, but in 1927 the Guaranty Trust Co. of New York evolved what is today known as the American Depositary Receipt, known more simply in the market as ADR's.* The ADR's provided answers for most of the problems that the overseas investor faced.

Basically, the ADR is a substitution certificate for the foreign bearer share. It works in this fashion. When a foreign security becomes widely held and traded, one of the leading international banks or trust companies will decide to issue ADR's for that company's stock. The Morgan Guaranty Trust Co. of New York issues about three-quarters of the ADR's outstanding and is acknowledged to be the leader in this field. (Indeed, one foreign securities dealer somewhat ironically dubbed all others in the field as "greengrocers.") ADR's are also issued by the Belgian-American Banking Corporation; Bankers' Trust Co., Chemical Bank New York Trust Co., The Chase Manhattan Bank, Empire Trust, The First National Bank of Jersey City, The First National City Bank of New York, Irving Trust Co., The Marine Midland Trust Co. of New York, and Schroder Trust Co. The bank may or may not consult the company involved before it goes ahead; most of the time it does talk to the firm concerned, but occasionally, as was the case with *Olivetti,* ADR's will be issued despite its objections. Once shares are deposited with the bank's overseas branch, affiliate or custodian—that agency acts as either nominee if the shares are in registered form or custodian if they are bearer—the home office is then notified by the foreign office of such a delivery. The bank in the United States will then issue the negotiable receipt (the ADR's), which simply stand for the number of shares deposited abroad. From then on, the ADR can be bought, sold, or held almost as simply as any domestic stock certificate.

* R. E. Moxley, "The ADR: An Instrument of International Finance and a Tool of Arbitrage," *Villanova Law Review,* Vol. 8 (Fall, 1962), pp. 19–42.

Though it is not in the province of the investor, ADR's readily lend themselves to two- or three-way arbitrage, and arbitrageurs do take advantage of this situation. For instance, a stock with an international following is bought in Amsterdam and a broker entrusts the shares to the Depositary's Amsterdam Correspondent. It then comes to his attention that the ADR's of this security are selling at a premium in New York. He may either sell the ADR's in New York or buy more stock in Amsterdam, leave it with the Depositary's Correspondent and have a further lot of ADR's issued. Similarly, he could sell the ADR's short in New York and then go through the process of having them made up.

The reverse process is also possible. If the price is better in Amsterdam than in New York, the arbitrageur or investor will sell the underlying shares, undoing his ADR's and any others that come his way by simply returning them to the New York Depositary. It should be noted that any securities or ADR's whose price gets out of line are quickly forced back in by international arbitrageurs.

There is, however, a point that the issuing banks would like to make clear for the investor's benefit: the process of issuing ADR's is essentially a service to the financial community, not a value judgment as to the quality of the company's shares. The only reason for the bank to be involved in this business—one, they claim, that hardly pays its way—is as a service to their clients.

Once issued, the holders of the ADR's are informed by the Depositary of annual reports, the reorganization of the corporation, dividends, rights issues, and other pertinent information. The bank will sell his rights, if the new shares are not registered with the SEC, collect his dividends, and convert the proceeds to dollars or any other currency for that matter. In brief, the bank plays much the same role as the local broker. ADR's are, of course, not gratuitous, Depositaries charging between $3 and $5 per 100 shares to issue them or to unmake them. The cost is based on the foreign market price of the shares deposited: when the price is at or under $5 per share, then the cost is $3 per 100 ADR's; when the price of shares is between $5 and $10, then it is $4; and finally if the share is more than $10 the cost is $5 per 100 ADR's. Prices are a dollar per 100 cheaper if the ADR's were issued before the Securities Act of 1933.

On top of that, there is a small charge of about 1 cent per share per dividend. These costs are negligible in the long run, but do account for the slightly higher price for the ADR's compared with the underlying shares.

Currently, there are approximately 200 foreign companies, most of them European, but also a scattering of South African, Australian, and Japanese firms that have ADR's. Since the foreign shares tend to have different price ranges than do American securities—the average share of the New York Stock Exchange is about $50; that on the American Stock Exchange about $15—ADR's take this into consideration. Swiss shares tend to be rather high priced, often costing several hundred dollars per share. English shares on the other hand are quite cheap; some of the best British companies selling for less than $10 a share. ADR's attempt to round out a manageable lot by either representing fractional ownership of an expensive stock or consolidated ownership of low denomination shares. British Motors Corporation Ltd., for instance, sells for approximately $2 an ordinary share in London. The Irving Trust in New York issues 1 ADR to 10 ordinary shares, selling for roughly $20. In this way, foreign stocks are brought into line with American securities prices. Most foreign stocks, however, have ADR's issued against them on a 1-to-1 basis. Sometimes two different banks will issue ADR's for one company, such as in the case of the Dresdner Bank. In this instance, both the Morgan Guaranty and the Chemical Bank New York Trust Company perform the identical service for the same price. Apparently, there is enough business for both depositaries and usually there is no difference in actual trading as both ADR's represent like amounts. Once in a rare while they do not. For instance, ADR's of Chase Manhattan on "Shell" Transport & Trading Co. Ltd. represent 8 English ordinary shares, whereas the Irving Trust ADR's stand for only 4 English ordinary shares.

There are twenty-six foreign securities listed on the New York Stock Exchange and half of these are Canadian issues. These twenty-six companies accounted for 2 per cent of the volume in 1963 or about 23 million shares. If bonds are included, the New York Stock Exchange can boast of 253 foreign securities valued at about $9 billion. Some of the foreign stocks are ADR's, some are not. Where does the difference lie?

European and foreign corporations that came to the United States for capital, such as Royal Dutch Petroleum of Holland in 1954, complied with SEC and Stock Exchange regulations for listing. Such listing requirements were almost as detailed as for an American company. This direct listing did away with the substitution certificate, the ADR's, and registered the original security in the buyer's name. Besides Royal Dutch, the following European companies are listed on the New York Stock Exchange: Electric and Musical Industries, Ltd., K.L.M. Royal Dutch Airlines, Montecatini Mining & Chemical Co., Schlumberger, NV, "Shell" Transport & Trading Co., Ltd., Unilever Ltd. and Unilever NV. Some foreign securities are listed on regional Exchanges.

Still other European and foreign companies are traded in the United States through the use of negotiable receipts—ADR's. In order to have these ADR's listed, they and the underlying securities must be registered with the SEC under the Securities Exchange Act of 1934, and of course, the particular Exchange. Certain regulations, such as disclosure of insider holdings, are not required of foreign firms. Consequently, somewhat less formal information is immediately available on these companies, though a good research department should have most of the important facts.

The bulk of ADR's are traded in the over-the-counter market, though some over-the-counter houses do not deal in foreign shares.

ADR's are an extremely useful, but limited tool. Though there are ADR's for 200 companies, this is but a small fraction of potentially interesting investments. The London Stock Exchange alone has 10,000 companies listed. Even if the issuing banks do not openly approve of the companies behind the ADR's, their participation suggests that the companies' securities are widely held, traded, and readily quoted. In other words, they are stable companies. Conversely, they may have less of a potential for growth than many companies that have no ADR's.

Another consideration points up the limitations of ADR's. Some

European companies tend to reward their stockholders with frequent rights issues rather than high dividends. Large dividends might bring higher wage demands from labor and difficulties from tax officials. If the rights mean a distribution of company stock that is not registered with the SEC the Depositary will sell the rights, if it can, and pass the proceeds on to the ADR holder. In the long run the rights might be more valuable than the immediate proceeds, but the ADR holder has no option in this matter due to the Securities Act of 1933. Subscription rights are available from foreign banks for Americans that wish to exercise these rights abroad. This necessitates a brokerage or bank account in a foreign country to take care of the mechanics. Unless one follows foreign financial journals with regularity, a holder of foreign rights through ADR's will only know about it after they have been sold and he receives a check from the bank.

FOREIGN SECURITIES IN NEW YORK

The business side of the foreign securities industry begins at the working end of a telephone line. There is no physical foreign securities market in a sense that there are commodity markets or Stock Exchanges for domestic securities. Foreign securities are traded in much the same way as are over-the-counter stock—on the telephone. Therefore, habitués of boardrooms never see the over-the-counter markets, or for that matter the mechanics of foreign trading. Both, nevertheless, do have loci. At one time, trading took place in smoke-filled backrooms that had little air, less light, but much noise. Today, with the surge in foreign securities during the last few years, these dens have turned into lushly carpeted, beautifully appointed electronic havens, but still situated in the back offices. The only thing that has not been banished—though they've tried—is the noise.

Though there are many thousands of brokerage houses throughout the United States, there are only a dozen or two brokerage houses, traders, and foreign banks that actually trade in foreign shares or have any knowledge of foreign markets. All of them are within a stone's throw of Wall Street proper.

Foreign securities may be purchased through any brokerage house. (Under certain state blue-sky laws, brokers are forbidden to advertise shares of companies that have not met state registration requirements. Blue-sky laws—drafted in the 1930s—vary, but their general intention is to protect the public by requiring full disclosure. Since the notion of full disclosure is a relative concept, varying widely even from state to state, few foreign companies will take the trouble to meet them, though they may have met federal regulations. Moreover, except for the giants, few European companies were interested in American capital or ownership. Blue-sky laws do not enjoin the investor from purchasing foreign stocks; they merely restrain the broker from soliciting them.) Unless a brokerage house deals in foreign issues, it will have to call upon one of the foreign securities dealers that primarily "make the market" in those particular foreign stocks. Indeed, the whole foreign securities business in the United States revolves about these dealers who stand ready to buy and sell every conceivable overseas share. Thanks to these houses, foreign stocks can be appropriated or repatriated with ease. They *are* the foreign securities business.

"Making the market" is less a mystery than it sounds. These firms have staffs of professional traders, known as arbitrageurs, who arbitrate among markets, ironing out price differences for their own profit. Domestic arbitrage is an old business in the United States, and a few Wall Street houses have found their fortunes in it. But before the Second World War, international arbitrage and foreign securities were pretty much the exclusive province of Carl Marks. Marks bought and sold just about anything that came his way, from a South American agricultural bond to the Russian Kerenski Loan 5 per cent 1917. The latter is still being kicked around and recently was quoted at one-quarter bid, one-half asked. Marks, until he died a few years ago, knew more about foreign paper than perhaps anyone else, though he modestly kept it to himself. In fact, he took the trouble to publish a book on the subject: a two and one-half pound, three hundred-page opus bound in green covers, titled in gilt *What I Know About Foreign Securities*. The book had three hundred *blank* pages.

Since the house of Marks was one of the earliest in the business, the traders are somewhat senior to those of other houses. In fact, there are two distinct generations in the foreign securities business.

When World War II ended, the business was inactive, to say the least. Not only was the outlook for Europe bleak, but Europe was a maze of monetary restrictions. It was no place for investment dollars since there was little likelihood of being able to redeem them. All securities were traded against block currencies and these currencies were almost worthless. For instance the franc was worth 1/200th of a cent. As Europe stabilized its currencies and dealt with the chronic postwar inflation, these securities increased in value. Not only were the currencies worth more, but plant assets also appreciated.

During the next ten years there was little foreign portfolio investing and almost no new blood went into the securities business, domestic or foreign. European refugees, brokers, and arbitrageurs that had come to the United States either before the war or immediately thereafter, supplied the two necessities for the business. The traders had techniques and banking connections and knew the foreign markets, while the refugees had brought with them their bearer securities or deposit books to their blocked bank accounts. Both helped to rejuvenate the American foreign securities business.

By the end of the forties a few Wall Street houses set up foreign departments. One house bought Philips as their first foreign security when it was pointed out that its price-earnings ratio was roughly half that of General Electric. Another began their foreign trading desk in 1952, but one of their first trades lost them a thousand dollars. They thought they would make a small killing by buying a stock in London and selling it in New York since there was a considerable price difference. To their chagrin, it was soon apparent that London stock was ex-dividend while New York stock was cum-dividend. This was but the price of experience, for soon the company's foreign desk became one of the most successful on the Street.

Thus today's arbitrageurs are either men in their fifties or sixties, whose families were in the banking business for generations, or very young men who have come into the business in the last five or ten years. The difference is more than chronological. The older Europeans spent their youth apprenticing in the world's financial capitals, steeping themselves in languages and business lore. In comparison, the younger traders are mostly Americans who have had little experience abroad but lengthy on-the-job training. A good trader—young or old —is immensely valuable to the firm and most firms know it. In a good year he will receive a bonus that is equivalent to his annual salary and often that is in five figures.

What makes a good arbitrageur? Undoubtedly, it's a rather special skill, for arbitrage requires a facility with numbers, a phenomenal recall, a willingness to take risks, and a fascination with the business. At the end of the day when the financial community is apt to do some comparison shopping, a caller may request a dozen quotes. Traders will respond with a string of prices, citing merely the names of the stock and the fractional change. An *aide memoire* is about, but he may not use it.

Prices are usually determined by the chief trader or one of the managing partners. Once determined, all traders will deal at this limit until conditions change. These prices form long and cryptic lists and, depending on the firm, are posted in various fashions. One firm has a large green blackboard, dotted with colorful magnetic tags. At a glance one can see most actively traded stocks. Red indicates which stocks have ADR's outstanding; blue is used when ADR's are not on a 1-to-1 basis. There are also different colors of chalk, pink and yellow, and wooden X's to mark stocks that have gone ex-dividend. To facilitate changes in this mass of numbers, the erasers are cut down to junior size, good for blotting out one figure at a time. Another large foreign securities house solves the problem in a more novel if less colorful fashion. Two lantern machines—the kind used in junior high school science classes—project the quotations on huge screens on the wall. When a quotation is changed the two boys who attend the projectors erase the figure and write in the new one. An enormous hand, projected to giant size, neatly corrects the quote. The effect is bizarre; literally the handwriting on the wall. Other firms, less cinematically inclined, merely use mimeographed lists.

Mnemonic devices vary with the firm, but other equipment is standard. Each trader's turret is provided with stacks of finely sharpened pencils, a calculating machine, binoculars to see the lists of quotations, and a magnifying glass for the fine print.

Common also to all trading floors is the high degree of tension. Though chairs are provided, traders rarely sit. The more hectic the pace, the fewer mistakes is a truism in the field. As proof, traders point to their most active day in recent history, the day after the British general election in 1959. Many people had speculated that the Conservatives would win. They did. When the arbitrageurs came to work, their switchboards were blinking like Christmas trees. English industrials were running and everyone wanted to jump on the band wagon. In quick time, trading reached a frenetic pace. A visiting English broker, on a busman's holiday, was put to work despite a broken arm. Chairs remained untouched all day, errors were almost nonexistent, and profits were never greater. Soon after the Labor victory of 1964 and subsequent sterling crisis there was activity of a different sort as Americans unloaded English securities.

Bid and Ask

High in a Wall Street office building commanding an imposing view of the lower New York harbor, an immaculately dressed foreign banker summed up his forty years of experience in buying and selling the world's currencies and securities. His philosophy, he confided, was disarmingly simple: "Every once in a while I must remind myself to sell it for a little bit more than I bought it."

This might be an appropriate prologue for arbitrage, the heart of the foreign securities business. Arbitrage, according to the definition in Webster's dictionary, is purchasing in one market for immediate sale in another at a higher price. While the essence remains the same, the art of arbitrage has become more complex and competitive due to modern communications techniques. The market is no longer a secretive operation or a singlehanded business.

"Making the market" has its own law; the first proposition is to be on friendly terms with competitors—they are one's best customers. Trading posts consist of a series of small turrets with 100 or more private lines to banks and brokers. There is no switchboard, but each trader can take or transfer calls directly. A prospective buyer or seller is at the other end of a blinking light; telephone bells have been banned from the trading desks. The caller—who it is is clear both from his voice (it's a very small industry) and from the location on the telephone deck—requests a quotation on *Siemens and Halske AG*. He doesn't indicate whether he is buying or selling. The arbitrageur responds with the bid and asked prices, "70½—1¼," meaning, "I'll buy one hundred shares at the lower figure, and sell to you at the higher." If the caller makes a counter-offer or checks the competition and calls back five minutes later, the trade need not be consummated at the original price. The trader can deal at the counter offer, but is perfectly free not to. Once the caller does accept his price, he *must* deal at least one hundred shares, or fifty shares of a foreign insurance company.

The trader's art is an amalgam of instinct and knowledge. For instance, suppose the voice at the other end says: "Fine, I'll take forty thousand shares." The arbitrageur must calculate rapidly, taking into account who is making the offer, his own firm's inventory of the stock, at what price he can purchase the remaining shares needed, the length of time it will take him to do this, particularly if he must round them up in Europe, etc. Should he deal or not? Will the customer call around and spoil the market by raising prices? Once the competition is alerted, it may be impossible to obtain stock. Will accepting the offer—even at a small loss—mean enticing this institution's business away from a rival broker? All these questions must be decided before the final click that ends the conversation.

Above all, a trader must know his markets. European markets are more precarious—"thinner," in the jargon of the Street—than U.S. ones; the volume is much smaller and a sizable order can boost prices as much as 25 per cent if not properly handled. The arbitrageur must know how to stagger his purchases; when he buys is as important as where.

A change in the mechanics of arbitrage has brought with it some alteration in its day-to-day practice. In fact, of the dozen or so arbitrage houses, two or three distinct philosophies emerge. In the pre-electronic era, arbitrageurs worked with smaller volume but for greater price spreads. Consequently, the older members of the art still retain an inclination to make a number of points. Younger colleagues and newer houses are satisfied with fractions of points instead of a handful of points. They, therefore, give more consideration to volume. This difference is basic and gives rise to further variations.

Just as it is impossible to draw a definitive line between speculating and investing, both being a part of the whole, so arbitrage has many facets. Classic arbitrage is completed, if not simultaneously, at least in one day, the day being twenty-four hours long to allow for the opening and closing of every market in the world. Wall Street traders try to make it a practice to be free and clear of most of their deals by the end of the day. When they are not, they are long or short for purposes of gambling, speculating, or *tendency*. Tendency is by far the dominant practice in arbitrage trading.

For instance, an Amsterdam affiliate or branch office cables its New York office at 3:30 P.M., 10 A.M. New York time, that Amsterdam and Swiss brokers and bankers are advising their clients to switch from Philips' (Gloeilampenfabrieken) to Royal Dutch Petroleum, two industrial giants in the Netherlands. The reasons are at first not very clear, but there are indications that Royal Dutch may be raising its dividends. At the time of the cable there are no hard facts, since the board of directors will not meet for a few weeks. However, the investing community, acting on faith, hope, and charity, since Royal Dutch appears to have had a good year, takes the fly like a trout. Almost simultaneously, cables from Europe and flashes on the trans-lux screen (since it is a listed stock) indicate that sales are mounting, as is volume. Traders decide for themselves which way the market will eventually go and what they want to do. In practice, arbitrageurs are not concerned over the short-term or long-term price of a security they trade. Nor, if they are going to be successful, personally "like" a particular stock. Whether the market is rising or falling has little bearing on their business.

Essentially, they are doing one of two things: either buying and selling securities in which they have no inventory, or only a small one; or trading for periods longer than one day. The latter technique is less pure arbitrage than the former, since this kind of trading is often motivated by calculated risks, speculation, or outright gambling. Arbitrage that is completed within a day or so is usually based on tendency. When word first came on Royal Dutch, the trading houses quickly sensed a tendency and started to buy Royal Dutch, realizing as word spread that it could easily be sold at a higher, hence profitable, price. In this kind of operation a house might lose money, but the likelihood is not very great provided that they be free of most stocks by the end of the day. If the house decides to accumulate an inventory of Royal Dutch, whether this be overnight or over a month on the assumption that its price will be considerably higher later on, the house is not trading on tendency, but on other factors, compounded no doubt by wishful thinking. Here the risks are greater, but the gains may be greater too.

Tendency traders may of course try it the other way. Instead of assuming that Royal Dutch will appreciate, they might decide, on the basis of other information or disenchantment with the high prices of international oils or the rising terrorist activities in the Venezuelan and Saudi Arabian oilfields that are sources for Royal Dutch, or the shaky political situation, or whatever, that an opposite price movement is in the cards. They then sell Royal Dutch short and hope for a declining market so that they can replace the borrowed stocks they sold at lower prices. Again this tendency trading can be emphasized to the point of gambling.

By and large, most foreign traders undo 80 to 95 per cent of their daily business. While a few long-term speculators make and lose fortunes with frustrating regularity, most houses are conservatively operated with too much of the partners' moneys at stake to be run like a pari-mutuel window. "The margin of profit," recalled one partner, "is not what it used to be. But then there is ten times the volume."

While the work sounds easy, it is an extraordinarily complex business. In fact, during the Wall Street boom years of 1959–1961 a number of over-the-counter houses started to trade foreign securities. Their flings were short-lived. Remembering, as good financiers should, "to sell it for a little bit more than they bought it," they usually made money on any given trade and could show a gross profit at the end of the day. Only one factor had not been fully accounted for: the basic costs of the business. They left the field when it became obvious that profits were too slim to cover fixed costs—some of them quite intangible.

Brokerage houses that are in the business of making foreign securities markets naturally make money. In fact, eight or nine days out of ten they usually end up in the plus column. However, the trading of foreign securities usually constitutes but a small percentage of a house's business. Though this has been growing in absolute terms over the past years, houses that had specialized in foreign business are now broadening their domestic efforts to present images of well rounded concerns.

The costs and complications of this arcane business begin quite early on any working day and even on some days and nights not meant for laboring. Since Europe is five or six hours ahead of New York, traders can count on many an early rising at five or six in the morning to find out what the trends are abroad or to complete trades that remained unfinished from the previous day. Upon arriving at their offices, one of the first things that traders will do is to calculate what are the prevailing foreign exchange rates for the day. Within the past few years they have been fairly stable, but this has not always been the case. Money rates will fluctuate for little apparent reason. Given a small political crisis, a run on a country's gold supply, or an unfavorable balance-of-trade position and a significant difference will shortly manifest itself. If another French government falls, the French franc will go from five to perhaps six or seven to the dollar. Consequently, traders must adjust their money parities, for any trade in foreign stocks is one that entails two elements: the actual shares and potentially the foreign money the shares represent. Once the parities are figured, the traders make a note on their inventory and which stocks are to be sold ex- or cum-dividends.

No two houses have identical communication systems. Some have expensive networks of local brokerage houses through which they can funnel stocks throughout the country. Others have but one or two offices in Boston or Chicago or Los Angeles. The same is true abroad —some have offices or affiliates in every financial capital, while others, only in London or Zurich. Many stockbrokers have offices abroad, but their function is usually to sell American securities to Europeans, not the other way around. These offices are quite convenient for travelers in executing "give ups"; that is, selling one's shares through a different brokerage house from which they were purchased. Ties with Canada are most common and Canadian arbitrage is arbitrage at its purest. At the Canadian desk sits a trader with open telephone lines to the Toronto and Montreal Exchanges. Sitting at the foot of this inverted isosceles triangle, he simultaneously buys and sells as price fluctuations eddy about him. His headset, his phones, the Canadian and New York tapes, and his cigar are the tools of his trade.

In dealing with other parts of the world, traders rely on a more elaborate wire system. Direct telephone calls are used, but they present problems of their own, the first but not necessarily the most important one being cost. A minimum call to the Continent costs $15.00 the regular way.* In itself, the call is not excessively expensive, though it is cheaper to call from the Continent to the United States since there is no federal tax, but it does add to the cost of an order. Every brokerage house has its own figure, but it is widely agreed that the mechanics of an execution cost approximately $15.00. A $15.00 call would make arbitrage on 200 shares at a gain of a quarter point hardly worthwhile. Besides the relatively high costs of telephoning, printed cables are easier to work with, give time to reflect, and are less likely to cause errors—the printed word being safer than the spoken word.

Cables are faster than telephone switchboards. Cables come in a variety of styles: the telex may even be an open line connecting the overseas offices directly and exclusively, or the newer dial telex that can cross through a whole network of similar machines, much in the same fashion as a telephone. Most offices have both, enabling the staffs to converse by typewriter. If there is a good deal of information to be transmitted overnight, such as excerpts from the financial press,

---

* Shortly after Telstar was orbited, the first special order was executed on September 5, 1962. A large French Bank, *Credit Lyonnais,* placed an order with the Paris office of Merrill Lynch, Pierce, Fenner & Smith for one hundred shares of, of course, AT&T. The order was relayed via Telstar and for another ten minutes French and American securities were traded through the Cosmos. Once continuous satellite service is maintained, this will prove to be yet another way to trade.

the operator merely prepunches a paper tape. This is then fed into the machine which may work all night, unattended. Direct lines or private wires are instantaneous though a dial telex may have a slight delay if the party is busy. Other cable machines, such as Western Union, are also used, but are somewhat slower since messages are passed through a clearing house—the Federal Communications Commission prohibits any priorities—and then through a foreign cable company for distribution. All cable machines are leased at no mean cost, either monthly, by the word, or by the tap. Since every tap is worth two cents, traders have taken to inventing their own financial cable-ese—unintelligible to the uninitiated.

Armed with this mass of electronic array, not to mention automatic billing machines, electric adding machines, the Dow-Jones news ticker, and hotplates to keep the coffee warm, by the end of the day the trading floor is snowed under with used carbon paper, the morning newspapers, both read and unread, miles of ticker tape, doodlings, foreign financial papers, incompleted order slips, and the wrappings from lunch. Traders rarely have the time to eat out and hot corned beef sandwiches are the specialité de la Street. Trading usually picks up and the beef grows cold, much to the chagrin of the arbitrageurs. For some inexplicable reason, foreign agiotage gets increasingly hectic after two o'clock. By this time not only are European Exchanges long closed, but the swing shift is retiring for supper. How does one undo the large block of Elliott-Automation or Source Perrier when fewer and fewer traders are about? For this contingency many European houses work two shifts to cover the close of the New York market at 3:30 P.M. Nevertheless, it becomes more difficult as the afternoon wears on and more than one broker or banker has had to excuse himself from a dinner party for the sake of business.

For the arbitrageur Europe is not the only place to reverse his play after the market closes. In the Far East, say Sydney or Hong Kong, the brokerage houses open their doors for a couple of hours of business after the evening movies to receive New York's closing prices even though it is still, on the calendar, the previous day. By the time the New York trader leaves his office—surprisingly late compared to other Wall Street professionals—he can consider his day nine-tenths over. Before retiring, he may take a quick look at the early editions of the morning newspapers for the latest earnings reports and other financial news, have a glimpse at the eleven o'clock TV news and then perhaps cable to Europe an order to be executed when trading starts all over again. The figures on General Electric didn't live up to expectations and he wants to unload his inventory before the New York market starts to operate. He may sleep peacefully through the night provided some French broker doesn't cable him to buy all the Michelin he can lay his hands on because its earning figures were better than anticipated.

CAPITAL MARKETS AND TAXES

Integration or uniform practices may not be imminent, but Europe's capital markets are undergoing changes and reforms. These have been triggered by the growing need for greater equity financing and pressures brought by the U.S. Treasury. In addition, the real shortage of long-term capital in the fifties still exists in Europe today, though the nature of the problem has changed somewhat. Due to high costs of borrowing money in most European nations—Switzerland is a notable exception—it was not only cheaper but easier and faster to tap the ample resources of Wall Street.* The effect of European reliance on Wall Street was twofold: it established the United States as a leading international financial center; and constituted a lucrative business for the American securities industry. On the other hand, the plethora of borrowers was one of many factors contributing to the problematic balance-of-payments position confronting the United States. But for 1957, the balance of payments has run large deficits since 1950.

The curious aspect of these deficits and the drain on gold is that they arose from a position of strength rather than from weakness. The United States had to play too large a role in overseas financing aside from and in addition to its official loans and grants of economic and military assistance. Furthermore, additional strain was placed

* U.S., Congress, Joint Economic Committee, *Economic Policies and Practices: Paper No. 3, A Description and Analysis of Certain European Capital Markets,* 88th Congress, 2d Session, 1964, pp. 1–13.

upon the dollar since it had come to be used as the major reserve currency. Europe's extraordinary period of growth and prosperity accumulated an excess of external reserves of dollars in many European countries. This created an active Eurodollar market. ("They are U. S. dollars that have gone abroad to live and work under foreign jurisdictions, earning interest for their owners.")* More significantly the strain upon the U.S. balance of payments eventually led to what was tantamount to the suspension of dollar-to-gold convertibility at the behest of the American Treasury. By use of elaborate swap agreements, holdings of foreign currencies through the IMF and other ad hoc arrangements, the United States was in effect borrowing from these creditor nations on a short-term basis to support long-term capital exports to these very same countries. A commentator in the *Financial Times* remarked that this is "one of the silliest aspects of the international financial scene."

Another curious aspect of this balance-of-payments drain was that though the European nations were borrowing long-term while lending short-term funds they were not necessarily impoverishing the United States. One international bank has written that "in the whole period since 1950, Western Europe has—through short-term investment of its massive dollar earnings—put more capital into the U.S. than it has taken out through long-term borrowing."†

When the balance-of-payments position worsened in 1962 and beginning of 1963—the second quarter of 1963 saw the deficit rise to an unprecedented $4.6 billion calculating on an annual basis—the administration proposed an interest-equalization tax. In the Treasury's words, "The tax is designed to aid our balance-of-payments position by restraining the heavy and accelerated demand on our capital market from other industrialized countries." By levying a tax on American purchasers of foreign securities of developed countries, other than those specifically exempt, the Treasury was singling out one of many causes of the payments deficits.

The interest-equalization tax is a temporary excise tax, in a sense an import tariff, that effects all nonexempt foreign securities purchased

* Norris O. Johnson, *Eurodollars in the New International Money Market* (New York: First National City Bank, 1964), p. 4.

† *The Morgan Guaranty Survey* (New York: The Morgan Guaranty Trust Company, October, 1963), p. 8.

by Americans from non-Americans from July 19, 1963 (August 17, 1963 for listed securities) through December 31, 1965. Americans purchasing foreign securities from other Americans are tax-exempt. In other words, the bulk of foreign securities owned by U.S. citizens or under U.S. control through American Depositary Receipts can be traded without fear of incurring a tax liability. Purchases of foreign stock from non-American sources requires the payment of a 15 per cent tax on the stock's actual value at time of transfer. The tax on foreign debt obligations varies from 15 per cent on those with a maturity of 28½ years or more, down to 2.75 per cent for those with a maturity of 3 to 3½ years. Bonds with a shorter maturity are tax-exempt. The aim of the tax is to reduce the rate of return on foreign securities by approximately 1 per cent per year. By making it more expensive for the foreign seller, the Treasury hopes to decrease the number of foreign securities and cut the payments deficits.

There are many exemptions in the law, but the most significant to private investors is probably the one on the securities of "less-developed-country corporations" and the obligations of less-developed nations. Investors can get prior rulings from the Internal Revenue Service on potential purchases, to be certain; but the law provides that all European countries are subject to the tax with the exception of Finland, Iceland, Ireland, Portugal, and Greece. There are, of course, no tax liabilities if one sells American-owned foreign securities to foreign purchasers.

This tax took over a year to pass, but its effects were immediate since it had a retroactive provision. In the third quarter of 1963 the flotation of foreign debt and the purchase of foreign securities from abroad fell sharply. Many of these foreign securities owned by Americans went to a slight premium. In the case of a few securities the premium became quite sizable since the supply of the stock was obviously limited. For example, Royal Dutch Petroleum shares that were domestically owned sold for approximately a dollar more per share than the foreign-owned shares. However, when Royal Dutch announced new oil finds in the Middle East the premium jumped to almost 15 per cent, or to the point where it would have cost no more to buy the foreign-owned shares and pay the tax.

When the tax was finally passed in September 1964, it was far from clear that the balance-of-payments position was in any radically better shape, though undeniably the threat of the tax had caused a moderate improvement. In 1960, the balance-of-payments deficit was $3.9 billion; in 1961 it was $2.4 billion; in 1962, $2.2 billion; and in 1963, $1.9 billion, though the increase in the second quarter of that year to $4.6 billion on an annual basis prompted the Treasury to propose the interest-equalization tax. Indications based on the first three quarters of 1964 suggest that the deficit for the year will surpass $2 billion. Indeed, an average of the deficits since 1958 through 1964 indicates an average deficit of $2.7 billion. While the interest-equalization tax has had some effect, the outflow of private capital still continues at a level of some $5.5 billion. Indeed, a fair case can be made out against the interest equalization tax as detrimental to American interests in the long run.

The tax has been criticized from a variety of viewpoints. First of all the tax was poorly planned and executed. Besides the countless amendments and numerous exceptions to the original proposals which were appended in the course of the year it took to enact it, the administration of the tax has been frought with problems. The threat, and eventual passage of the levy, of course, slowed down the purchase of foreign-owned securities by Americans—at least through official channels. The tax is a form of currency restriction without the formalities of currency controls. But obviously watertight compartmentalization of the currency is farther than the Treasury wishes to go. Whether the tax would be effective in the face of bullish foreign markets and a bearish American market—in other words, a reversal of trends which dominated 1963 and 1964—remains in the realm of conjecture.

Moreover, there are many questionable and arbitrary aspects to the law. While it penalizes investment bankers and private, small- and medium-sized investors, it does nothing to limit the outflow of funds by commercial banks (though there is an amendment that gives the President power to include commercial banks if it appears that their loans have taken the place of equity flotations for foreign companies) and large corporate investors or wealthy individuals. With long- and short-term bank loans and direct investments exempt (over

10 per cent of the voting equity for the purposes of the law), only a small percentage—approximately 10 per cent—of private capital exports are subject to the tax. Early indications are that tax-exempt sources are increasing their export of private capital.

Another puzzling aspect is the self-defeating quality of the levy. Foreign investments, whether they be of direct or portfolio variety, are not lost expenditures. In the long run they return to the United States considerably more dollars than the original investment. The *Wall Street Journal* illustrated this point, observing that "from 1958 through 1962 income from all private foreign investments nearly offset the aggregate net outflow for new investment, and in 1962 exceeded it. In the future this income, unless the government succeeds in reducing it could well be a strong support of our balance-of-payments position."* If this tax is renewed and remains in force for any length of time, it will undoubtedly cut down on a profitable source of income for the United States.

Another effect might be to reduce America's influence and power as a center of international finance. The London *Times* remarked that "like London [New York] will be reduced as an international capital market virtually to entrepôt trade."† Though this judgment may be somewhat drastic, these barriers are not conducive to increased international intercourse. The United States has also been charged with hypocrisy since the tax goes against long-standing articles of faith: increase of trade, the liberalization of currency convertibility, and freer capital movements. An editorial in the *New York Times* commented that:

This is inconsistent with the position of the United States as the world's banker and with the long-standing objectives of lowering barriers to trade and capital movements. Instead it suggests that we are regressing toward direct controls over capital, which led to the breakdown of international finance a generation ago. . . . [The tax] cannot eliminate the deficit, but could lead to a return to the financial nightmare of the nineteen thirties, when each power resorted to unilateral "beggar thy neighbor" policies that effectively disrupted trade and brought economic stagnation.**

* *The Wall Street Journal,* February 13, 1964.
† *The London Times,* July 29, 1963.
** *The New York Times,* July 25, 1963.

Without doubt this has encouraged other nations to follow with capital curbs to suit their own needs. The Germans have passed a dividend tax on foreign purchasers of German fixed-interest securities to keep foreign money out of their overheated economy. On the other hand, the new English Labor government no sooner came to power in October 1964, than they immediately established a 15 per cent import surcharge.

Another law which may effect an investor in foreign securities is the Securities Act Amendments of 1964. Among other things, this act calls for fuller disclosure of financial information for foreign securities traded in the over-the-counter market. The object of the new regulation is to afford the American investor approximately the same information on foreign securities he now enjoys with listed American companies. In other words, the requisites for foreign firms whose securities are traded in the United States might include publishing of annual and semi-annual reports, insider trading, and proxy dealings. This raises a whole series of questions—not the least of which is the problem of enforcement. In view of the inherent difficulties, the SEC has exempted all foreign concerns from these requirements till the end of November 1965. Whether the exemption will be extended or the requirements enforced remains to be seen. If European concerns find that they need financing which is unobtainable in their home markets, they will probably comply with Wall Street's demand for information. If not, the SEC obviously has no jurisdiction.

Europe's capital markets have been in a stage of transition and flux since the U.S. Treasury proposed its interest-equalization tax. In 1963 most European countries floated fewer stock issues than in 1962, but there was a noticeable increase in bond financing. A study by the Chase Manhattan Bank noted that "the $10.3 billion of new capital raised in the eight European countries last year came close to the U.S. level. This performance of the European capital markets is remarkable considering the fact that the combined national income of these eight European countries is still only half of the national income in the United States.*

* *Report on Western Europe* (New York: The Chase Manhattan Bank, April–May, 1964), p. 4.

In other words, it is misleading to think that Europe is incapable of financing her own industries. Though these capital markets are shackled by high interest rates, inflationary overtones, capital issues committees, and other factors, they do have a broad absorptive capacity. Many of the foreign flotations in the New York market rather quickly find their way back to their native lands.

Some experimentation with new forms of financing has taken place recently. One of the most successful thus far has been the unit-of-account. The dollar and the unit-of-account are on a par since they both represent the same value of gold. Debt obligations in units-of-account are designed to cover seventeen Western European currencies. Consequently, loans can be made in one currency but repaid in another. The object of this is to safeguard all parties against any sharp fluctuations in the value of the money lent or borrowed. Moreover, such loans can be floated in every financial center in Europe, thus tapping the resources of over 300 million people.

Another form of financing coming into greater use are dollar bonds issued in Europe. American investment bankers use their resources and techniques to float bonds denominated in dollars. From July 1963 to July 1964 over $325 million were issued with the pace picking up after the interest-equalization tax became law.

CONCLUSION

Americans will undoubtedly continue to be interested in Europe's direction and policies and involved with her actions for generations to come. There are forces within this dynamic and expansive Continent that make European states competitors, clients, and complementary citizens of the Western world. The mutual interpenetration between European and American ideas and techniques should not be ignored by an alert investor.

Prospects and projections for Europe appear promising indeed. By 1975 the population will have grown to an estimated 342 million people; the EEC will have 191 million, EFTA 99 million with the remainder in the other European states. The GNP will be an estimated $600 billion or 90 per cent more than 1960. Obviously, there will be greater demand for a wide spectrum of goods; heavy machinery, consumer appliances, automobiles, housing and construction. Service industries can also be expected to grow quickly with greater demand in everything from nursery to geriatric care. Indeed, $1,260 billion will be invested in basic industry and public works while another $545 billion may be channeled into housing.*

Although Europe may not quite reach the 1960 standard of living of the United States by 1975, it will be getting close to it. Undoubtedly each nation's prosperity will reflect each nation's tastes and preferences. The Americanization of Europe is an inaccurate cliché. More to the point perhaps are the modern industrial and technical forces that have pulled a sometimes recalcitrant Europe into the second half of the twentieth century. The similarities may be more striking, but the differences will remain more lasting.

Besides the potential growth and prosperity of the Continent there is another factor to ponder. Until the national business cycle is abolished, European economies are likely to be at different stages of expansion and contraction. Growth rates, dividends, interest rates, and stock market behavior may run parallel at moments, but rarely concurrently for any length of time. As long as the national state or a limited trading bloc remains sovereign in its political decisions, economic plans, and fiscal and monetary policies, the securities markets will anticipate and mirror these contrasts. Therefore, European economies represent alternative investment opportunities. A discriminating investor should consider moving part of his funds from one country to another, as he would from a less profitable to a more profitable company. With the waxing and waning of bull and bear markets, the better part of wisdom dictates a geographic diversification as well as an industrial diversification.

Investing abroad is not without its perils. However, the 2,500 American business concerns that have established some form of new operation in Europe since 1958 attest to the fact that in the long run *not* investing abroad may prove more costly.

* Arnold B. Barach, *The New Europe and Its Economic Future* (New York: The Twentieth Century Fund, 1964), pp. 24, 113.

APPENDIX I

Exchange Rates of European Currencies
(for One U.S. Dollar)

Country	Currency and Fractional Divisions	Approximate Rate as of December 31, 1964
Austria	Schilling (Sch.)=100 Groschen	26.00
Belgium	Franc (BF)=100 Centimes	50.00
Denmark	Krone (DKR)=100 Ore	6.90
Finland	Markka (FMK)=100 Pennia	3.17
France	Franc (FF)=100 Centimes	4.90
Germany	Deutsche Mark (DM)=100 Pfennige	4.00
Greece	Drachma (DR)=100 Lepta	30.00
Italy	Lire (L)=100 Centesimi	625.00
Netherlands	Guilder (Gld.)=100 Cents	3.60
Norway	Krone (NKR)=100 Ore	7.15
Portugal	Escudo (Esc.)=100 Centavos	28.60
Spain	Peseta (Pse.)=100 Centimos	60.00
Sweden	Krona (SKR)=100 Ore	5.17
Switzerland	Franc (SF)=100 Centimes (Rappen)	4.32
United Kingdom	Pound Sterling (£)=20 Shillings (S.) 20 Shillings (S.)=240 Pence (d.)=	.357

APPENDIX II

The Major Publicly-held Corporations of Europe

Company	Industry
1. Shell	Petroleum products
2. Imperial Chemical Industries	Chemicals, metals
3. British Petroleum	Petroleum products
4. F. W. Woolworth	Merchandising
5. Marks and Spencer	Merchandising
6. Distillers Company	Distilleries, chemicals
7. Burmah Oil Company	Petroleum products
8. Great Universal Stores	Merchandising
9. Courtaulds	Textiles
10. Unilever	Food processing, fats and oils
11. British American Tobacco Co.	Tobacco
12. Royal Insurance Company	Insurance
13. Imperial Tobacco Company	Tobacco
14. Guest Keen and Nettlefolds	Iron and steel, engineering
15. Prudential Assurance Company	Insurance
16. Barclays Bank	Banking
17. Plessey	Radio components
18. Associated Portland Cement Mfrs.	Cement
19. Midland Bank	Banking
20. British Motor Company	Automobiles
21. Turner and Newall	Asbestos, plastics
22. J. & P. Coats, Patons & Baldwins	Textiles
23. Allied Breweries	Breweries
24. United Drapery Stores	Merchandising
25. General Accident Fire and Life	Insurance
26. Legal and General Assurance	Insurance
27. International Publishing Co.	Publishing
28. Lloyds Banks	Banking
29. British Insulated Callender's Cables	Cables, electrical equipment

GREAT BRITAIN: FIFTY LARGEST COMPANIES[a]

Company	Industry
30. Tube Investments	Iron and steel, engineering
31. Boots Pure Drug Company	Pharmaceuticals
32. Rank Hovis McDougall	Food products
33. Commercial Union Insurance	Insurance
34. National Provincial Bank	Banking
35. Dunlop Rubber Company	Banking
36. Leyland Motors	Automobiles
37. Reed Paper Group	Paper products
38. Metal Box Company	Containers, packaging
39. Rio Tinto-Zinc Corporation	Mining, chemicals, steel
40. Arthur Guinness Son and Co.	Brewing
41. Reckitt and Colman Holdings	Food products, pharmaceuticals
42. Bowater Paper Corporation	Paper products
43. Beecham Group	Pharmaceuticals
44. Bass Mitchells and Butlers	Brewing
45. Sears Holdings	Machinery, shipbuilding, footwear
46. Rank Organization	Motion pictures, office equipment
47. British Oxygen Company	Gases, chemicals
48. Associated Electrical Industries	Electrical equipment
49. Watney Mann	Brewing
50. General Electric Company	Electrical equipment

[a] In order of share capitailzation, 1964.

FRANCE: FIFTY LARGEST COMPANIES[a]

Company	Industry
1. Rhone-Poulenc	Chemicals
2. Air Liquide	Chemicals
3. Saint-Gobain	Glass, chemicals
4. Générale d'Électricité	Electric utility
5. Française des Pétroles	Petroleum products
6. Esso-Standard	Petroleum products
7. Michelin	Rubber
8. Pétroles d'Aquitaine	Petroleum products
9. Pechiney	Aluminum
10. Ugine	Metals
11. Nouvelles Galeries Réunies	Department stores
12. Française de Raffinage	Petroleum products
13. Hachette	Publishing
14. Usinor	Steel, cement
15. Beghin	Sugar refining and cellulose

France: Fifty Largest Companies[a]

Company	Industry
16. Générale des Eaux	Water works
17. Machines Bull	Electronic equipment
18. Pont-a-Mousson	Iron and Steel
19. Printemps	Department stores
20. C.S.F.—Générale de T.S.F.	Electrical and electronic equipment
21. Shell Française	Petroleum products
22. Financière de Suez	Financial holding company
23. Crédit Foncier de France	Official long-term credit agency
24. Lyonnaise des Eaux	Water works
25. Kuhlmann	Chemicals
26. Wendel	Steel
27. Simca-Auto	Automobiles
28. Roussel-Uclaf	Pharmaceuticals
29. Citroen	Automobiles
30. Ciments Lafarge	Cement
31. Pétroles BP	Petroleum products
32. Galeries Lafayette	Department stores
33. Banque de Paris	Banking
34. Radiotechnique	Radio components
35. Peugeot	Automobiles
36. Boussois	Glass, chemicals
37. Pricel	Paper and pulp holding company
38. Cellulose du Pin	Paper and pulp
39. Sidelor	Steel
40. Thomson-Houston	Electrical equipment
41. Progil	Chemicals, tanning
42. Lorraine-Escaut	Iron and steel
43. Perrier	Mineral water
44. Trefimetaux	Steel, metals
45. Bazar de l'Hotel de Ville	Department stores
46. Compagnie Bancaire	Bank holding company
47. Casino	Food products
48. Forges et Aciéries du Nord et de l'Est	Iron and steel
49. Denain-Anzin	Iron and steel
50. Crédit National	Official medium-term industrial loan agency

[a] In order of share capitalization, 1963.

BELGIUM: TWENTY LEADING COMPANIES

Company	Industry
1. ARBED	Iron and steel
2. Banque de Bruxelles	Banking
3. Banque Nationale de Belgique	Banking
4. Banque de la Société Générale de Belgique	Banking
5. Belge Azote	Chemicals, gasses
6. Cimenteries et Briqueteries Réunies	Cement, construction material
7. Cockerill-Ougrée	Metallurgy
8. Espérance Longdoz	Metallurgy
9. Fabrique Nationale d'Armes de Guerre	Armaments
10. Financière des Caoutchoucs	Rubber plantations
11. Industries Chimiques	Chemical holding company
12. Innovation	Department stores
13. Métallurgie Hoboken	Nonferrous metals
14. Pétrofina	Petroleum products
15. Photo-Produits Gevaert	Chemicals, photographic products
16. Sidro	Electric utility
17. Sofina	Transportation
18. Union Chimique Belge (UCB)	Chemicals
19. Union Minière du Haut Katanga	Congo mining
20. Wagon-Lits	International railways

SWITZERLAND: TEN LARGEST COMPANIES[a]

Company	Industry
1. Credit Suisse	Banking
2. Société de Banque Suisse	Banking
3. Union de Banques Suisses	Banking
4. Nestlé Alimentana	Food products
5. Banque Populaire Suisse	Banking
6. Aluminium Suisse	Aluminum
7. CIBA	Chemicals
8. Aar et Tessin, S.A., d'Électricité	Electric utility
9. Brown, Boveri & Cie.	Electrical equipment
10. Swissair	Airline

[a] In order of share capitalization, 1964.

THE NETHERLANDS: TEN LARGEST COMPANIES[a]

Company	Industry
1. Royal Dutch Petroleum	Petroleum products
2. Philips' Incandescent Lamp Works	Electrical appliances
3. Unilever	Food products, fats and oils
4. Amsterdamsche-Rotterdamsche Bank	Banking
5. AKU (Algemene Kunstzijde Unie)	Chemicals, textiles
6. KLM (Royal Dutch Airlines)	Airline
7. Algemene Bank Nederland	Banking
8. Hoogovens	Iron and steel
9. Scheepvart Unie	Shipping holding company
10. Koninklijke Zout-Ketjen	Salt, chemicals

[a] In order of share capitalization, 1964.

GERMANY: FIFTY LARGEST INDUSTRIAL COMPANIES[a]

Company	Industry
1. Volkswagenwerk	Automobiles
2. Siemens	Electrical equipment
3. Daimler-Benz	Automobiles
4. Krupp	Steel, machinery
5. Gutehoffnungshütte	Steel, machinery
6. Esso	Petroleum products
7. Farben Bayer	Chemicals
8. Rheinische Stahlwerke	Coal, steel, machinery
9. AEG	Electrical equipment
10. Farbwerke Hoechst	Chemicals
11. Shell	Petroleum products
12. BASF	Chemicals
13. Opel	Automobiles
14. Mannesmann	Machinery, iron
15. Gelsenkirchener Bergwerks	Coal, petroleum
16. Salzgitter	Steel, machinery
17. Unilever	Food products, fats and oils
18. Bosch	Electrical equipment
19. August Thyssen-Hütte	Iron and steel
20. Ford	Automobiles
21. B. P. Benzin und Petroleum	Petroleum products
22. Metallgesellschaft	Nonferrous metals

GERMANY: FIFTY LARGEST INDUSTRIAL COMPANIES[a]

Company	Industry
23. Hoesch	Coal, steel, machinery
24. Deutsche Erdöl	Petroleum products
25. Klöckner-Werke	Iron and steel
26. Phoenix-Rheinrohr	Iron and steel
27. Klöckner-Humboldt-Deutz	Engines, machinery
28. Dortmund-Hörder Hüttenunion	Iron and steel
29. Henkel	Detergents, chemicals
30. Mobil Oil	Petroleum products
31. Vereinigte Glanzstoff	Chemicals, textiles
32. Degussa	Metals, chemicals
33. Wintershall	Chemicals
34. Demag	Machinery
35. Brown, Boveri	Electrical equipment
36. Reemtsma	Tobacco
37. Continental Gummi-Werke	Rubber
38. Saarbergwerke	Mining
39. Scholven Chemie	Chemicals
40. Hüttenwerk Oberhausen	Coal and steel
41. Brinkmann	Tobacco
42. I.B.M.	Electrical machinery
43. Felten & Guilleaume	Metals, cables
44. Rheinische Braunkohlenwerke	Coal mining
45. Preussag	Petroleum, machinery
46. Bergwerksges. Hibernia	Mining, iron, steel
47. Eschweiler B.-V.	Coal and steel
48. Standard Electrik Lorenz	Electronic equipment
49. Alldephi	Electrical equipment
50. Stahlwerke Südwestfalen	Iron and steel

[a] Arranged by total sales, 1963.

AUSTRIA: TEN LARGEST INDUSTRIAL COMPANIES[a]

Company	Industry
1. Steyr-Daimler-Puch	Motors, ball bearings
2. Veitscher Magnesitwerke	Mines
3. Semperit Österreichisch-Amerikanische Gummiwerke	Rubber
4. Perlmooser Zementwerke	Cement
5. Oesterreichische Brau	Brewing
6. Leipnik-Lundenburger Zuckerfabriken	Sugar refining

AUSTRIA: TEN LARGEST INDUSTRIAL COMPANIES

Company	Industry
7. Steyrermühl Papierfabriks- und Verlags	Paper and pulp, publishing
8. Kleinmünchner Baumwoll- Spinnereien	Textiles
9. Leykam-Josefsthal	Paper and pulp, cellulose
10. Felten & Guilleaume	Electrical cables, metals

ª In order of share capitalization, 1964.

SWEDEN: TWENTY LARGEST INDUSTRIAL COMPANIESª

Company	Industry
1. SKF, AB Svenska Kullager- fabriken	Ball bearings, roller bearings
2. ASEA, Allmänna Svenska Elektriska AB	Electrical equipment
3. AB Volvo	Automobiles, trucks, buses
4. LM, Telefon AB L M Ericsson	Telephone equipment
5. LKAB, Luossavaara-Kiirun- avaara AB	Mining and refining of iron ore
6. Alfa-Laval	Dairy machines, centrifuges
7. AB Skånska Cementgjuteriet	Constructions
8. Stora Kopparbergs Bergslags AB	Mining, steel works, pulp, wood products
9. Svenska Tändsticksaktiebolaget	Matches
10. AB Scania-Vabis	Automobiles and engines
11. AB Electrolux	Household appliances
12. SCA, Svenska Cellulosa	Paper, pulp, wood products
13. Uddeholms AB	Steel works, paper, pulp, wood products
14. SAAB, Svenska Aeroplan AB	Automobiles, aircrafts
15. AB Svenska Metallverken	Semifinished metal products
16. AB Bofors	Steel, defence material
17. AGA, Svenska AB Gasacku- mulator	Lighthouses, signal lights, radio, TV
18. AB Atlas Copco	Compressors, pneumatic tools
19. Sandvikens Jernverks AB	Iron and steel
20. TGO, Trafik AB Grängesberg- Oxelösund	Iron mining and manufacturing

ª Arranged by total sales, 1961.

DENMARK: TEN LARGEST COMPANIES[a]

Company	Industry
1. Landmandsbank	Banking
2. Kjøbenhavn Telefon	Telephone system
3. Handelsbank	Banking
4. Foreningen Dampskibsselskab (United Steamship Company)	Shipping
5. Østasiatisk Kompagni	Plantations: rubber, teak
6. Privatbank	Banking
7. Jydsk Telefon	Telephone system
8. Burmeister & Wain	Shipyard
9. Danske Sukkerfabrikker	Sugar Refining
10. Det Danske Luftfartsselskab	Airline

[a] In order of share capitalization, 1964.

NORWAY: TEN LARGEST COMPANIES[a]

Company	Industry
1. Norsk Hydro	Electric utility
2. Borregaard	Paper and pulp, chemicals, fibers
3. Christiania Bank og Kreditkasse	Banking
4. Den norske Creditbank	Banking
5. Bergens Privatbank	Banking
6. Storebrand	Insurance
7. Christiania Spigerverk	Iron and steel
8. Forretningsbanken	Banking
9. Orkla Grube-Aktiebolag	Industrial holding company
10. Bjølvefossen	Iron and steel, metals

[a] In order of share capitalization, 1963.

FINLAND: TEN LARGEST COMPANIES[a]

Company	Industry
1. Enso-Gutzeit	Paper and pulp, wood products, newsprint
2. Kymmene	Wood products, chemicals
3. Kansallis-Osake-Pankki	Banking
4. Ab Nordiska Föreningsbanken	Banking
5. Wärtsilä-koncernen	Iron and steel, shipbuilding

FINLAND: TEN LARGEST COMPANIES

Company	Industry
6. Yhtyneet Paperitehtaat (United Paper Mills)	Paper and pulp, wood products
7. Kesko	Wholesale merchandising
8. Oy Tampella	Textiles, electrical equipment
9. Pargas Kalkbergs	Mines, building material
10. Outokumpu Oy	Nonferrous metals

a In order of share capitalization, 1963.

ITALY: FIFTY LARGEST INDUSTRIAL COMPANIES[a]

Company	Industry
1. Fiat	Automobiles
2. Edison (Group)	Industrial holding company
3. Esso Standard of Italy	Petroleum products
4. Italsider	Iron and steel
5. Shell of Italy	Petroleum products
6. Montecatini	Chemicals
7. Pirelli	Rubber
8. La Rinascente	Department stores
9. Ing. C. Olivetti & C.	Office machines
10. Snia Viscosa	Synthetic fibers
11. Alfa Romeo	Automobiles, engineering
12. B. P. Italy	Petroleum products
13. Dalmine	Metallurgy
14. Alitalia	Airline
15. Total	Petroleum products
16. O. M.	Electrical machinery
17. Acciaierie e Ferriere Lombarde Falck	Metallurgy
18. Rai—Radiotelevisione	Radio and television
19. Stipel	Telephone equipment
20. Lancia & C.	Automobiles, mechanical engineering
21. Rhodiatoce	Synthetic fibers
22. Eridania	Sugar refining, distilling
23. Mobil Oil of Italy	Petroleum products
24. API—Anonima Petroli Italy	Petroleum products
25. Innocenti	Metallurgy
26. Egidio Galbani	Dairy products, meats
27. Fina Italy	Petroleum products
28. Teti	Telephone equipment

ITALY: FIFTY LARGEST INDUSTRIAL COMPANIES[a]

Company	Industry
29. Italcementi	Cement
30. Gruppo Breda	Industrial holding company
31. Cantieri Riuniti dell'Adriatico	Railroad equipment, office machinery
32. Caltex of Italy	Petroleum products
33. Manifattura Lane G. Marzotto & Figli	Wool
34. Carlo Erba	Chemicals
35. P. Ferrero	Food products, candy
36. Piaggio	Machinery
37. Motta	Food products
38. Nuovo Pignone	Machinery
39. Châtillon	Synthetic fibers
40. Italiana Industria Zuccheri	Sugar refining, distilling
41. Ercole Marelli & C.	Machinery, electrical equipment
42. Cartiere Burgo	Construction, electric power, timber products
43. C. G. E.—Compagnia Generale Elettricità	Electric utility
44. Mondadori Editore	Publishing
45. Italgas	Gas
46. Compagnia Singer	Machinery
47. Telecomunicazioni Siemens	Electrical equipment
48. Farmaceutici Italia	Chemicals
49. Ansaldo San Giorgio	Machinery
50. Set	Telephone equipment

[a] Arranged by total sales, 1963.

SPAIN: TWENTY LARGEST COMPANIES[a]

Company	Industry
1. Telefónica Nacional de España	Telephone system
2. Empressa Nacional Siderúgica (ENSIDESA)	Iron and steel
3. IBERDUERO	Electric utility
4. Hidroeléctrica Española	Electric utility
5. Altos Hornos de Vizcaya	Iron and steel
6. Fuerzas Eléctricas de Cataluña (FECSA)	Electric utility
7. Fuerzas Eléctricas del Noroeste (FENOSA)	Electric utility

SPAIN: TWENTY LARGEST COMPANIES[a]

Company	Industry
8. Compañia Arrendataria del Monopolio de Petróleos (CAMPSA)	Petroleum products
9. Sevillana de Eléctricidad	Electric utility
10. Unión Eléctricidad Madrileña	Electric utility
11. Unión Española de Explosivos	Chemicals
12. Cros	Chemicals
13. Española de Petróleos	Petroleum products
14. Hidroeléctrica del Cantábrico	Electric utility
15. Española de Construcción Naval	Military construction, naval facilities
16. Banco Hispano Americano	Banking
17. Metalúrgica Duro-Felguera	Metallurgy, mining
18. Banco Español de Crédito	Banking
19. General Azucarera de España	Sugar refining, distilling
20. Babcock & Wilcox	Machinery, boiler makers

[a] In order of share capitalization, 1963.

PORTUGAL: TEN LARGEST COMPANIES[a]

Company	Industry
1. Banco de Portugal	Banking
2. Banco Nacional Ultramarino	Banking
3. Banco de Angola	Banking
4. Banco Espirito Santo e Comercial de Lisboa	Banking
5. Siderurgia Nacional	Iron and steel
6. Hidro-Eléctrica do Cávado	Electric utility
7. Hidro-Eléctrica do Douro	Electric utility
8. SACOR—Soc. Anónima Concessionária da Refinação de Petróleos em Portugal	Petroleum products
9. Companhias Reunidas Gas e Electricidade	Gas and electric utility
10. SONEFE—Sociedade Nacional de Estudo e Financiamento de Empreendimentos Ultramarinos	Overseas development corporation

[a] Arranged by asset value, 1963.

GREECE: TEN LARGEST COMPANIES[a]

Company	*Industry*
1. National Bank of Greece	Banking
2. Bank of Greece	Banking
3. Chemical Products & Fertilizers	Chemicals
4. Ionian and Popular Bank of Greece	Banking
5. Commercial Bank of Greece	Banking
6. Piraiki-Patraiki Cotton Industry	Textiles
7. Hellenic Shipyards Company	Shipyards
8. FIX Breweries	Brewing
9. Hellenic Electric Railways	Railroad
10. Hellenic Paper Mills	Paper and pulp

[a] In order of share capitalization, 1964.

APPENDIX III

General Sources of Information

A staggering number of books reporting on every aspect of the European scene has been published in the last decade. The following few publications provide a general Pan-European background of the varied topics under discussion.

I. Books

BARACH, ARNOLD B. *The New Europe and its Economic Future*. New York: The Twentieth Century Fund, 1964.

BENOIT, EMILE. *Europe at Sixes and Sevens*. New York: Columbia University Press, 1961.

BLOOM, SOLOMON F. *Europe and America: The Western World in Modern Times*. New York: Harcourt, Brace & World, Inc. 1961.

DELL, SIDNEY. *Trade Blocs and Common Markets*. New York: Alfred A. Knopf, 1963.

DENIAU, JEAN F. *The Common Market*. New York: Frederick A. Praeger, 1960.

DEWHURST, FREDERIC J., *et al. Europe's Needs and Resources*. New York: The Twentieth Century Fund, 1961.

FEDERATION OF BRITISH INDUSTRIES. *Taxation in Western Europe* (Annually). London: Federation of British Industries.

FRIEDMANN, WOLFGANG G. AND PUGH, RICHARD C. (eds.). *Legal Aspects of Foreign Investment*. Boston and Toronto: Little, Brown and Company, 1959.

GOTTMANN, JEAN. *A Geography of Europe*. New York: Henry Holt and Company, 1954.

GRANICK, DAVID. *The European Executive*. Garden City, New York: Doubleday & Company, Inc., 1962.

GUNTHER, JOHN. *Inside Europe Today*. New York: Harper & Row, 1962.

HALLSTEIN, WALTER. *United Europe: Challenge and Opportunity*. Cambridge, Massachusetts: Harvard University Press, 1962.

HOMER, SIDNEY. *A History of Interest Rates*. New Brunswick, New Jersey: Rutgers University Press, 1963.

JOHNSON, NORRIS O. *Eurodollars in the New International Market*. New York: First National City Bank, 1964.

KITZINGER, U. W. *The Politics and Economics of European Integration*. New York: Frederick A. Praeger, 1963.

LICHTHEIM, GEORGE. *The New Europe*. New York: Frederick A. Praeger, 1963.

MADDISON, ANGUS. *Economic Growth in the West: Comparative Experience in Europe and North America.* New York: The Twentieth Century Fund, 1964.

SAYERS, R. S. (ed.). *Banking In Western Europe.* Oxford: Clarendon Press, 1962.

SPRAY, DAVID E. (ed.). *The Principal Stock Exchanges of the World.* Washington, D.C.: International Economic Publishers, 1964.

WASSERMAN, MAX J., HULTMAN, CHARLES W., and ZSOLDOS, LASZLO. *International Finance.* New York: Simmons-Boardman Publishing Corporation, 1963.

Who Owns Whom (Annually: United Kingdom and Continental Editions). London: O. W. Roskill & Co. (Reports) Ltd.

Official Reports, Bank Studies and Business Services

Congressional committees in recent years have produced many valuable reports on Western Europe. Two excellent general surveys are:

U.S. Congress, Joint Economic Committee. *Economic Policy in Western Europe.* 85th Congress, 2d Session, 1959.

U.S. Congress, Joint Economic Committee. *Economic Policies and Practices: Paper No. 3, A Description and Analysis of Certain European Capital Markets.* 88th Congress, 2d Session, 1964.

Studies of the European economies are far too numerous to cite, but one should bear in mind the works of the Organization for Economic Cooperation and Development; the European Economic Community; the European Free Trade Association. Furthermore, every European central bank publishes an annual report—frequently in English. The central bankers' organization, the Bank for International Settlements, also publishes an authoritative yearly review.

With but a few exceptions, private banks in the United States and Europe publish some variety of economic or financial information. The quality naturally differs from bank to bank; perhaps the best work comes from the special study groups established as joint enterprises by several banks.

Specialized private business services are also a source of excellent financial intelligence. These services usually charge substantial subscription fees. Besides the well-known foreign research of Moody's and Standard & Poor's, Business International Corporation publishes extensive reports both in the United States and in Switzerland. The Gallatin Service of the American Heritage Publishing Company publishes an annual reference encyclopedia and a fortnightly letter of current international business developments. In Europe the Economist Intelligence Unit publishes a series of quarterly economic reviews on individual nations. Opera Mundi-Europe, a European literary syndicate, publishes a weekly Common Market Newsletter in Paris, though an English edition is distributed by the London *Times*. The *London Letter* is another European weekly publication, though printed in the United States, which discusses international business and finance.

INDEX